PLANTING**CHURCHES**
in the 21st century

PLANTING**CHURCHES**
in the 21st century

A GUIDE FOR THOSE WHO WANT FRESH PERSPECTIVES AND NEW IDEAS FOR CREATING CONGREGATIONS

STUART MURRAY

Herald Press

Scottdale, Pennsylvania
Waterloo, Ontario

Library of Congress Cataloging-in-Publication Data
Murray, Stuart, 1956-
    Planting churches in the 21st century : a guide for those who want fresh perspectives
and new ideas for creating congregations : a framework for practitioners / Stuart
Murray.—North American ed.
        p. cm.
    Rev. ed. of: Planting churches. 2008.
    Includes bibliographical references (p.   ).
    ISBN 978-0-8361-9424-1 (pbk.)
    1. Church development, New. I. Murray, Stuart, 1956- Planting churches. II. Title.
    BV652.24.M87 2010
    254'.1—dc22

                                                    2010002651

Environmental Savings

Mennonite Publishing Network saved the following resources by printing the pages of this book on
chlorine free paper made with 30% post-consumer waste.

Trees	Water	Solid Waste	Greenhouse Gases
About 18 trees	18,954 gallons	1,719 pounds	5,224 pounds CO2

Environmental impact estimates were made using the Environmental Defense Fund Paper
Calculator. For more information visit http://www.papercalculator.org.

Scriptures taken from *The Holy Bible, New International Version*®, NIV®. Copyright
© 1973, 1978, 1984 by Biblica, Inc.™ Used by permission of Zondervan. All rights
reserved worldwide. www.zondervan.com

This North American edition of *Planting Churches* is based on the version first published
in 2008 by Paternoster, an imprint of Authentic, 9 Holdom Avenue, Bletchley, Milton
Keynes, MK1 1QR, U.K. This edition is published by agreement with Paternoster. In
relation to the UK edition, the right of Stuart Murray to be identified as the Author of
this Work has been asserted by him in accordance with the Copyright, Designs, and
Patents Act 1988.

PLANTING CHURCHES IN THE 21ST CENTURY
Copyright © 2010 by Herald Press, Scottdale, PA 15683
  Released simultaneously in Canada by Herald Press,
  Waterloo, Ont. N2L 6H7. All rights reserved
Library of Congress Control Number: 2010002651
International Standard Book Number: 978-0-8361-9424-1
Printed in the United States of America
Cover by Reuben Graham

15 14 13 12 11 10   10 9 8 7 6 5 4 3 2 1

To order or request information please call 1-800-245-7894 or visit
www.heraldpress.com.

To Neil, Emma, and Joel

CONTENTS

Foreword 9
Introduction 11

1. Planting Churches Today 13

2. Planting Churches: Why? 29

3. Planting Churches: How? 53

4. Planting Churches: Where? 83

5. Planting Churches: When? 109

6. Planting Churches: What? 133

7. Planting Churches: Who? 161

8. Planting Churches: What Next? 185

Appendix 211
Notes 215
Author 227

FOREWORD

Church Planting is in the dock. The lawyer for the prosecution has just sat down, having given a lengthy treatise on why Church Planting is not only outmoded and irrelevant, but, in fact, a very real danger to society. Why plant more manifestations of communities that seem to have so little to do with the life of Jesus? Why perpetuate an institution that has distorted the message of the gospel? The atmosphere in the courtroom is listless and bored—no one is much interested in this case—it seems so nineties. A few picketed the entrance with boards that read, "Life is not long enough!" They were mainly those who had been hurt and damaged by aggressive church-planting campaigns in the past that had either decimated their churches or failed to deliver on promises.

Stuart Murray gets to his feet and begins a systematic defense of the accused. He does not gloss over the mistakes of the past, but carefully outlines what has been learned along the way that now makes Church Planting a reformed character. It is not right to consign her to oblivion. In her new approaches and guises, he argues, she has much to offer to our society and to the kingdom of God. The mood in the courtroom changes, and some begin listening intently. Church Planting tentatively raises her head for the first time in the proceedings and there is a gleam of quiet hope in her eyes.

This book presents an extremely helpful summary of the key questions that need to be faced by those considering church planting anew. Stuart Murray writes and speaks with consistent logic and clarity. When he gave some of the lectures that form the substance of this book in Melbourne, Australia, in 2007, someone commented that he had a gift of "being an iron fist in a velvet glove." He has a way of tackling the most difficult subjects and challenging the most sacred cows of Christian culture, which enables people to begin to see things differently. This is important when tackling a subject such as church planting, because the topic evokes some strong emotions at both ends of the spectrum and a deal of indifference in the middle. This book will help people to shift their positions so that in the end it is the kingdom that is served.

At the Melbourne conference, we sought to bring together those committed to the church-growth style of church planting and those who were seeking to pioneer different ways of being church; we believed that these groups have much to offer each other. This book is one of the first to straddle that divide between the more organic, emerging church approach and the need to be strategic and intentional about founding Christian communities in specific locations. It is important that we listen and learn from one another, so that together we can support each other in forming communities that are authentic expressions of the life of Christ in our contemporary society.

My hope is that *Planting Churches in the 21st Century* will be the stimulus for many to ask serious questions about what church and evangelism mean today. The book is geared specifically for those who are considering planting churches, as individuals or as agencies, and should be seen as essential reading before anyone embarks on such a venture. However, its relevance is to a broader audience. This book should encourage all churchgoers to think about their context, their practices, and their methods of communication.

I am a firm believer that we need to be planting new Christian communities of faith in all sorts of contexts and places. Some of these communities will look like the mental image we already have of church; others will make us wonder how we define *church*, but it seems essential that, at a time when many of the familiar church institutions are declining, we keep encouraging a variety of inclusive, welcoming communities in which Jesus can be seen. This is a time for humble, grace-filled experimentation, and Stuart Murray has provided us with a much-needed guide book as we explore new possibilities and seek to engage our wider community with the love of God. If we read and learn, we can avoid the mistakes of the past and be aware of some of the pitfalls of the present, and, with faith and hope, enter the future of God's beckoning.

Anne Wilkinson-Hayes
Melbourne, Australia

INTRODUCTION

Why have I written this book? Because I am convinced that church planting is crucial for the continuing mission of the church and the health of the Christian community. Because I believe church planters need to think more carefully about what we are doing than we have sometimes done. Because most books on church planting are out of print, out of date, or written for a different context than where I find myself in post-Christendom Europe. Because church planters and those who deploy and support them cannot easily access the experience accumulated over the past twenty years. Because those who are pioneering fresh expressions of church or are involved in emerging churches, whether or not they regard this as church planting, are also creating new Christian communities and can learn from this experience too.

I have been involved in church planting for more than thirty years. In January 1978, leading a small mission team in East London, I stumbled into this as a new church started in my home. I spent the next twelve years leading a multiethnic church that grew to about three hundred adults and children. During most of the 1990s I directed the church planting and evangelism course at Spurgeon's College in South London. In 1997, I founded Urban Expression,[1] an inner-city church-planting agency with teams now in London, Manchester, and Glasgow (and a partner agency in Holland). Throughout the past twenty years I have acted as a coach, mentor, trainer, and consultant to church planters, emerging churches, fresh expressions of church, denominational leaders, and mission agencies in a dozen nations and two dozen denominations.

I have also written five books on church planting. Why write a sixth? Because I am frequently asked to recommend a book that provides a framework for practitioners to think through what they are doing or planning—and I have not known what to suggest. I have been hoping for the past three or four years that someone would write this book, but nothing has emerged, so finally I decided to write it myself.

I hope this book will be a resource for those who deploy and support church planters; for church leaders in inherited and emerging churches; for training institutions and mission agencies; and for church planters and members of church-planting teams.

This book is not a step-by-step guide. Each chapter (except the first) addresses a specific question, but the chapters can be read in any order. It does not deal with every practical issue, but identifies strategic questions and offers a framework for reflection, prayer, and action. It recognizes that there are many different reasons for planting churches. And it explores the dynamics of several approaches to church planting. It is not prescriptive but encourages creativity and contextual sensitivity. And it draws on experience I have gained from conversations with many church planters and more recently pioneers involved with fresh expressions and emerging churches.

I am grateful to many friends, colleagues, and former students for insights that have surely been woven into this book, even if I cannot recall who said what. I am especially grateful to those who have read through the manuscript—George Lings, Andrew Grinnell, Juliet Kilpin, Anne Wilkinson-Hayes, Trisha Dale, and my wife, Sian. Their suggestions and comments were very helpful (and they bear no responsibility for the inadequacies that remain). Particular thanks to Anne for writing the foreword and for the invitation to teach a church-planting course in Melbourne in 2007 that finally galvanized me to start writing.

1

PLANTING **CHURCHES TODAY**

In 1998, at the beginning of *Church Planting: Laying Foundations*, I wrote, "There are many reasons *not* to plant churches in Britain at the end of the twentieth century."[1] This was an odd opening gambit for a book that advocated church planting and provided theological foundations for this practice. But the church-planting movement, launched with such fanfare in 1992, was by 1998 already running into serious difficulties in Britain. Church planting was apparently not a panacea for a declining church, a guaranteed church-growth mechanism, or even "the most effective means of evangelism under heaven."[2]

Several hundred new churches had been planted between 1992 and 1998 (not the thousands anticipated, but still a cause for celebration). Most denominations had endorsed church planting as a legitimate component of their mission strategies. And many church planters had adopted a code of practice that meant church planting was now usually characterized by consultation and partnership rather than competition or unilateral action.[3] These were significant gains.

But many new churches in Britain struggled: some never gelled, and closed after a few years; others persisted but did not thrive; some grew rapidly through transfers but made few inroads in the community they were meant to serve. Galvanized by the challenge of starting twenty thousand new churches by the year 2000, church planters had focused on speed and quantity rather than quality, on how many churches to plant rather than what kind of church to plant. Observers and consultants discerned recurrent problems: superficial or nonexistent research; inadequate training and preparation; serious leadership deficiencies; going public too early; relying on attractional forms of evangelism; prioritizing church rather than mission; unrealistic expectations; and insensitivity to their cultural context.[4]

Even where new churches seemed to be doing well, two strategic defects were apparent. First, most churches were planted by entrepreneurs in their own locality with no reference to wider mission priorities, exacerbating the disparity between different regions. Second, much planting was actually "cloning" and represented missed opportunities to explore fresh ways of incarnating the gospel in a changing and increasingly diverse context.

Advocates of church planting in Britain embarked on a period of reflection. Some denominations stopped planting altogether while they reviewed their recent experience and laid firmer foundations for future initiatives. In most denominations, the rate of planting slowed to pre-1992 levels, although some younger networks continued to plant vigorously. There were occasional attempts to pool insights from several denominations and learn lessons from the past few years.[5] But between 1998 and 2005 church planting in Britain had a much lower profile.

Meanwhile, other possibilities were capturing the imagination of those who had thought church planting was on the cutting edge of mission. Some were inspired by visits to two American mega-churches, Willow Creek Community Church in Chicago and Saddleback Valley Community Church in California, introducing into British churches their "seeker-sensitive" and "purpose-driven" approaches.[6] Others became convinced that "cell church" models (imported from East Asia or Latin America) offered better prospects for making disciples.[7] More popular than either of these imports was the home-grown Alpha course,[8] which inherited from church planting the accolade of being "the most effective means of evangelism under heaven," at least in recent memory. Other "process evangelism" courses emerged, each with their distinctive elements. None of these developments required church planting.

New churches were still being planted during these years, but quietly and unobtrusively as small groups of Christians reflected on an emerging culture that seemed to require fresh expressions of faith, church, and mission. Those who discovered these initiatives and realized something new was happening labeled them "emerging church" or "fresh expressions."[9] Many of these groups choose not to use the term "church planting" to describe what they are doing.

Church-Planting RIP?

So has church planting had its day? Should we allow it to rest in peace as a courageous but flawed strategy that failed to deliver what it promised in the 1990s? Is the language of church planting still usable, or does it carry too much unhelpful baggage? In what should we invest the limited resources of a declining church in a complex culture?

"Church Planting RIP" was the title of the opening session of a church-planting course I taught in Melbourne in 2007. Those who planned this course were aware that church planting has very different resonances nowadays than it had fifteen years earlier. Before we explored the practicalities of church planting, it was necessary to justify the existence of a church-planting course.

Another challenge those who teach on church-planting courses encounter is the dearth of books on the subject to which students can be pointed. Most books on church planting in Britain were published during the first half of the 1990s and are out of print and rather dated.[10] There is a glut of books on emerging churches and fresh expressions of church, but these rarely draw on the experience of church planters or explore contemporary applications of church-planting principles and practices. From my conversations with church planters and mission strategists in several European nations, it is evident that church-planting literature is also scarce there. Even in America, where church planting remains popular, few books on the subject have been published recently (and the different context means these are of limited value in Europe).[11]

This dearth of literature is not a problem, of course, if church planting is passé and there is no way of justifying training courses on the subject. An unusual chorus of voices can be heard expressing this conviction:

- Ex-church planters whose dreams and expectations were unfulfilled and who were unsupported in their struggles.
- Denominational mission strategists who are wary of investing their diminishing resources in a strategy that fell short of what was anticipated.
- Some church leaders with a sacramental ecclesiology or, alternatively, a mega-church vision who regard church planting as unsophisticated and amateurish.
- Those who have little patience with congregational forms of church and propose more liquid and informal expressions of Christian community.
- Emerging church pioneers who regard church planting as programmatic, goals-driven, modernistic, and culturally insensitive.

But these are not the only voices. Denominational leaders in several

European nations have recently initiated church-planting strategies—strategies that can have implications for North American readers as well. The number of church-planting ventures in Britain has been increasing since 2005. New church-planting networks have emerged,[12] new church-planting courses have been developed, and the first church-planting congress in Britain since 1995 took place in 2006.[13] There are also some deliberate attempts to cross-fertilize the experience and insights of church planters and emerging churches.[14]

I remain convinced that, far from having had its day and being allowed to rest in peace, church planting is a crucial component in any mission strategy in our post-Christendom[15] Western societies. Church planting in the 1990s fell short of fulfilling its potential but, if we can learn from that decade and discover forms of church planting that are contextually sensitive, missionally attuned, and ecclesially imaginative, church planting may yet make a valuable contribution.

George Lings and I concluded the following after reviewing the very mixed results of church planting in the 1990s:

> Church planting continues to represent a vital response to the missionary challenges of contemporary culture. Indeed, unless we believe existing churches are flexible enough to embrace the changes needed to retain our present members, let alone reach out effectively to those beyond our congregations, planting is crucial. And unless we resign ourselves to mission and ministry only among the very limited proportion of the population for whom most churches seem even remotely relevant, planting is essential.[16]

I cannot imagine how we can respond to the diverse missionary challenges of the twenty-first century, or even survive as a Christian community, without the stimulus of church planting and the opportunities this offers to explore fresh ways to incarnate the gospel in a changing context.

We acknowledged, however, that only certain forms of planting would be helpful:

- Planting that reflects deeply and continually on the cultural context in which churches are planted.
- Planting that pays attention to the criticisms of those for whom present forms of church are not working.
- Planting that attempts to incarnate the gospel into areas and people groups beyond the reach of existing churches.

- Planting that refuses unthinkingly to replicate models of church or imperialistically to impose models on communities.
- Planting that encourages creative engagement with diverse communities and allows this to inspire theological and ecclesiological developments.
- Planting that is not isolationist but open to share insights with and receive critique from the wider church.

My intention in this book, then, is to provide a framework for practitioners as they set about this kind of planting. *Church Planting: Laying Foundations*, as the title indicates, focused on theological, biblical, historical, cultural, missional, and ecclesial foundations. While some of what I wrote in 1998—especially the cultural analysis and the section on emerging forms of church—has inevitably dated while the theological and missional material seem to have worn quite well. Indeed, the theological subjects on which I concentrated (*missio Dei*, incarnation, and the kingdom of God) are frequently encountered today in the emerging church conversation.

So I do not intend to review these foundational issues at length here, although they will inform the discussion of various matters in this and later chapters. The focus of this book is strategic and practical, rather than theological, addressing issues that church planters—and those who deploy them—need to consider as they assess opportunities for planting and as they embark on the planting process.

The Language of Church Planting

Is the language of "church planting" worth retaining? Can it be detached from various assumptions, expectations, strategies, priorities, and other baggage that are now regarded with understandable suspicion, and redeemed for use in a different context and a different ethos? My response to this question is evident from the title of this book, but I recognize that there are serious problems with the way the language has been used and that a period of rehabilitation will be necessary if "church planting" is again to convey images of adventure, exploration, provisionality, creativity, gentleness, and humility rather than imperialism, imposition, colonization, insensitivity, and marketing.

Why has the language of church planting fallen out of favor in some circles?

- Some are concerned that the notion of "planting" is inherently imperialistic. Even though the imagery is horticultural and indicates a natural process, the application has often been colonial—a predetermined model of church imported and imposed on a community. This is particularly so if a large planting team arrives to meet publicly as church and starts at once and without consultation.
- Some are concerned that "church planting" reinforces an ecclesiocentric approach to mission, in which the formation and growth of congregations takes precedence over other dimensions of mission. Anglican church planter Bob Hopkins has said, "We must stop starting with church," but some question whether this is feasible if we continue to use "church planting" language.
- Some are concerned that the language discourages reflection on what it means to be church today. Those who embark on planting churches can make assumptions about what they are planting based on personal preference and uncritical adoption of familiar or well-marketed models. Even those who reject a "cloning" approach may adopt an alternative model without thinking deeply enough about ecclesial or contextual issues.
- Some are concerned that the language of "church planting" encourages pioneers to establish new congregations rather than missional communities. These missional communities may have some ecclesial characteristics but are not required to carry the full weight of congregational expectations. "Fresh expressions" of church and "missional clusters" may be preferable in many contexts to new congregations.

These are significant concerns, some of which we will explore in later chapters, but I am not persuaded that rejecting the language of "church planting" is the best way to address them. For four reasons I propose that we continue to use this language while we work on issues raised by its critics.

First, the language of "church planting" has been used for many centuries to describe the process of reproducing Christian communities in diverse cultures and contexts. There is even a Latin phrase for this, *plantatio ecclesiae,* which adds gravitas if nothing else! Christians in many traditions, Catholic and Orthodox as well as Protestant, are familiar with this term, so it offers a common language with which to discuss practice and share insights. Abandoning it because we disapprove of certain forms of church planting may hinder discussions that could lead to better practice emerging.

Second, the imagery of "church planting" has deep biblical roots. Planting, watering, and harvesting are images various biblical writers employ to describe the means by which the kingdom of God advances, the good news of Jesus spreads, and churches are formed. In relation to planting churches, although the phrase itself is not used, the classic passage is probably 1 Corinthians 3:6-9, in which Paul tells the church in Corinth that he planted the seed and Apollos watered it, but God made it grow. In light of this passage we may prefer to talk of planting seeds and trusting God for what grows rather than planting churches, if this latter phrase conveys imposition and franchising, but I am loath to move too far away from this biblical imagery.

Third, alternative terms have their own limitations. The phrase "fresh expressions" is very popular in Anglican and Methodist circles in Britain but is much less familiar in other traditions and entirely unknown in many other nations. It is a useful phrase for the reasons set out in the *Mission-shaped Church* report,[17] but it is not comprehensive enough to cover all forms of church planting and is often used to describe new initiatives in existing churches that are unlikely to become new churches. The phrase "emerging church," on the other hand, has rapidly achieved international familiarity (though not in Africa, Asia, and Latin America, where church planting is rampant) and helpfully signals the issues of cultural sensitivity and contextual awareness. But the term lacks missional intentionality and may already be associated with certain styles of church in fairly limited cultural contexts. And it is surely too early for either of these newly coined phrases to replace a historic term like "church planting."[18]

Fourth, abandoning "church planting" may hinder those involved in emerging churches, fresh expressions, and other mission initiatives from drawing on the hard-won experience of church planters. However new and different these initiatives are in style, ethos, and approach, they do involve the formation of Christian communities and so have more in common with church planting than some may wish to acknowledge. Critical engagement with recent and historic forms of church planting may offer contemporary pioneers many useful insights and help them avoid unnecessarily repeating mistakes that have dogged church planters over the years.

The *Mission-shaped Church* report, which began as an investigation into church planting over the previous ten years and morphed into a discussion of fresh expressions and emerging churches, offers an attractive definition of church planting, which addresses some of the concerns expressed above:

> Church planting is the process by which a seed of the life and message of Jesus embodied by a community of Christians is immersed for mission reasons in a particular cultural or geographical context. The intended consequence is that it roots there, coming to life as a new indigenous body of Christian disciples well suited to continue in mission.[19]

The report also advocates the use of *church planting* as a verb to describe a process but expresses doubt about the legitimacy of using *church plant* as a noun. It is my intention to abide by this distinction throughout this book. But I will continue to use the language of *church planting*, although I do so aware of the concerns that have been expressed and in many places indicating how these concerns affect church planting practice.

The Scope of Church Planting

A further concern relates not to the language of church planting but to its scope. How are we to understand church planting in relation to other dimensions of mission, including evangelism, community development, interfaith and cross-cultural communication, the transformation of culture, peace-making, creation care, and missiological reflection on the interaction of gospel and culture? With the benefit of hindsight it seems church planting in the 1990s was very narrowly focused and that the theological foundation of *missio Dei* was often not in place.

Church Planting and Evangelism

The limited scope of church planting was evident from the popularity of its accolade: "the most effective means of evangelism under heaven." Not only was this claim untested by comparative research into other evangelistic activities, but few questioned the assumption that church planting was essentially a means of evangelism. British church planting was widely promoted as the primary means by which the aims of the Decade of Evangelism might be achieved. Most conferences, books, courses, and manuals on church planting endorsed an approach to mission that prioritized evangelism and dismissed other aspects of mission as secondary or even unhelpful distractions. This defective missiology can be attributed, at least in part, to the strong connection between church planting in the early 1990s and the "church growth" school of missiology.[20] But it also reflected the dominant influence of evangelicals in the church-planting movement and the extent to which these evangelicals had not yet embraced a more holistic understanding of mission.

Another reason why many emerging churches avoid the language of church planting is their distaste for this narrow understanding of mission and the evangelistic practices that accompanied it. The allergic reaction to evangelism apparent in some emerging churches and their concentration instead on other aspects of mission represents an understandable desire to distance themselves from activities perceived as inauthentic and manipulative. Uncorrected, however, this opposite missional imbalance will mean they are parasitic on the evangelizing churches they criticize and may eventually lead to their demise. Church planting may not be merely a "means of evangelism," but evangelism and church planting are both essential aspects of holistic mission.

Church Planting and "Success"

The narrow scope of church planting can also be detected in the anticipated outcomes and "success" criteria often applied to church planting in the 1990s. Church planters, sending churches, and denominational funders alike expected growing congregations, increasing financial self-sufficiency, and plenty of ecclesial activity. If these outcomes were evident, questions were rarely asked about who was involved and why, whether the new church was strategically located, how it was impacting the local community, what kind of church had been planted and why, whether indigenous leadership was emerging, or what those involved in the planting process had learned about themselves and the gospel.

But these are precisely the questions we need to ask about church planting. Many of the churches planted in the 1990s mainly attracted other Christians and so were much less evangelistically effective than is sometimes suggested. Most were in fairly affluent, well-churched suburban areas rather than low-income housing or inner-city or rural communities— not for strategic reasons but because this was within the comfort zone of those involved in the planting process—and so were able to ignore issues of poverty, deprivation, and injustice. Too many were clones of the sending churches and discouraged, wittingly or unwittingly, questions about the nature and purpose of the church that was being planted. Few seized the opportunity to engage in serious theological reflection on the culture in which they were planting and how to contextualize the gospel in the local community.

Many emerging churches and a new generation of church planters are much less reluctant to ask these probing questions. They are not operating within a "church growth" paradigm but a "cross-cultural mission" paradigm. Their missiology is multifaceted, they practice cultural exegesis and contextual theology, and they are not in thrall to imposed success criteria, goals, and time frames. Some are planting at the interface between the church and postmodern culture or into marginalized subcultures and networks. Others are planting in neighborhoods suffering the effects of multiple forms of poverty and deprivation.

Incarnational Versus Attractional

Concerns about the narrow scope of church planting also figure in the conversation about "attractional" and "incarnational" approaches to mission that has occupied some emerging churches and mission strategists recently. Critics castigate the inherited model of church, betraying its Christendom roots, as dualistic and attractional, intent on extracting people out of "the world" into a separate entity—"the church"—which becomes their new family, community, and culture and which occupies an inordinate amount of their disposable time and resources. Church planting, they argue, simply replicates this model and demands an even greater level of commitment to it. They advocate instead a missional approach to church that is incarnational and resources Christians to live out their faith in their daily lives, networks of relationships, workplaces, neighborhoods, and interest groups.[21] An incarnational approach, they insist, is relational rather than programmatic, affirming and redemptive of culture, whole-life-oriented rather than segmented into sacred and secular components, and modeled on the life and ministry of Jesus.[22]

This critique of attractional mission and dualistic forms of church is, like the rejection of manipulative evangelism, timely and insightful. Many inherited churches do operate in this way, and church planting has often exported these unhelpful models and expectations rather than questioning their legitimacy. But the terms *attractional* and *incarnational* may not be the most helpful, and it may be unnecessary to remain locked into the polarity they convey. Furthermore, not all dualism is unhealthy: the church/world dualism runs through the New Testament as the Israel/nations dualism runs through the Old Testament. The biblical story involves God calling out a distinctive community as well as dispersing it. The people of God are to be "light" as well as "salt," gathered as well as scattered, invitational as well as incarnational, attractive as well as authentic. There is a "come" as well as a "go" dimension in mission.[23]

The Christendom era, sometimes blamed for the attractional approach, can be interpreted instead as an attempt to transform an entire society incarnationally *without* the witness of a distinctive community. The outcome was a weak and compromised church rather than a sanctified culture. In our post-Christendom context, we must not make the same mistake. We need distinctive and countercultural expressions of church more than ever if we are to sustain authentic incarnational mission.

Christendom was a continent-wide and millennium-long project to incarnate the gospel in the cultures that emerged from the ruins of the Roman Empire. The Bible was translated into different languages. The gospel was explained through images that were familiar in a feudal and hierarchical society. The parish system ensured everyone had access to a local church. Christian faith was communicated via culturally attuned festivals and ceremonies, art and architecture, music and sculpture.

So what went wrong? Christendom overemphasized one aspect of incarnational mission at the expense of another. Incarnational mission means *both* identifying with our culture *and* living counterculturally. Andrew Walls argues that authentic mission involves "the indigenizing principle" and "the pilgrim principle."[24] The missionary task is to encourage the emergence of indigenous churches in every culture, rather than imposing alien forms of church or extracting converts from their culture. But it is also to represent and embody the story and purposes of God, encouraging converts to discern and challenge dimensions of their own culture that are not consistent with the values of God's kingdom.

Christendom was strong on the indigenizing principle but weak on the pilgrim principle. The gospel was inculturated but compromised. Christendom meant the domestication of the church rather than the transformation of the empire. We must be very careful lest we slip into this distorted understanding of incarnational mission. We need to identify with our social and cultural context, affirm all we can, and avoid unnecessary dualism, but we also need to offer and live out countercultural values rooted in the story that shapes us as the people of God.

Perhaps, then, the issue is not best represented as attractional versus incarnational but as attractional versus "extractional" or incarnational versus "impositional." A missional church will be wary of extracting people from their community and creating a ghetto, but it will want to attract people to Jesus by the way that it (albeit imperfectly) embodies the values of God's kingdom. A missional church will recognize that few today will respond to invitations to church events, so its priority will be to equip its members to incarnate the gospel in all areas of society. But a truly missional church will be both incarnational and attractional, culturally attuned and countercultural. Bryan Stone insists that ecclesiology and evangelism cannot be separated: "the embodiment *is* the heralding; the medium *is* the message; incarnation *is* invitation."[25] Incarnational mission is energized and authenticated by attractive churches that are, in Lesslie Newbigin's oft-quoted phrase, the "hermeneutic of the gospel."[26]

Belonging, Believing, and Behaving

A related issue, which is much more familiar today than in the 1990s (although the reality was already present), is the complex interaction in a post-Christendom culture between believing, belonging, and behaving. Many emerging churches encourage "belonging before believing" and are wary of erecting boundaries between those who are in the church and those who are not. They are critical of inherited churches and church planters who continue to work with such boundaries. In practice, however, if not always in theory, many church planters have operated in a similar way to emerging churches, sometimes to the disquiet of their sponsors, especially if the behaving component lags too far behind the belonging and believing components.

This may be interpreted as a further expression of an incarnational rather than attractional (or better extractional) stance, though it could be argued that this is really an attractional strategy and that a truly incarnational approach (if Jesus is the model) will engage more robustly with beliefs and behavior. However we understand this, it will be some time before the fruits of this approach are seen. Will belonging eventually lead to believing? If not, what kind of church will emerge, and will it be sustainable? But many church planters today operate with a "belonging before believing" model and are hesitant about claiming members for their new church—to the frustration of denominational leaders who want figures on their report forms—preferring to celebrate the relationships the new church has in the community and its influence for good there.

The scope of church planting, then, must not be narrowly construed as setting up church services in new locations. The calling of church planters is to incarnate the gospel in the diverse neighborhoods and networks that comprise contemporary society and to develop contextually appropriate forms of mission, community, and worship. The formation of a distinct congregation that meets regularly in a designated place may be much further down the track than church planters have often assumed. It may also look very different from the expectations of those who deploy and support them—and from the expectations of the planters themselves. Church planting begins with discovering what God is doing in a community and joining in.

The Context of Church Planting

This discussion about the scope of church planting leads naturally into the final issue we will consider in this chapter. Church planting does not take place in a vacuum but in specific cultural and social contexts, which are themselves located within historical and global developments. This has significant implications for a practitioner's resource book, which are not easily resolved. Any attempt at presenting generic principles needs to be surrounded by caveats if it is not to be misleading, whereas covering multiple contexts one after the other soon becomes tendentious.

Church planting in new housing developments is substantially different from planting in traditional rural villages and from planting in multiethnic, inner-city communities and from planting in monochrome government housing and from planting in clubs in city centers and from planting in affluent suburban areas, and so on. Some of the church-planting literature in the 1990s was sensitive to these differences, but much assumed that the same principles applied anywhere and gave little attention to contextual issues. Since the majority of church planting was taking place in suburban or similar cultural contexts, this was usually the context church-planting books assumed as normative. Similarly, as most church planting in the early 1990s focused on geographical communities, books and training courses generally offered guidance on church planting in neighborhoods.

These assumptions and choices were understandable. However, they had the unintended but missionally damaging consequence of reinforcing the prejudice toward planting in such settings and disempowering those who were considering planting elsewhere. This then created a vicious circle when church planters who were inspired and helped by these resources planted successfully in suburban communities and wrote further books about their experience, reinforcing still more strongly the message that this was where church planters should go if they wanted to succeed.

Church planters determined to operate in other contexts have strug-

gled to apply insights from these books or have concluded that the principles
they teach do not work. Where, until very recently, did a church planter find
resources on planting into social networks rather than local neighborhoods?
Where are the resources on cross-cultural planting in areas with large other-
faith communities? How does a small church-planting team draw on training
material that assumes far more resources and personnel than they have?
What guidance is available for those wanting to work ecumenically to plant
churches in rural communities or new housing developments? Some inner-
city church planters have discarded their church-planting books in despair,
turning instead to resources produced by cross-cultural church planters on
other continents, with whom they feel greater affinity and whose experience
and guidance seem easier to apply.

In a diverse and rapidly evolving culture, we will need a range of new
resources on church planting in various contexts if we are to equip emerging
church planters properly. No one book or training program will do, nor
will any one consultant or trainer have sufficient expertise. Any resources
will need to be updated regularly if they are not to become obsolete.

An option that was not readily available in the early 1990s is to
disseminate and update resources via websites and blogs. Undoubtedly the
emerging church has sustained momentum, encouraged new initiatives,
and shared insights widely through these media, although the many books
written by and about emerging churches suggest that books will remain an
important resource in this ongoing conversation. The online knowledge
bank Share, which Fresh Expressions is developing in partnership with
Church Army, offers resources that many church planters will find helpful
and might indicate the way forward for the development of a comparable
church-planting online resource.[27]

This book, then, is not an attempt to do justice to these multiple church-
planting contexts. But it does take seriously this contextual diversity and
tries to reflect this in the resources it offers to practitioners. There are, I
believe, many transferable principles and skills, so much of what follows
will be generic in nature, but there will also be numerous cautions scattered
throughout the text, and indications that these principles and skills need
to be applied very differently in different situations. In particular, I have
tried to spell out the implications of using other models of church planting
than the mother/daughter model that was dominant in the 1990s and in
most church-planting literature of that era. And I have borne in mind the
likelihood that some practitioners are working in social networks rather
than geographical neighborhoods.

One further question concerns the wider historical and global developments that form the backdrop to specific contexts within which new churches are planted. Is it legitimate to write a book on church planting or any aspect of mission without reflecting on these? But how can these be integrated into a book for practitioners that is primarily concerned with strategic issues and the process of church planting? The simple answer is that they cannot be without producing an enormous tome and becoming eclectic and simplistic—choosing elements the author believes are significant and skating quickly over the surface of these. I have no intention of falling into this trap.

There are many resources available to church planters who want to keep appraised of wider cultural and social developments. So this element is omitted, as are several other important subjects—all of them relevant to church planters—including principles of community development, models of evangelism, making disciples, the spiritual life of a church planter, and the practice of corporate worship. On these subjects too there are many other resources available, so there is no need to feature them in this book.[28]

But if the cultural context affects the kinds of churches we plant, it also influences those who plant them. For some church planters (especially those who disown this term), this chapter has already confirmed their fears that this book is going to complicate things and deflect them from simply praying for God's guidance and inspiration. For others, who are interested in what emerges organically and are very suspicious of anything that remotely resembles planning, the following chapters look much too organized and schematic.

But this is not a manual or step-by-step guide to church planting. It does not pretend to be comprehensive, but attempts to address many of the questions church planters and those who deploy and support them ask—or should be asking. It is not an alternative to prayer, as I hope will be evident in many chapters, but fuel for prayerful discernment. Nor do I want to take the mystery or the fun out of church planting. But I have witnessed too many poorly planned ventures fail and have sat with too many heartbroken practitioners to endorse the idea that prayer precludes the need for planning or to accept that organizational and organic approaches to pioneering are incompatible.

● ● ●

Questions for Further Reflection

Each chapter will end with some questions intended to stimulate further reflection as well as sum up some of the key points.

1. How much do you know about the recent history of church planting in your country? Would it be worth your while finding out more? If so, how would you go about this?

2. Is the language of "church planting" worth retaining? If not, what language would you suggest instead? How do you respond to the definition of church planting quoted from the *Mission-shaped Church* report?

3. How would you respond to those who argue that evangelism should be the priority for church planters and that other aspects of mission must wait until a church is formed?

4. If you are involved in church planting, what does "success" mean to you? What do you think it means to those who support, fund, or pray for you?

5. In what contexts do you think you would or would not thrive as a church planter? How should you weigh your preferred mission context against the strategic priorities?

6. Which of the following features of the wider cultural context do you regard as the most significant for church planters: consumerism, secularization, individualism, a surveillance society, the therapeutic culture, the culture of violence, tribalism, alternative spiritualities, post-Christendom, the communications revolution, interfaith relations, post-commitment culture, spectatorism, globalization, urbanization or postmodernity? Or what would your own list contain?

2

PLANTING **CHURCHES: WHY?**

Why do mission agencies, churches, and denominations decide to plant churches? What are the motives and expectations of church planters? Why are new churches and new kinds of church emerging? Why are hundreds of churches creating fresh expressions of church? What stirs the imagination and energizes the commitment of the pioneers? What does it take to move from vision to reality?

There are many different, though often overlapping, reasons for planting churches. Most people involved point to the leading of the Holy Spirit, mediated through Scripture, prophecy, or prayer, as the dominant factor. But this conviction of God's call to action is usually accompanied by some understanding of why a church should be planted. Most motives are honorable, although questionable motives are also sometimes evident. But there may be different expectations in relation to what kind of church should be planted, how the planting process will be evaluated, and what impact it will have on participants and on others.

I have encountered many situations where divergent expectations have caused confusion and strained relationships, distorting or jeopardizing the planting process. These different perceptions are difficult to integrate once the initiative is underway, so it is worth taking time to clarify motives and anticipated outcomes early in the process.

This chapter surveys many reasons for planting churches. It does not rank them in order of validity or missional significance but affirms and celebrates the scope and potential of church planting. Church planters and those who deploy them may find it helpful to work through this chapter and reflect on which reason or combination of reasons (including others not mentioned here) motivates them. Some sections also highlight strategic issues that are particularly relevant to certain forms of church planting.

Planting Churches in New Housing Developments

Although the overall population of Britain and much of the Western world is at present increasing only slowly, changing patterns of family life and the increasing number of single-person households have put huge pressure on the available housing stock. Recent projections have suggested a much greater increase in the overall population within the next twenty-five years. Consequently in Britain there are plans to build hundreds of thousands of homes, including whole new towns, especially in the south and east of England. Such housing developments are not unprecedented: several new towns have been built in the past few decades. But the rate of construction seems likely to increase. New towns are being built on "green field" sites, despite environmental concerns and local opposition, and many towns and villages are expanding beyond their historic boundaries.

I have participated in several consultations about planting churches in such communities and have spent time with many church planters working in these contexts. This seems to be the least controversial reason for church planting. Denominational representatives will debate many ecclesial and logistical issues (often at great length), but there is widespread agreement that church planting is essential in new housing developments. Although any housing development is technically within an existing Anglican parish, most Anglicans agree with their ecumenical conversation-partners that in practice this community is outside the scope of existing churches.

Church planting in new housing developments happens in three main ways:

- Christians moving into the community discover one another and decide to start a new church in a home or community building.
- A nearby church, especially if it has members moving into the new community, plants a house group and grows a church from this.
- Ecumenical discussions produce a plan to establish a church in the community and initiate negotiations with the developers for land on which to place a church building. There are different forms of ecumenical church planting: establishing a formal partnership from the outset; one denomination taking the lead and inviting others to join in; sharing a building but holding separate services; denominational cells in a multidenominational church; or grass-roots cooperation without a formal ecumenical partnership.

Especially in larger housing developments, all three kinds of initiatives may take place in the same period, with or without much consultation. Sometimes, once they become aware of each other, there is sufficient commonality of vision and mutual trust for resources to be pooled. Quite often, though, this outcome is frustrated by disagreements over theology or ecclesiology, vested interests, or personality clashes.

What issues should we consider when planting churches in new housing developments?

- How quickly will the new homes be built and how reliable are the projections of the developers? I visited a church planter who had moved into a development area during its first phase but was frustrated when construction stalled and he had few neighbors. He eventually gave up and moved out.

- What, if any, community buildings will be provided and at what stage (developers tend for economic reasons to build these last)? There may be no suitable meeting place for a church if numbers are too large for a home. The most popular solution I have encountered is a strategically placed Portacabin, though others have braved a dentist's waiting room or decided simply to meet in several home-sized groups.

- Will planting ecumenically be worth the complications? There are some obvious advantages: greater resources of personnel and finance; an opportunity to avoid importing old divisions into a new community; and a single entity for developers to deal with (they will often refuse to negotiate with more than one church). But ecumenical church planting has been plagued with difficulties: it has often been slow, cumbersome, rancorous, and lacking missional focus. Recently, though, I have encountered ecumenical initiatives operating with a much lighter touch as denominational representatives have trusted each other and have urged local Christians to get on with starting a new church rather than insisting on resolving all the constitutional issues first.

- What will the church's role be in this housing development? Some planters focus on evangelism and starting services, making friends and offering practical help to attract people into the church. Others explore opportunities for the church to manage community facilities or partner with other agencies in providing community resources. I was deeply impressed by one church planter who moved in very early and became the community networker and a highly valued contact point for new residents.

Planting Churches in Areas with Growing Populations

New churches are needed on "brown field" as well as "green field" sites. In many urban areas, industrial and commercial buildings are being converted into homes; new houses are being built on former wasteland; and population density is increasing as properties are occupied by larger families. Sometimes there are already churches there, perhaps several of different traditions and denominations, so church planting may be unnecessary. A better mission strategy may be to support and strengthen their witness and ministry. But the amount of population growth may be enough to justify the planting of new churches, especially if the existing churches are some distance geographically or culturally from the growing points in the community.

The initiative and resources for this kind of church planting may come from the following:

- A local church with sufficient personnel to establish a new congregation or fresh expression of church in the area where the population is growing.
- A church elsewhere in the city that feels some cultural affinity to people who are moving into the area or growing in numbers there. Examples I am familiar with include an upper-middle-class Anglican church planting into a gentrified, gated community on the riverfront and an African Baptist church planting into an area where African families were increasing in number.
- A mission agency deploying a church-planting team after researching the area and consulting with existing churches.

Two significant caveats should be registered before embarking on church planting for this reason. First, those responsible for planting another church in this area should do all they can to avoid weakening other churches and to discourage transfers from those churches. Second, if the new church serves a different section of the community than is present in the older churches, old and new churches alike face the challenge of discovering ways to transcend rather than mirror cultural or social fragmentation. How we address these issues will reveal much about our motives and expectations.

Planting Churches More Locally

Even where the population is relatively stable, a church-planting policy may be the most effective way of incarnating the gospel and serving the community. A common scenario is where a church recognizes that there is a neighborhood or low-income housing project nearby with which it has fewer connections than the rest of its "patch." The church may have known this for some time, or a community survey may reveal the situation. Sometimes the few church members who do live there urge the church to get involved locally.

There may be physical, mental, or cultural barriers preventing stronger links between the church and this section of the community. Main roads, railway lines, parks, and rivers may not appear to be insurmountable obstacles, but community surveys reveal the "mental maps" that often restrict people's normal movements.[1] In communities that are heavily dependent on public transport, bus routes and venues within easy walking distance are essential for any agency offering resources or inviting participation. I recently visited a couple planting a church in a government housing project only a few hundred yards from the church building where they were members. The barrier here was cultural—the very expensive cars in the church parking lot each Sunday intimidated those who lived in the housing project.

During the 1990s, many churches planted new churches within their community to bring church closer to where people lived, shopped, worked, or relaxed and to discover more culturally appropriate ways of engaging in mission. "More effective penetration of the parish" was one of the reasons given at a conference in the early 1990s for Anglican church planting,[2] reflecting the fact that many urban parishes contain a much higher (and more varied) population than when parish boundaries were drawn. The term "saturation church planting" became familiar in the 1990s to those influenced by the international DAWN organization, which advocated planting a church within reach of every thousand to fifteen hundred people.[3]

In the previous chapter, we noted that many emerging churches are focusing on networks rather than neighborhood. Especially in urban areas, many people travel long distances to shop, meet friends, visit family, go clubbing, play or watch sports, and participate in a range of interest groups. Where they live is only one small, maybe quite unimportant, component in their network of relationships. Planting churches into social networks will be an important dimension in any contemporary mission strategy. But in some parts of the country, especially in poorer communities, people may have few networks beyond the local neighborhood. Understanding how local communities work and planting churches more locally is also essential.

Planting Churches to Replace Churches That Have Closed

During the 1990s, despite the surge in church planting, many more churches closed than opened. The persistent decline in church membership in Britain over several decades has resulted in many churches becoming nonviable and either amalgamating or ceasing to exist. In some areas, despite closures, there are still many churches, and the need to plant more churches is not apparent. Indeed, in some communities there are too many churches competing for too few people—a result of excessive church-planting efforts and ingrained denominationalism in an earlier era. Some judicious "church pruning" would be helpful in these situations.

In other areas, churches have closed because of social and economic changes. Declining employment opportunities may have resulted in a diminishing population, which can no longer sustain the churches it once could. Or a burgeoning "holiday homes" market may have decimated the local community, replacing them with a transient population with other weekend priorities than church attendance. Not every church that closes needs to be replaced.

But, especially in inner-city and rural areas, closure may mean that communities are now seriously under-churched and that church planting is essential. In Urban Expression and our sister agency, Rural Expression,[4] we use the unwieldy term *under-churched* to avoid giving unnecessary offense to denominations that claim national coverage through their parish system (especially the Church of England and the Church of Scotland). Our experience has been that many parish priests readily accept that their parish is under-churched and have welcomed the proposal of a church-planting team. We will continue to use this term rather than the more threatening term *unchurched*.

However, at some point—and hopefully soon—the myth of national coverage will surely need to be exposed as a vestige of the Christendom era. Anglican church planting has been hamstrung long enough by ecclesiastical protectionism. Bolting together many rural parishes and burning out overstretched parish priests is an unwise pastoral strategy and no kind of mission strategy. And many parish priests in inner-city areas have long since effectively abandoned whole swathes of the population in order to retain their own sanity.

If we plant churches to replace those that have closed, we should not assume that these will necessarily be in the same precise locations, which may now be inappropriate and one of the reasons the church closed. Changing road systems, for instance, have made some church buildings almost inaccessible. These may be contexts in which we should consider fresh expressions of church, although in some rural and inner-city communities, ecclesial innovation may be suspect rather than attractive.

Planting Churches to Offset Ineffective Churches

Churches are sometimes planted in communities in which there are already churches that, in the judgment of the church planters or those who deploy them, are ineffective and contributing little or nothing to the task of mission.

This is a controversial and problematic motive that critics of church planting may seize upon as evidence that church planting is arrogant, competitive, and insensitive. Although church planting in the 1990s was far more consultative and cooperative than previously, there were still too many instances of church-planting teams arriving unannounced in an area and, explicitly or implicitly, writing off existing churches as irrelevant. Sadly I still encounter church planters who feel no compunction about riding roughshod over the hurt feelings of long-serving ministers and passing judgment on congregations they have not met, and whose notion of "consultation" is distributing invitations to the launch event of a new church.

But we must beware of going too far in the opposite direction and becoming sentimental and uncritical. It is dangerous and irresponsible to interpret the existence of a church building or congregation as evidence that the mission of God is advancing. Judgmental attitudes must be avoided, but we may need to exercise judgment for the sake of under-churched communities. Churches that are inward-looking, morally compromised, narrow-minded, unwelcoming, culturally irrelevant or spiritually moribund (whatever their size, style, or theology) may not be incarnating the gospel authentically in their community and may need to be discounted when we are considering church planting.

This is not a judgment that we dare reach lightly or from a distance. More may be going on beneath the surface than is apparent; the church may be engaged in aspects of mission that we value less highly than we should; and, by the grace of God, churches can change. And if we do plant a new church nearby, maintaining a humble and open attitude rather than conveying disdain, this new church might even be a catalyst for renewal in the older church.

Planting Churches to Disciple New Christians

While some church planting is motivated by a desire to evangelize a neighborhood or network, there are also examples of church planting that attempt to nurture, encourage and disciple those who have responded to evangelistic initiatives. Sometimes such church planting is reluctant rather than enthusiastic and initiated only after heart searching and exhausting other alternatives. My own early experience of church planting was motivated in part by trying unsuccessfully to integrate some very new Christians into other churches that were culturally too distant; I realized they needed a different kind of church.

A difficulty some churches using the Alpha course encounter is a mismatch between the ethos and spirituality of the course and that of the sponsoring church. Though the course may have been advertised as an opportunity to see what church is like, the differences between the course and regular church services are glaringly obvious. After struggling but failing to persuade those who have come to faith in Christ through Alpha to join the church, some have planted a different kind of church that resonates better with the ethos of the course and is better able to help new believers become disciples.

Evangelistic agencies and youth mission agencies have also planted churches recently to care for and disciple new and young Christians. Their deep reluctance over many years to take this step was partly so as not to seem to be competing with the churches from whom they drew support, and partly so as not to be distracted from what they saw as their primary calling. Some have concluded, however, that the culture gap between most churches and many new Christians, especially postmodern teenagers, is too great to bridge, so church planting is the only option.

Planting Churches to Reach Unchurched People

Some churches are planted to engage with people at an earlier stage than when they have become Christians. There are problems with the terms *unchurched* and *dechurched* (not least their implicit assumptions that church involvement rather than faith in Christ is the primary issue and that being "churched" is normal in post-Christendom culture). But these terms highlight an increasingly significant mission concern: in previous generations the vast majority of people in Western societies had some connection with the churches and were perceived by those churches as "latent Christians" to be wooed back and urged to become "active Christians." Relatively few had no understanding of the Christian faith and no church links at all (although in some poor urban communities this was more often the case). But today in the West the dechurched sector of the population is shrinking rapidly and the unchurched sector is expanding. Many churches are reasonably effective at engaging with the dechurched but have little clue how to reach the unchurched.

Some church planters have become convinced that the best, maybe the only, way to reach unchurched people is to plant churches that operate with very different assumptions and develop different approaches toward those who have no prior experience of church and not the slightest interest in joining existing churches. I know two people who were ministers of thriving churches but who are now self-supporting church planters. They are not dismissive of their previous churches or of the ability of these churches to reach dechurched people, but they did not believe their churches could reach unchurched people. Longing to do so, both embarked on courageous pioneering ministries that are incarnational rather than invitational.

Unchurched people can be found in all socioeconomic groups and all regions, but the greatest concentration of these is in poor urban communities. Inner-city church planters may, therefore, be pioneering on behalf of others as they explore fresh ways of engaging with individuals and families who may be two or three generations away from any kind of church involvement. Denominations and church-planting agencies may be tempted to avoid the challenge of these communities, but an authentic missionary strategy will surely prioritize them.

Planting Churches to Relocate and Redistribute Christians

A common criticism of church planting is that new churches often take Christians from other churches rather than reaching people with no church connections. "Transfer growth" is dismissed as both illegitimate and misleading in any attempt to evaluate the success of church-planting strategies. Undoubtedly many new churches have grown in this way, as members of nearby churches have decamped in search of a more congenial expression of church or to find fresh opportunities for mission and ministry. Some church planters have been very wary of this dynamic and have acted responsibly, consulting with other church leaders and agreeing with them how to process would-be transfers. Others have refused to accept transfers from nearby churches, fearing distraction from their mission. Sadly some have encouraged transfers without consultation, usually because they are convinced their church is more authentic than others, and have wreaked havoc in other churches.

However, redistributing Christians is a legitimate reason for church planting. A serious problem in Britain, from a strategic and missional perspective, is that Christians are very unevenly distributed across the country. In some areas we are numerous (especially in southern provincial towns and in suburban areas). There are other areas (especially in the inner city, some rural communities and in housing projects) where we are thin on the ground. The difference can be as much as 12 to 15 percent of the population in one area compared to 0.5 to 1 percent in another. In inner urban areas, this has been exacerbated by the flight of Christians out of the cities over several decades and the closure of the churches they once attended. There has been movement in the opposite direction more recently through the gentrification of inner-city communities; and the planting of many vibrant and growing churches in diverse ethnic communities has changed the face of Christianity in London and some other cities. But the imbalance persists, hindering our mission and bringing into question the scope and depth of our discipleship.

Church planting is one way to relocate and redistribute Christians into areas with fewer Christians, significant social needs and many mission opportunities. But this will happen only if larger churches in well-churched areas encourage and release their members to respond to this challenge rather than planting yet another suburban church nearby. This is a more demanding form of church planting: it will mean moving home, learning to live in a different community, rethinking issues of gospel and culture, reimagining church and mission, maybe even learning a new language. Stimulating and supporting this kind of church planting has been a priority for mission agencies such as NEO, Eden, and Urban Expression.[5]

Planting Churches to Engage with Emerging Culture

However reluctant emerging churches may be to label their activities "church planting," many of them represent attempts to engage with shifts in contemporary culture and to find authentic ways of incarnating the gospel in the culture that is emerging. The diffuse nature of the emerging church "conversation" and the diverse expressions of church that are taking shape indicate that there is ongoing discussion about the characteristics of this emerging culture and how the gospel intersects with it. Although postmodernity is by far the most influential conversation partner, other features of contemporary Western society also inform this debate. Implicit— and sometimes explicit—within this conversation is the suggestion that inherited forms of church have become locked into patterns and ways of thinking derived from the Christendom era and the fading culture of modernity.

The emerging church is still emerging, so it is too early to assess its engagement with the emerging culture. But we can note some common themes and convictions:[6]

- There is no expectation that one new model of church will emerge. In a plural and rapidly changing culture, many expressions of church will be needed.
- The increasing culture gap between the churches and the rest of society needs to be closed, which will mean churches that are less dualistic and more open-edged.
- There are rich resources from past eras and in many Christian traditions that can be reclaimed and recontextualized to nourish Christians today.
- There is very little interest in numerical growth as a measure of success (this way of thinking is regarded as typically modernist); authenticity and cultural resonance are more significant indicators of faithfulness.
- There are deeper issues to explore than the shape and style of churches, not least the contextualizing of the gospel, the nature of discipleship, and the parameters of mission.

Observers and critics note that most emerging churches are currently reaching only those who are already Christians, albeit often no longer involved in other churches, rather than those with no prior Christian faith. Others remark that they generally emphasize cultural attunement rather than being countercultural—some worry about this, but others regard this as an appropriate first stage for missional communities engaging with an emerging culture. Some critics also question whether postmodernity is as significant as is claimed and ask whether Western societies really are experiencing a radical culture shift. Many in the emerging church, though, are convinced that it is better to surf the incoming breakers than to find ourselves washed up on the shore as the tide recedes.

This new wave of church planting coincided with the period of soul searching prompted by the stalling of the 1990s church-planting movement. Whatever other factors influenced its emergence, the urgency of the question, What kind of church? or more fundamentally, What do we mean by church? was influential. Some earlier church planters had wrestled with these questions and had reflected on the implications of various cultural factors for the churches they were planting, but the emerging church represents a deeper level of engagement with such issues. Most church planters I meet today, whether or not they identify with the emerging church, are increasingly sensitive to cultural dynamics.

Planting Churches to Embody Ecclesial Convictions

But not all church planters ascribe as much significance to cultural and contextual factors. Some want above all to embody certain convictions in the churches they plant. Numerous house churches have been planted in the past forty years to embody convictions about the role of charismatic gifts, apostolic ministry, and nonreligious Christianity. New networks or denominations have resulted (including Pioneer, New Frontiers, and Salt and Light). In the past few years, a new wave of house churches has emerged, expressing the conviction that church should be simple, participative, and easily reproducible. Other church-planting movements with clear ecclesial convictions include Vineyard and the Jesus Army. And a few churches have recently been planted as "peace churches" or to embody Anabaptist convictions.[7]

Planting churches to embody ecclesial convictions is not, of course, a new phenomenon. The early history of most denominations is largely characterized by this form of church planting. Baptist churches were planted in the seventeenth century because their views on religious liberty, church government, and the meaning of baptism were deemed important enough to require the planting of new churches. New denominations, including Elim and the Assemblies of God, emerged in the first half of the twentieth century in response to the conviction of many Christians about (among other things) baptism in the Spirit and divine healing.

What begins as an expression of deep convictions, however, can soon give way to fixed and unreflective ecclesial patterns. Some church planters simply assume that the model of church they embrace is nonnegotiable and transferable, with only minimal adjustments, into any context. They are wary of paying attention to cultural or contextual factors, not only because this slows down the process and risks loss of momentum, but also because they are committed to ecclesial principles and practices they regard as biblical and essential. Furthermore, although some criticize them for adopting a franchising approach to church planting, they argue that they are achieving more than most supposedly culture-sensitive emerging churches (depending, of course, on which measurement of "success" is used).

Denominational leaders propose from time to time that a new church representing their own ecclesial convictions and bearing their label should be planted in towns lacking this particular brand. If this proposal is based on research and consultation that confirms the need for more churches there and if it is motivated by a missional desire to incarnate another expression of the gospel, this may be appropriate. If it is motivated primarily by denominational expansionism, we need to ask serious questions.

We may have similar questions about some of the less missional emerging churches, in which the primary motivation appears to be creating a community that meets the needs and expresses the values of its founding members and their close friends. Some argue that authenticity is essential and that others will in time join a healthy community that enjoys being together. But there is a danger of such groups postponing mission indefinitely and prioritizing their own ecclesial preferences. They may function as therapy groups for ex-members of other churches who have become disillusioned and burned out, but will they at some point move beyond this and engage with others?

All church planters carry with them some ecclesial convictions—nobody starts with an entirely blank canvas—and these convictions are not to be lightly overturned. But I have been particularly impressed by church planters I have met who are prepared to question their convictions, wrestle with contextual issues for the sake of mission, and engage in an ongoing two-way conversation between their context and their convictions.[8] I have been even more impressed by church planters who have planted a church that does not suit their own preferences but which they are convinced is a more appropriate expression of the gospel in their context.

Planting Churches into Specific Cultures and Networks

We have already mentioned the need for church planting into both neighborhoods and networks, and during the 1990s there were already examples of churches being planted into networks of relationships rather than neighborhoods. In the past few years there have been many more examples of such church planting, including the following:[9]

- Workplace churches that aim to incarnate the gospel and encourage discipleship in the places where people work, rather than where they live. Recognizing that many people spend much of their time and invest much of their creative energy at work, and have little of either left after commuting home, these churches provide friendship and support, and resources that are rarely available in neighborhood churches, for those who see their workplace as the main mission context.

- Churches planted in clubs, leisure centers, cafés, arts cooperatives, restaurants, and various other places to which people go or belong not because of where they live but because of who they know and what interests they share. These churches are often expressions of the incarnational rather than attractional approach to mission discussed in the previous chapter. They require of church planters very different skills and priorities.

- Churches emerging within subcultures that have not felt welcome in existing churches and know that their taste in music, dress code, passions, interests, and way of life are not affirmed in most churches. Examples include Goth churches, churches among travelers, in the sci-fi community, the surfing community, the homeless community, and many more.

- Churches planted in various ethnic communities that enable people to worship in their own heart language, share their faith with other members of the community in culturally sensitive ways, and become disciples of Jesus without denigrating their own culture. London has witnessed an explosion of such churches in the past twenty years.

- Hidden communities of people from Muslim backgrounds who are followers of Jesus but choose to remain within their family, cultural, and mosque environment. Such communities, part of an "insider movement" that resists the need to become Westernized in order to follow Jesus, are proliferating in various nations within and beyond Europe.[10]

This practice of planting customized churches around the lifestyles, interests, aspirations, needs, cultural backgrounds, and meeting places of quite narrowly defined groups has, not surprisingly, attracted criticism[11]— to whom one might respond a little mischievously that many churches already appear to be customized to suit white, middle-aged, middle-class churchgoers who sing hymns from the nineteenth century and speak a language that is impenetrable to outsiders.

However, there are serious questions to be asked about these initiatives. Is it legitimate to plant churches that are homogeneous by design (rather than default)? Although in theory anyone may be welcome, in practice they are unlikely to connect with many outside their specific remit. Does this matter? Is such a homogeneous mission strategy contrary to the gospel we proclaim of the Christ who broke down the dividing wall of hostility between different communities?[12] Are homogeneous communities places where discipleship is fostered if we do not learn to relate to those who are different from us?[13] What about the effect on families whose members belong to different churches? Are customized churches sustainable, and does this matter? What about the next generation, which may not want to belong to the same kind of church as their parents? Do customized churches risk straying into syncretism and ethical compromise in an attempt to contextualize the gospel? Or can church planters humbly acknowledge their limitations and be realistic about who they can and cannot reach? Can partnerships be forged between these churches and other different kinds of churches for the benefit of all?

These are valid concerns and questions that church planters and those who deploy and support them will want to consider carefully, before any initiatives begin and as they take shape. But it may be that only such cross-cultural church planting and focused churches of this kind will be effective in connecting with various subcultures that are distant from the prevailing cultural norms of most churches and capable of incarnating the gospel in ways that make sense to them. And it may be in these frontier situations that we learn more about the grace of God, the power of the gospel, our own blinkered views, and the ways we too have compromised with social norms and the dominant culture.

Planting Fresh Expressions of Church

It is clear that in a diverse and increasingly customized society, where we expect a range of options in all spheres of life, no one church suits everyone. Whether or not we think this cultural obsession with multiple options is helpful (or even if what purports to be choice really is), we need to consider how to respond to this aspect of our culture. We might decide to challenge it by resisting the temptation to develop diverse churches. Or we might judge that such diversity is an appropriate contextual response—although, as indicated above, how such churches relate to others is important in light of the biblical vision of a reconciling gospel and a united church.[14]

Of course, there are already in most urban and suburban areas many kinds of churches, some of which were deliberately designed to be different from others in the locality (but there are fewer options in rural communities).

Church planting enables us to create new churches that offer an even wider range of options: large and small, formal and informal, drawing on various traditions, with diverse styles of leadership, approaches to mission, patterns of worship, and expressions of community. Many church planters believe that creating a fresh expression of church will enable them to connect with people who do not find existing options congenial.

Since 2000, there has been an explosion of fresh expressions of church, especially within Anglican and Methodist circles. Some of these fresh expressions are built around existing groups or activities in church buildings and are attempts to move away from the model of expecting people to transition from these groups to the main church services. Instead, these groups and activities are invested with ecclesial significance and develop into fresh expressions of church. Other fresh expressions are new initiatives, within or beyond the church premises, that hope to engage with sections of the community with which the church has few connections. In his *Encounters on the Edge* series, George Lings has told the stories of many creative, fresh expressions, within which the various motives noted in this chapter are apparent.[15]

Relatively few fresh expressions have yet achieved full ecclesial status (and some may not want this), but many churches now have two or more "ecclesial communities" that represent their desire to express the gospel in ways that make sense to a wider range of people. Time will tell whether these fresh expressions will evolve into new churches, withdraw back into the churches that initiated them, or persist as a flexible and multifaceted approach to church and mission.

How do "fresh expressions" differ from "emerging churches"? Both are recent phenomena and are still evolving, so this question is difficult to answer. There is considerable overlap and the term used may depend on the preferences of those involved rather than differentiating characteristics. But it may be fair to suggest that many emerging churches have looser links (or no link at all) with inherited churches, whereas fresh expressions are usually connected in some way with inherited churches. Martin Robinson has proposed three categories: church planting within denominations, church planting on the edge of church, and church planting beyond the churches.[16] The latter two categories may equate roughly (though only roughly) to fresh expressions and emerging churches.

This may be the place to note an unintended consequence of church planting, rather than a motive for planting or an expected outcome. Research indicates that, as well as transfers from other churches and people discovering Christian faith for the first time, a significant proportion of those who join newly planted churches were once members of a church but had not been there for some time (often many years).[17] Why do they join a new church? There is perhaps something attractive about a church with no history that offers a chance to start again. I recall sitting next to a woman at the first meeting of a new church in London who told me she had dropped out of church life years ago but had discovered this new church within her low-income housing community. She saw this as God giving her a second chance to follow Jesus.

Church planters who are aware of this dynamic may encourage it, looking out for former church members and inviting them to make a fresh commitment. But this may be a distraction from the primary purpose of the new church. The planting team may become embroiled in demanding pastoral ministry as they counsel those who often bring with them unresolved issues and considerable pain. I have talked with church planters who deeply regretted allowing their focus to shift from mission in the community—not least because many of those they had spent hours with soon became disenchanted with their new church and left once more.

Planting Churches to Pioneer on Behalf of the Church

There are limits to the kind of changes, the extent of change, and the speed of change that we can introduce into inherited churches without causing pastoral damage. This may be deeply frustrating for those who are eager to pioneer new ideas, but wise church leaders recognize the danger signs and seek a balance between innovation and conservation. Churches, like all institutions and communities, cannot cope with constant or excessive change. Evolution, rather than revolution, is normally required.

But in a time of rapid and disorientating culture shift and in the context of declining and closing churches, will evolution suffice? And do we risk alienating our most creative and courageous people if we do not release them to take risks and push the boundaries? Quite often such people find opportunities through their jobs, in the community, or in mission agencies, and these may be the best contexts for them to use their gifts and energy. But we surely need some of these pioneers to help us discover new ways of being church and engaging in mission in a changing world.

Church planting offers opportunities for pioneering and innovation— opportunities to try things that would not be feasible in established churches because of restrictive traditions, buildings, constitutions, and expectations. Those who would otherwise be champing at the bit can be given freedom to take risks, to experiment, to follow hunches, to respond to the Spirit's leading, to explore new patterns of Christian community, new forms of worship, and new approaches to mission. Such entrepreneurial leaders need to be held accountable, but they also need support and encouragement— and channels through which they can share what they are learning with others.

Church planting can be perceived as setting up "ecclesial laboratories" on behalf of local churches or denominations. Experimental forms of church and mission can be tested and evaluated; those that seem promising and in some measure transferable can inform and stimulate the evolution of other churches. Those that seem less promising can either be tested further or discarded.[18] In effect, church planting allows other churches to continue as they are, or evolve only gradually, while pioneers test new and riskier possibilities on their behalf. Risk-taking implies the possibility of failure and the apparent wasting of time, money, and effort. We must take great care to ensure that pioneers know they are operating in an environment where it is acceptable to "fail," and we need to put processes in place to help them and others learn from their experiences. Better still, we may choose to redefine "success" and "failure," recognizing that learning from experiments, whatever their outcome, is a form of success.

Pioneering is for the benefit of others. Church planters are acting not as lone rangers but as scouts, exploring new territory on behalf of the denomination or network to which they belong. This is why it is so crucial that strong links are forged and maintained between denominations and their church planters. It is also why denominations and networks need to deploy and support church planters, not just to help create new churches but to learn all they can from their experiences.

A good example of this kind of partnership was the Cutting Edge project of the Anglican Diocese of Oxford, which ended in 2007 after several years of supporting pioneering initiatives and learning from their experiences. The diocese provided authorization, some funding, support, and accountability for several pioneers, each of whom was committed to planting a fresh expression of church. Regular accompaniment and opportunities to share with one another and with a diocesan steering group ensured that the wider church benefited from the experiences of the pioneers it had deployed.[19]

"Planting churches to pioneer on behalf of the church" will not, and should not, be the sole or primary motivation for church planting. Any church-planting initiative needs to have integrity in its own right. But denominational leaders would be foolish not to seize or create opportunities to learn from church planters as they pioneer new churches. As Stuart Christine wrote in one of the most popular church-planting books of the 1990s,

> Creative church planting that discovers new ways of being the Body of Christ in a changing world will help keep the sinews of our denominations supple and more able to respond sensitively and vigorously to the as yet unforeseen challenges of tomorrow's world . . . New churches, and the fresh theological insights that they generate, counter the tendency to ecclesiological ossification that turns structures into strictures.[20]

The church-planting movement of the 1990s stalled and fell short of expectations, but one crucial outcome was that, across the denominations, church planting achieved recognition as a legitimate missional activity. The challenge today is to move beyond legitimacy to normality. Church planting enables churches and denominations to experience the natural rhythm of reproduction and renewal that saves them from stagnation, decline, and death. Biblical and historical evidence suggests that renewal usually comes from the margins, so church planting can be understood as a process by which the inherited church is renewed by the emerging church, the mainstream from the margins. Of course, renewal can occur without church planting, but church planting is an unusually potent stimulus.

Planting Churches to Release Gifted People

It is not just pioneers who may need to be released into church planting. In many larger churches, there are simply not enough opportunities for people to use their God-given gifts or develop their leadership potential. I have had conversations with ministers of larger churches who were concerned about this but could not see a way forward and conversations with members of larger churches who could find no role and were deeply frustrated. Undoubtedly some people join larger churches so that they do *not* need to be actively involved—because their gifts are used in other spheres of life or because they need or prefer undemanding experiences of church. But others have untapped resources and underused gifts that need to be released for their own spiritual development and for the sake of mission.

Church planting is not the only way to release these gifted people, nor should this be the primary reason for church planting, but it does offer many fresh opportunities. There are tasks associated with the church-planting process that require a range of skills: research, strategic planning, team-building, training, intercession, community surveying, forging links with community groups and other agencies, evangelism, administration, finding a suitable meeting place, budgeting, and reimagining church, to name only a few. As the new church is planted, other gifts will be needed, giving opportunities to those who could not exercise these before. The third-best pianist or fifth-best Bible teacher in a large church may feel redundant, but she is a precious gift to a newly planted church.[21] And if the new church is not a clone but an opportunity for creativity and innovation, many more gifted people can be released and their talents unlocked. Many emerging churches have created space for people with a range of artistic gifts that have previously lain dormant.

Planting Churches to Resolve Internal Issues

Church planting is not always considered for purely missional reasons. There are often internal factors involved and sometimes other agendas that may be more or less hidden. These do not necessarily invalidate a church-planting initiative or jeopardize the outcome—indeed, sometimes these factors combine with missional motives to galvanize a church to action. But if church planting is an attempt to avert attention from unresolved issues, it can cause serious relational and institutional damage.

Sometimes church planting is considered as a solution to a cramped church building.[22] If the church has outgrown its facilities and this is hampering its ministry and limiting its development, action is needed. Church planting is not the only option and may not be the first to be investigated. Some buildings can be extended or redesigned. Congregations with sufficient resources may choose to relocate or rebuild. Church members living at a distance may be encouraged to join a more local church. But church planting is another option, releasing space and diversifying ministry and mission by sending out teams to plant new churches.

Sometimes church planting is considered in order to reduce the size of the congregation. Although many church leaders and some church members regard numerical growth as desirable, larger churches can be problematic. Especially when a church has grown rapidly, many of its members will be very aware of the losses as well as the gains, and some will be troubled by the increasingly impersonal and institutional nature of what is emerging. Some may question whether large churches are legitimate and wonder how much of the New Testament teaching on church life can realistically be applied in large congregations.[23] They do not regard the proliferation of small groups to compensate for these deficiencies as adequate. Church planting offers occasional or regular opportunities to adopt a multichurch rather than mega-church approach.

Sometimes church planting is considered as a way of reducing or eliminating tension in a church. This tension may focus on personalities, theological differences, divergent views of mission or worship, or other issues. Left unresolved, this tension will over time become damaging, inhibiting, and destructive. But if attempts to resolve it, find common ground, or construe it as a healthy tension have failed, an alternative way forward might be to plant a new church in which some can pursue a different theology, understanding of worship, or approach to mission. This sounds suspiciously like a "church split" rather than a church-planting initiative, and it is fraught with danger. But if all involved honor each other, respect their divergent views, and maintain strong and open relationships, it may be worth considering—especially if there are other missional reasons for church planting in this situation. This is obviously not a recommended approach to church planting, but it is undoubtedly a factor in many situations. I have often discovered this when I have heard the inside story of church-planting initiatives that do not mention this element when they tell their story in public.

There are, of course, other less honorable reasons why churches are planted. Ambitious church leaders may decide to "get a church plant under their belt" because it will enhance their CV (as one distraught couple reported to me after failing to dissuade their minister from embarking on a disastrous initiative). Aspiring church leaders may get involved in church planting to have a church of their own to lead. Church leaders may plant more churches to extend their sphere of influence and increase their prestige. On occasions, churches have been planted to distract attention from serious problems in the life of a church or its leader (akin to invading another country to distract attention from domestic political difficulties).

Planting Churches to Stimulate Denominational Growth

This final reason for planting churches may also be perceived as less honorable than others if it amounts to no more than institutional expansionism. But evidence has been gathered from various contexts indicating that denominations or networks of churches that initiate church-planting strategies are more likely to be growing than those that do not. There are probably two reasons for this.

First, younger churches tend to grow more quickly than older churches.

Inevitably, there are exceptions to this rule: some older churches experience periods of renewal that lead to rapid growth and some new churches lack missional focus and stagnate. But generally a church is at its peak in terms of its growth potential during its first decade. Several factors may be involved: younger churches may be more wholeheartedly committed to mission as their raison d'être and more attuned to the needs and potential of the community; they may have more members involved in mission rather than in maintenance activities that often proliferate as groups age; they may be more flexible in their approach, more willing to take risks, less culturally disconnected and less intimidating to join; they may meet in buildings shared with other community groups, making it easier to build relationships and form partnerships; and they may be contexts within which gifts can be released and skills sharpened, inspiring people to serve the church and the community with passion and commitment. Planting new churches gives denominations a growing edge.

Second, church planting may stimulate other churches or even the whole denomination to embrace more missional perspectives and encourage faith that growth is possible. Church planting may seem counterintuitive in a declining denomination, but investing personnel and resources in such initiatives may do more to halt decline and stimulate growth than efforts to turn around existing churches or rationalization and reorganization processes. If our motivation for church planting is no more than saving a denomination, this is clearly deficient, but if our motivation is to galvanize faith and renew vision within a network of churches so that many of these churches experience renewal and fresh growth, that seems to be an honorable reason for planting churches.

Planting Churches for Many Reasons

This chapter has explored many reasons for planting churches. I have chosen not to group them neatly into categories, such a "missional motives," "geographical motives," "cultural motives," and "ecclesial motives." Readers who would prefer such a categorization can no doubt construct this without difficulty (and might find this exercise instructive). Instead, I have tried to reflect the complex environment within which church planters are operating today and the various ways in which church planters and those who deploy them describe their intentions. The overlap between different sections in this chapter is deliberate.

In my experience, church planting happens when a number of these reasons for planting coincide. Sometimes church planters and those who deploy them may have different, but not incompatible, reasons for planting. For example, church planters may be motivated by concern for a network or neighborhood, and perceive any impact on their sponsoring denomination as a by-product, whereas their denominational leaders may be interested in exploring new ecclesial possibilities and be indifferent about where these possibilities are tested out.

Some of the reasons we have examined are "pull" factors as mission agencies or churches respond to challenges and opportunities; others are "push" factors as denominations or churches recognize church planting as a means of resolving issues or releasing potential. When "push" and "pull" factors are aligned, they may create enough momentum to plant a new church. And God's grace seems remarkably able to cope with mixed motives and diverse agendas, as people become involved in church planting for different reasons.

Having said all this, though, it is the missional motives for church planting that we should prioritize if church planting is not to be domesticated or co-opted. Whatever the benefits of church planting for churches, denominations, or church planters, the primary reason for planting new churches is to participate in God's mission within the neighborhoods and networks where the gospel is not at present effectively incarnated.

Planting Churches in Response to God's Call

This brings us to the final reason for planting churches and to the only sufficient reason. Is God calling an individual, church, denomination, or mission agency to get involved in church planting? Is God calling us to a particular community at a particular time? Is God inviting us to reimagine church in a changing culture? Is church planting just our idea or God's?

I do not believe that this most important question makes redundant the material we have explored in this chapter. The various reasons for planting churches we have surveyed are factors that we bring to God in prayer as we ask for insight and confirmation or as we try to understand why God might be inviting us into church planting. And as communities or groups pray together about this, they may reach agreement as to what they believe God is saying to them, even if different individuals are inspired by different expectations.

How do we discern the call of God to plant churches? In the same way we hope to hear God speaking to us on other issues—a combination of prayerful listening, reflection on Scripture, conversations with others, attentiveness to our context, openness to the voice of God through others.

I have noted how often a "word of prophecy" or a vision seems to play a significant role, if not in the final decision to plant, at least in encouraging people to explore the possibility of planting. But this may reflect the charismatic spirituality of many of those who were involved in church planting in the 1990s. Different traditions will emphasize different ways of hearing from God.

Planting churches is an exciting adventure of faith, and there are multiple reasons for us to endorse this mission strategy and participate in it, but it is far too demanding to embark on unless we are as confident as we can be that we are responding to the call of God.

Questions for Further Reflection

1. As you consider these many different motives for planting churches, which inspire you and which leave you cold?
2. Do you regard any of these reasons for church planting as illegitimate? If so, why?
3. Have you come across or can you think of any other reasons for planting churches?
4. If most churches are planted by other local churches, rather than by denominations or mission agencies, what reasons are likely to be dominant? Does this matter?
5. How would you decide whether God was calling you to become involved in church planting?

3

PLANTING **CHURCHES: HOW?**

Just as there are many different *reasons* for planting churches, so there are many different *ways* of planting churches. Often, however, mission agencies, churches, and even church planters seem unaware of this and adopt the approach with which they are most familiar without examining other possibilities. By far the most popular approach in Britain in the 1990s was the "mother/daughter" model (see below)—so much so that for many people this was assumed to be the only way to plant a church.[1]

But this limited perspective can have damaging consequences:

- Using an inappropriate model of church planting can hinder what might otherwise be a promising venture.
- Equating church planting with one particular approach may convince us that we cannot plant a church, whereas we might not squander this opportunity if we considered other models.
- Principles derived from church-planting initiatives that use a particular approach may be misapplied if we transfer these into a situation where another model is being used.

There is no one approach to church planting that fits every context. What matters is how the chosen model coheres with the motivation, resources, local context, and expectations of those involved. What matters even more is discerning which model the Spirit of God is indicating in any situation—and this discernment process is enriched by appreciating the range of possibilities.

Church-planting literature from the 1990s identifies various models of church planting[2] (although detailed guidance is offered for very few, with the emphasis overwhelmingly on the "mother/daughter" model). It also uses a range of images to describe these models. Perhaps the metaphor used most extensively is that of the "life cycle," with the stages of church planting likened to conception, prenatal, birth, postnatal, infancy, adolescence, maturity, and reproduction (and the "mother/daughter" symbolism). This communicates the idea that planting new churches is as natural for churches as parents having children. It also encourages planted churches in time to become planting churches. Horticultural imagery (sowing, watering, grafting, planting, "strawberry runners," and transplants) is also popular, again implying that church planting is a natural process rather than a marketing strategy or a franchising exercise. Some nautical images (the launch of a new church) and astronomical images (satellite churches) are also in evidence.

There is no agreed-upon terminology or standard way to categorize different models of church planting.[3] What follows is my attempt to set out the main approaches, using and adapting familiar imagery, and highlighting issues that arise when different models are used. I have presented this material to thousands of church leaders, theological students, and church planters in several nations, and I have found that their experiences of church planting usually fit snugly into one or another of the models I have outlined (although from time to time they describe a hybrid of two or more models). And, although some approaches are more familiar than others, even in small seminars participants are usually able between them to give examples that illustrate almost all of the models presented. However, as we investigate these models, it is worth emphasizing that each church-planting story has its own unique features. The purpose of categorization is not to preclude creativity but to indicate typical dynamics of different approaches, and lessons that church planters using these have learned.

So we will examine twelve approaches to church planting. In the first eight, the planting agency is a local church; the other four models have different starting points within the wider church. One other introductory point is that, although these are presented as twelve separate models and can operate independently, in some contexts some of these models may represent interim stages in the planting process.

Mother/Daughter

The most popular model of church planting involves a local church (the "mother church") deploying a group of its members to plant somewhere in the vicinity a new congregation (the "daughter church") with the expectation that in due course this will become a church that is no longer dependent on the planting church (see figure 3.1).

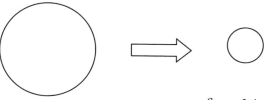

figure 3.1

This approach has several distinctive features:

- The team that plants the church is normally comprised exclusively of members of the planting church, who may be handpicked, volunteers, or a mixture of both. In some situations, a trained and paid team leader is imported. Often some members of the team already live in the neighborhood where the church is to be planted or are involved in the social network with which the church hopes to engage.
- The size of the team varies, depending on such factors as the size of the planting church, the extent of the neighborhood or network into which the new church is being planted, growth expectations, and the availability of suitable and envisioned personnel. The team may be as large as one hundred or just a handful but is typically twenty-five to thirty-five strong. Consequently, the team is often large enough to comprise the core of the new church and to start functioning as a church before anyone else joins.
- The daughter church is planted relatively close to the mother church, although far enough away to relate to a different section of the community. This means the planting team can retain strong links with the mother church. Most team members continue living where they are and avoid disruption to their jobs and schools for their children (though some who live further away may choose to move closer to where the church is being planted). This church-planting model is attractive and feasible to many more people than some other models that are more disruptive of family life.
- Despite the geographical closeness of the two churches and strong links between them, the intention is to plant a church that will become autonomous. The time frame within which this is anticipated will vary depending on local factors, as will the time frame within which this actually occurs: sometimes this is sooner than expected, sometimes later. But the goal is to plant a new church rather than an additional congregation.

One familiar scenario for mother/daughter planting is growing awareness that a particular part of the parish, neighborhood, or town (or a network of people in the area) appears to be beyond the reach of existing churches. The mother church investigates this, perhaps after abortive attempts to evangelize or develop community initiatives from a distance, and concludes that planting a new church is the best way forward. This decision is all the more likely if some church members live in this area or belong to this network and can form the basis for this venture.

Another scenario is sometimes designated the "expanding home group" model of church planting but is really a version of mother/daughter planting. Here the impetus for planting into a particular community comes from an existing home group, which meets in that neighborhood or participates in that network. The group is experiencing growth and has a deepening sense of missional responsibility for the community, which it shares with the mother church. The church responds by seconding more of its members (including some with particular gifts) to the home group and overseeing its expansion into a new church.

Because mother/daughter church planting is so common, it is worth pausing to reflect on its strengths and weaknesses. It has several advantages. First, it is a tried and tested model, so there are many churches and church planters with experience to pass on. There is no excuse for using this model without learning from them. Second, this is a relatively safe form of church planting, with support from experienced church leaders, adequate personnel (sometimes a ready-made congregation), financial and administrative backing, and a fallback position if needed. Third, because it does not require disruptive changes (of homes, jobs, schools, and so on), it has the capacity to mobilize a significant number of people. Fourth, if handled well, this model may have a positive impact on the planting church, releasing new vision and energy, and creating fresh opportunities for those who fill the gaps in the planting church.

However, there are also serious drawbacks, which may not cause major problems for any particular planting church but which diminish the missional potential of this approach to church planting. First, it is very demanding on the planting church if more than a handful of people are involved: only larger churches can use this approach, and few churches can plant out more than once or twice without suffering strain. Not only are many members given away each time, but church planting involves an upheaval, changed dynamics, reallocation of tasks, and other adjustments.[4] Second, the location of the new church is determined by where the planting church is and where church members live rather than by missional priorities, so the more we rely on this approach, the less strategic church planting is likely to be. Third, because the whole team comes from the same church and continues to draw extensively on resources and counsel from this church, the mother/daughter model often results in cloning rather than creative planting.[5]

This model, then, has made a huge contribution to the practice of church planting and will no doubt continue to be popular. But we will need other models if we are to release the gifts of members of smaller churches, plant new churches into areas and networks beyond the reach of larger churches, galvanize a church-planting movement, and develop a strategic approach that engages with the missional and ecclesial challenges of contemporary culture.[6]

Accidental Parenthood

Structurally this strangely named model is very similar to the mother/daughter model but the motivation for planting is more complex. As before, the initiative comes from a local church and the intended outcome is the emergence of an autonomous church in the vicinity of the planting church. Once again, all those involved come from this church and generally do not face significant disruption to other aspects of their lives. And, as before, there may be a mission focus as the team responds to the challenge of planting a church in a network or neighborhood not well served by the planting church or other churches (see figure 3.2).

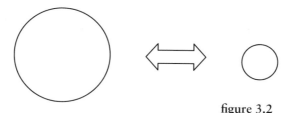

figure 3.2

However, mission is not the only motive and may not be the dominant one (however this venture is subsequently represented). This model is operative where the planting church is experiencing internal tensions, disagreements, and divergence of vision or expectations, a scenario we explored in the previous chapter. After attempts to resolve these problems and continue as a united church fail, it becomes clear that there are serious and persisting differences over substantive issues that threaten to damage the church and its witness in the community. Rather than allowing unresolved tensions to continue or to result in an acrimonious split, a decision is taken (usually after much prayer and heart-searching) to encourage one of the groups within the church to separate from it and form a new church in the vicinity.

This decision liberates them to develop a church that is in line with their convictions and allows those who remain to pursue a different vision without the previous tension. If this process is handled well, it holds out the prospect of two churches advancing in ways that seemed impossible in a single church. The two churches may also be able to affirm each other and maintain good relations now that points of tension no longer intrude into every conversation or decision. Much depends on the level of trust between the groups and their readiness to admit that the whole truth may not be on one side; the extent to which issues can be discussed openly, rather than being fudged; whether each group has a constructive vision rather than merely being reactive; the quality of leadership available in each group; and whether the primary concern is mission rather than ecclesial preferences.

The outcome is not always positive. Sometimes the new church flourishes and the old church declines. Sometimes the new church never gets established, flourishes for only a short time, or fragments, while the older church recovers and flourishes again. Sometimes members of the new church drift back to the old church. Sometimes, sadly, neither of the churches flourishes. I am familiar with examples of all these outcomes.

We need to acknowledge, of course, that this is not a recommended approach to church planting, that it is fraught with dangers, and that relational issues and mission questions need to be addressed if it is to have any hope of leading to a positive outcome. Indeed, the extent to which this may be legitimately regarded as church planting rather than a church split[7] depends on there being other motives than simply resolving tension, so that both churches are released for fresh engagement in mission. However, in some situations, all other ways forward seem at least as problematic, and I know numerous church-planting ventures that are officially described as mother/daughter but should really be classified under this heading.

Dispersion

Unlike the mother/daughter model and the accidental parenthood scenario, both of which have been quite common in Britain, church planting by dispersion has been unusual. But there are some contexts in which this may be the most effective approach. I have noticed in the past two years that more stories involving this model have been shared in church-planting courses, so perhaps its time is coming (see figure 3.3).

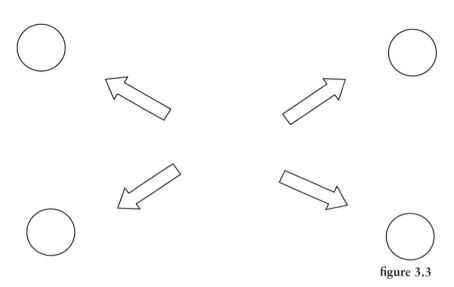

figure 3.3

The starting point is again a particular local church, and there are some similarities to the mother/daughter model, but there is one very significant difference: the planting church ceases to exist in its present form. *All* the members of the church are involved in forming new churches. The result of such a strategy is not a mother/daughter relationship between the planting church and a planted church but (if we continue to use the family analogy) a sister/sister relationship between a number of newly planted churches.

What factors might lead to such a radical dispersal of church members and the demise of the planting church?

- *Persecution.* In a context where continuing to meet together as a large church in a public place is too dangerous, dispersing into smaller churches that can meet in homes or other less public places may be a sensible strategy. Links between the dispersed churches can be maintained through relationships or by leaders visiting them regularly. But the original church ceases to exist as a single entity. Though persecution is not currently a factor in Britain, it is in many other nations, and we hear of inspiring examples of dispersed churches not only surviving but thriving spiritually and growing in numbers.

- *Strategic relocation.* Where a community experiences significant demographic and housing changes, a large church meeting in what used to be but is no longer a strategic central location may recognize that its mission would be enhanced if it divided itself into smaller churches located where the community now lives, works, or relaxes. Community development activities and contextual evangelism could both flourish in this dispersed framework.

- *Church and mission.* There has been a global rediscovery of smaller expressions of church (house church, home church, household church, base community, cell church, and so on) in recent years. Recognizing the potential of such models and their relevance to a postmodern culture that is deeply suspicious of institutional and hierarchical models, a large church may conclude that it will be more effective—pastorally and missionally—for it to disperse into smaller units, whether rooted in neighborhoods or in networks.

Although any church-planting initiative is a major undertaking for a church and requires prayerful discussion and wholehearted support, this model is unusually radical and will directly impact every member of the church. The implications need to be thought through and spelled out very carefully, and enough time given for everyone to come to terms with what is being proposed. If the church owns property, there may be issues about trust deeds and debates about what to do with the buildings. But if a church catches a vision of a new way of being church and a more effective way of engaging in mission, especially if many members already live in the areas to which the church will be dispersing, this model can be liberating.

Dispersion may take place in stages rather than all at once. There may be an initial dispersal into autonomous, though informally connected, churches that at some point (perhaps with changing circumstances) reconnect in a more formal way. There may, alternatively, be an initial dispersion into smaller units that remain formally part of one church (as in the multiple sites model below) but in time, develop into autonomous churches.

The popularity of the "cell church" model in recent years means that many churches are already moving in this direction, usually in order to become more effective in evangelism and to encourage their members to develop their gifts. Most of these churches would not regard this as church planting by dispersion, since the cells continue to relate together and still comprise one church, albeit with a different structure and focus. In some situations, however, this process develops to a point where some or all of the cells separate from the original church, expand, and become dispersed churches. In contexts where cell church values are affirmed but the structure is not working well, church planting by dispersion may be an (unintended) outcome of a cell church strategy.

Adoption

The models we have examined thus far describe church planting where only one church is involved at the outset. A new church is planted for various reasons, one of which is that there is no church engaging effectively with a particular network or neighborhood. But there are many situations where there is a church in the area but it is small, struggling, and seems unable to offer much to the community. We recognized in the previous chapter that this is a sensitive scenario when church planting is under discussion. Should we refrain from planting in this area because there is already a church there, albeit not very effective in mission? Or should we discount this church because it is largely disconnected from the community, and plant a new church regardless? Church planting by adoption represents a third way (see figure 3.4).

Church planting by adoption takes place when a church adopts another struggling church, nurtures and resources it, and enables it to rebuild and rediscover its missional potential, in effect becoming a new church. There are three main approaches to adoption church planting:

- *Grafting.* The adopting church seconds (temporarily or permanently) some of its members to the struggling church in the hope that this graft will bring renewed vision and energy and enable the church to recover and prosper.
- *Transplanting.* The adopting church seconds many more members than currently comprise the struggling church, in effect incorporating the struggling church into a newly planted church.
- *Fostering.* The struggling church gives up its independence and unites with the adopting church for a period of months or years. When the time seems right, the church is planted out again, augmented by some members of the adopting church.

The adoption process may be initiated by the struggling church, which realizes that it can no longer function independently and that its impact on the surrounding community is minimal. The initial approach may be for help with an aspect of ministry, rather than for adoption. At this stage the church may fiercely guard its autonomy but warmly welcome unconditional help. It may also be concerned mainly with its own survival or recovery. Mission concerns may or may not be present. And there may or may not be readiness to examine its culture and activities and consider changes.

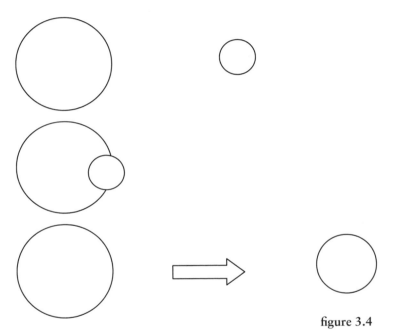

figure 3.4

Alternatively, the initiative may come from a larger church that is aware of the plight of a struggling church nearby. Its motivation may be to help that church recover confidence, grow in numbers, and engage once more in effective mission. It may also be interested in new opportunities for its own members to use their gifts and develop leadership skills or in finding new premises to extend its own mission activities. Unless there is substantial trust between the two churches, any initiative from the larger church is likely to provoke suspicion about being taken over or stripped of its assets.

A third possibility is a strategic initiative taken by a regional association, diocese, synod, network, or denomination. Rationalization of parish structures has been occurring among Anglicans for many years, merging churches in what may resemble the first stage of an adoption scenario. Generally these situations are retrenchments, not missional initiatives, and they have not led to churches being planted out again, but there is potential for such mergers to be missional and creative. Regional strategies could include church planting by adoption as a viable alternative to spreading diminishing resources more thinly.

The progression from any initial approach to church planting by adoption is likely to be slow and will require good will, honesty, and sensitivity on both sides. The struggling church will need to surrender its autonomy, and the adopting church will need to respect the other church's history but also challenge its members to embrace change. There are risks involved and no guaranteed outcomes. This is a complex and demanding approach to church planting, requiring a different skill set from most other models. Not all church planters are temperamentally suited to this: many would rather let the struggling church close and then plant again from scratch.

Planting from scratch will undoubtedly be simpler and may be the better option, but there are reasons to consider planting by adoption. These include historical and current links between the struggling church and the local community on which a reenergized church might build; suspicion of new initiatives in the community that might cause problems for church planting from scratch; the availability of suitable premises and possibly some financial resources; and enough personnel in the combined churches to embark on church planting, which might not be feasible for the larger church on its own. However, some of these factors can also be hindrances: the struggling church may have a poor reputation in the community; the premises may be unsuitable and expensive to maintain; and members of the struggling church may be unable or unwilling to embrace the necessary changes. There are, after all, reasons why the church is struggling.

Despite the complexities and inherent difficulties, this model of church planting has been used effectively in various contexts. Knowing this may encourage other churches to look carefully at this option and perhaps invest the time and energy in working through issues that are bound to arise. Inviting an outside facilitator, mediator, or consultant may help the two churches to assess the prospects and to develop an effective adoption process if they decide to go ahead.

But is this really a model of church planting, or is it better interpreted as an alternative to church planting? After all, the number of churches remains constant. But if the process is successful, there is growth rather than decline, a church that might otherwise have closed not only remains open but also finds new energy to engage in mission, and the adopted church may become a new church in all but name. Those who might otherwise have constituted the planting team for a new church are linked into an existing church and, together with renewed and reenvisioned members of that church, discover fresh ways of serving their local community.

Long-Distance

The previous models normally operate within the vicinity of the planting church (though planting by dispersion may involve a wider geographical area) and require relatively little disruption to other aspects of life for those involved. Planting churches locally dominated church planting in the 1990s.

But as we noted in assessing the strengths and weaknesses of the mother/daughter model, this raises serious strategic issues. Overdependence on entrepreneurial churches planting more churches in their vicinity hinders us from recruiting and deploying church-planting teams in under-churched communities or in contexts where social and spiritual needs are greater. A truly missional church-planting strategy would prioritize this.

Planting locally makes it likely that areas in which there are already strong churches will gain more, since these churches have the resources and personnel to plant out, whereas in areas where churches are weaker, fewer new churches will be planted. Although the local planting of more churches in relatively well-churched areas may be necessary to fill gaps and engage more effectively in mission, this actually exacerbates the disparity between communities in which churches are strong and communities in which churches are weak. Unless we think and act more strategically and employ church-planting models that allow us to plant beyond our local area, the present imbalance between church life in suburban and inner-city areas (for example) will become even greater.

I have had conversations with churches that were planning to plant another church locally but struggled to identify any neighborhood or network not already receiving attention from other churches. The choice they face is either to plant a church in competition with other churches or to look further afield. If denominations were to adopt a more strategic and regional approach to church planting and if churches were to take responsibility for mission beyond their own locality, it might be feasible for resources and personnel to be deployed in more imaginative, though also more demanding, ways (see figure 3.5).

Long-distance church planting[8] enables us to plant churches beyond our locality and into communities where churches are thin on the ground and new initiatives are needed to respond to mission opportunities. We can plant new churches ten, one hundred, or one thousand miles from the planting church.

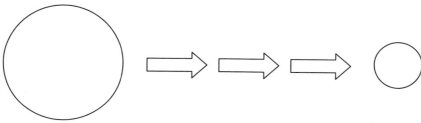

figure 3.5

The structure and motivation of long-distance church planting may be very similar to the mother/daughter model: planting team members all come from the planting church, and the aim is to plant an autonomous church. The major difference is location—long-distance church planting means that those involved very likely need to move, find new schools for their children, and perhaps change their jobs. A high degree of mobility and commitment is required, so planting teams tend to be smaller when the distance increases (although I know of one venture from the suburbs into inner London that involved thirty people).

There are three further differences. First, there is often a cross-cultural dimension, as the team moves into a different city, region, or even country. They may need to learn a new language as well as a new culture. Second, long-distance planting usually results in a new church being planted that is significantly different from the planting church: this is vital if it is to be contextual, but it may strain relations with the planting church. Third, given the distance involved and ecclesial differences that emerge, autonomy often comes sooner than when churches are planted locally.

This is a much riskier approach to church planting. Those who become involved uproot themselves from their present pattern of life and familiar community and embark on a missionary adventure. There is less support from the planting church and no obvious fallback position if things go awry. Except in some newer church networks, few people rise to this challenge, but perhaps we need to ask why and whether the risk-averse culture that permeates many churches incapacitates us and hinders us from responding to glaring social needs and significant mission opportunities.

Multiple Congregations

If the previous model enables church planting at a greater distance, this model envisages church planting at no distance at all, by situating new congregations in premises already used by the planting church (see figure 3.6).

Churches adopt this approach for various reasons:

- Some realize that their current expression of church engages only with a limited segment of the community and decide to plant different expressions of church in the hope of connecting with others. The type of church, rather than its location, is the issue, so there is no need to plant in a different location unless their building presents practical or cultural obstacles.
- Some recognize that their premises are nearing capacity when the whole church is together and decide that church planting is the most effective way of reducing pressure and releasing people into new spheres of mission and ministry. But the buildings are strategically located, well appointed, and capable of hosting several smaller congregations and other activities. Rather than planting churches in other buildings and multiplying administration and equipment costs, they plant further congregations within their own building so as not to lose the advantages of being a large church.
- Some acknowledge that efforts to persuade those who participate enthusiastically in midweek activities to become part of the Sunday congregation have failed. The alternative is to create fresh expressions of church around those midweek groups, so that a church with multiple congregations emerges.
- Some wrestle with the competing claims of diversity and unity in the church and plant multiple congregations as a way of holding these in creative tension. These congregations express the diversity of the church, but their partnership in the one building, expressed in various ways, encourages each group to cross ethnic, age, or other boundaries and relate to people who are different from them.

The reason for choosing this model of church planting will influence the outcome. If the primary motivation is logistical, the multiple congregations may be quite similar to each other—little more than duplicate services initially. But over time, diversity will appear as each congregation reflects those who comprise it and develops its own personality. If the main concern is mission and developing links with particular sections of the community or groups who use the building, each congregation will be intentionally designed for this purpose and may only be loosely connected to other congregations. But if the church is determined to express diversity within unity and encourages people to build relationships beyond their own relatively homogeneous congregation, it may invest significantly in developing intercongregational activities.

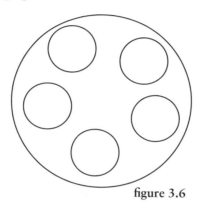

figure 3.6

There has recently been a dramatic increase in the number of churches planting multiple congregations following the publication of the *Mission-shaped Church* report, which endorsed a "mixed economy" and encouraged fresh expressions of church for the sake of mission. Although the term "fresh expressions" applies to various other forms of church planting as well as multiple congregations, this approach has been popular. Furthermore, smaller churches than previously are now using this model, so that the congregations that are emerging are also smaller and more varied in the way they function. The Churches of Christ community that hosted the conference in Melbourne mentioned in chapter 1 was only medium-sized but had several small congregations (including one called "Jebus" for those who knew little about the Christian faith).[9]

Many of these fresh expressions are so recent that they have not yet encountered issues that churches with multiple congregations have sometimes faced. These include practical matters, such as added pressure on facilities and equipment, time constraints if different congregations meet on the same day, and the sheer complexity of church life. There are also structural issues relating to leadership and accountability, raising and distributing finances, governance and decision making. And, if the congregations are not to become disconnected from each other, there are questions about how best to express the unity of a diverse church. Sharing meals together and joint mission activities offer better prospects than blended worship events, which often feel bland or artificial, and some churches also develop mixed house groups that draw members from various congregations.

While this approach has much to commend it, in principle and in practice, some questions are worth pondering:

- Can multiple congregations, especially diverse congregations, hold together over the years, or will they inevitably pull apart in search of greater autonomy, freedom to maneuver, and space in which to develop? Will missional or logistical issues lead some to leave the shared building and operate elsewhere?
- Will the original congregation that planted the others ever fully endorse the notion of "mixed economy" and accept that it is now just one among several equally valid expressions of church? Or will there be pressure for the younger congregations to acknowledge their derivative and semiecclesial status, encourage their members also to attend meetings of the original congregation, and recombine once they have finished "experimenting"?
- Does this model demonstrate the influence of "attractional" thinking? Rather than embracing church planting as an opportunity to incarnate the gospel beyond the comfort zone of the church building, more congregations are planted within this building to attract different kinds of people.[10] Or do attempts to plant new congregations around existing groups and activities indicate more "incarnational" ways of thinking?

A further question is whether multiple congregations really amount to church planting. Is it necessary for the congregations to be fully ecclesial, or at least to be moving toward this status, before we recognize them as planted churches? And does the use of the term *church* to designate a building as well as a community make it harder for us to accept a new congregation as a church if it shares a building with other congregations? Certainly many of the dynamics of other models of church planting are equally present here.

Multiple Sites

Another way of planting churches without losing the benefits of being a larger church is to develop congregations on multiple sites that are not autonomous but remain sub-units within a single church. Members of these congregations remain members of the planting church and meet sometimes in their separate congregations and sometimes as a whole church. This is less problematic than with multiple congregations because there is far less diversity among the various congregations. As with the previous model, this allows for economies of scale and shared resources across a number of congregations, though some additional costs are incurred because several buildings are used (see figure 3.7).

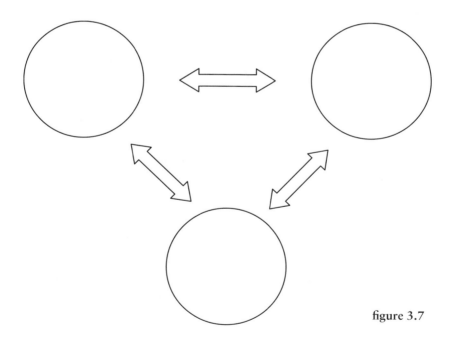

figure 3.7

Apart from these benefits, why else might churches consider using this model?

- This strategy is often precipitated by space constraints in the building used by the planting church. There is no desire to plant an autonomous church along the lines of the mother/daughter model, nor is there room for multiple congregations in the premises. The preferred option is to decant church members onto two or more sites while remaining one church.
- Another motive may be to locate church nearer to where people live. A multiple sites approach enables the church to operate in local community centers, schools, or other buildings in the vicinity. Multiple congregations on the same site would not achieve this kind of community penetration.
- In a relatively homogeneous area, there may be no apparent need to plant churches that are different from the planting church. The multiple sites model allows for a familiar model of church to be replicated in other locations with a minimum of fuss or ecclesial discussion.
- Where a church is strongly committed to its particular way of being church and wants to export this to other nearby locations without losing control or risking its ecclesial values and priorities being diluted or distorted, the multiple sites model achieves geographical diversification without ecclesial compromise.
- This model also requires fewer leaders than some other forms of church planting. The existing leadership can still oversee the whole church, albeit devolving some responsibilities to each congregation. A church operating on multiple sites may be very demanding on these few leaders, but this approach may make church planting feasible in churches with many people but limited leadership capacity.

Once again, the question arises as to whether this is really church planting if the multiple sites are simply different locations for the activities of a single church. The answer to this may depend on who is asking the question. From the perspective of the denomination or network to which the planting church belongs, there is still one church. This may also be the perspective of the planting church if it wants to underline its unity across the various sites. Alternatively, the church may suggest that it has planted new churches but without setting up separate ecclesial structures.

But from the perspective of the wider community and of those who join one of the congregations or are impacted by its mission activities, it will certainly seem that there is a new church in the area.

An interesting expression of this approach is the practice of church planting in rural areas by introducing a "mobile church," along the lines of a mobile library or mobile butcher. A church bus visits small villages and hamlets, and interacts with the local community on a certain day each week or month, before moving on to the next location.

But the questions we raised in relation to multiple congregations—Will they pull apart? Is it possible for each to be accorded ecclesial status? Is this approach too attractional?—apply also to multiple sites.

Satellite Congregations

As we reach the last of the eight models in which church planting is initiated by a church, these various models may be merging together and becoming indistinct. This is not entirely unhelpful for understanding them, as there are no definite dividing lines between them and some situations have features of more than one model. And, as we indicated at the start of this chapter, some initiatives develop through various stages and so may be classified under different headings as they move forward.

The model we are considering here falls somewhere between the multiple sites model and the mother/daughter model. It may be a transitional phase as a congregation develops its own characteristics and greater autonomy, or it may be a long-term model in its own right. This is a popular approach that is sometimes labeled "strawberry runner" or "radial" church planting (see figure 3.8).[11] It appeals especially to churches with an ecclesial preference for interdependence and networking rather than independence.[12]

Satellite congregations emerge when a planting church, motivated by the usual range of concerns, plants out some of its members to form new congregations in different places. These may differ markedly from each other and from the planting church (or the "home planet," to exploit the imagery further) and will normally operate in a semiautonomous manner. They continue to see themselves as expressions of the planting church in a way that is not apparent or the long-term intention with the mother/daughter model, but they have greater freedom than with the multiple-sites model to develop in different ways that are contextually appropriate.

One of the advantages of this model is that the satellite congregations can concentrate on mission and have the freedom to develop in ways that will enhance this. They need not carry the full weight of being autonomous churches but can rely on the planting church (sometimes known as the "resource church") for some aspects of church life and remain part of this church.

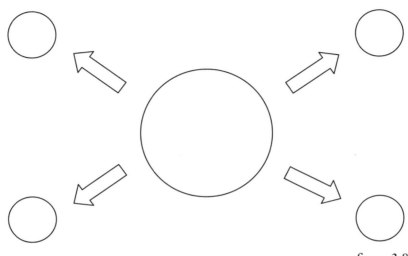

figure 3.8

One expression of this model is "cell planting." Cell churches usually emerge as existing churches restructure themselves, forming cells from existing members and then inviting others to join them. But with cell planting, members of the planting church invite friends or neighbors to help them form a new cell. This is a more incarnational approach to cell church.[13] Another expression of satellite congregations is "clusters," which Bob Hopkins defines as "creative mid-sized missional communities."[14] These clusters are larger than cell groups, mission-focused and able to be creative in ways that larger churches and cells find more difficult.

A popular structure in such networks of congregations involves the use of a three-level approach, often designated by the terms *cell*, *congregation*, and *celebration*. Cells may relate either to the satellite congregations or to the whole church network. As with the mother/daughter model, new congregations may emerge from expanding cell groups, although in this model there is less pressure for them to become self-sufficient. The unity of the church, despite the diversity of the satellite congregations, is expressed through regular celebrations. Church members are encouraged to participate in all three levels of church life, although they are more likely to do so if the activities at each level are quite different from each other in purpose and style (rather than congregations aspiring to be celebrations or applying cell principles).

Generally, each satellite congregation has its own leadership team, but there is also a church leadership team that oversees the whole network of congregations. The relationships between these groups of leaders are crucial to the health and development of this model of church planting. There are similarities to the multiple congregations model, which is also an attempt to enable creativity and diversity within a framework of partnership and shared resources. But satellite congregations do not operate within the same building as the planting church and may have greater freedom from ecclesial responsibilities.

As satellite congregations grow, their relationship with the planting church may evolve, so that the planting church is not perceived as different from the newer churches and the network develops as a partnership between equals. In some cases, however, the planting church continues to be regarded as a senior partner. The gravitational attraction that holds the satellite congregations together may or may not be strong enough to prevent ambition for autonomy, leading some congregations to take steps toward the outcome envisaged by the mother/daughter model. One of the key factors in this, as is the case with some of the other models, is the extent to which those who join a congregation also feel that they belong to the network of congregations of which it is a part. The other main factor is how differently congregations develop and the willingness of the planting church or network of congregations to live with diversity.[15]

Spontaneous/Emerging

All of the models we have examined involve careful planning over a reasonable period of time in order to plant a healthy new church without damaging the planting church. But churches are sometimes planted without a planting church and with minimal planning. Some are accidental, developing from mission projects or other activities; others are intentional but organic and independent of any planting agency. Such church planting was labeled "grass roots," "spontaneous," or even "nuclear fusion" in the 1990s: these initiatives were acknowledged but given little attention. After all, they comprised not so much a model of church planting as a collection of stories. Today the term "emerging churches" is used to describe many of these initiatives, and they receive much more attention (see figure 3.9).

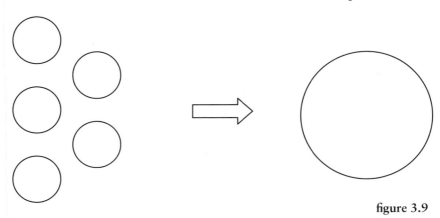

figure 3.9

Not all spontaneous church planting engages with emerging culture or participates in the "emerging church conversation" about Christian faith in postmodernity. Sometimes new churches emerge from growing relationships between Christians living in a particular area or who belong to a network of friends. If these relationships are accompanied by a mission concern for their friends or neighbors, if there appears to be room for a new church, and if there are some in the group with leadership abilities, a new church may be planted.

One context for spontaneous church planting is where several Christians are among those moving into a new housing development. Discovering one another and beginning to pray together may lead to the decision to form a new church together rather than to travel to other churches further away. Another situation is where Christians who have, for various reasons, become disaffected from other churches start meeting together, perhaps initially just for support and friendship, and out of this a new church develops. A third scenario is a mission project involving Christians from various churches out of which, intentionally or unintentionally, a new church emerges. This step may be taken reluctantly because of the cultural gap between other nearby churches and those whom the project is serving.

What emerges from these beginnings will vary according to contextual factors: the new church may remain independent or may reach out for support, accountability, and a wider network of relationships with an existing church, network, or denomination. Its prospects will depend to a large extent on the quality of leadership available and the range of gifts within the planting group. Because of its spontaneous origins, few if any of the group will have received any training or preparation for planting a new church, and its composition is determined by other factors than a mix of gifts and skills. However, strong relationships and shared vision and values can provide a firm foundation for a healthy new church.

In the sense that such churches are not planted by a church or other mission agency, they can be described as "emerging"—from particular contexts, from groups of friends, or from mission initiatives. But the term "emerging church" has in the past decade acquired other connotations:[16] theological reflection on postmodernity, attunement to emerging culture, ecclesial creativity, alternative approaches to worship, organic expressions of community, and a critique of inherited forms of church. Not only are there now many more emerging churches than the spontaneous ventures given scant attention in the 1990s, but some of these churches are pioneering missional and ecclesial approaches that may be influential in many other churches in the coming years.[17] Numerically they are still marginal, but they may represent a much more significant expression of church planting than most of the earlier examples of spontaneous planting. Nevertheless, the factors mentioned above in relation to the prospects of spontaneously planted churches (leadership capacity, mix of gifts, training, support, and networking) apply equally to emerging churches.

One further expression of spontaneous or emerging church planting is the phenomenon known as "simple church." Much less interested in engaging with emerging culture or the issues discussed in the "emerging church conversation," proponents and participants are interested in simplifying church and galvanizing a missional movement through creating lightweight and reproducible churches. Simple churches are usually small, home-based, and interactive. They require minimal structures and resources, and they multiply as members of these churches start new simple churches, which network together in regions or cities. Already popular in some parts of the United States, but drawing inspiration from movements in non-Western nations, simple church networks are emerging also in Britain.[18]

Pioneer Planter

Some new churches without links to existing churches do not just emerge but are planted by individual church planters.[19] These planters may operate independently; they may be deployed by and accountable to a denominational board or a mission agency; or they may be sent out and supported by their own church. There are numerous historical examples of missionary church planters. (Some were enthusiastic about planting churches; others did so reluctantly, wary of being distracted from other aspects of mission.) And there are many contemporary examples, especially in African and Asian contexts, but also in some European nations. In Belgium, for instance, almost all the new churches in the past thirty years owe their existence to pioneer church planters. In Britain, there have been relatively few such initiatives, although I knew one pioneer planter who planted a new church every few years throughout his life. Unlike other models we have examined in this chapter, the church planter (with or without spouse and children) starts without a team or core group (see figure 3.10).

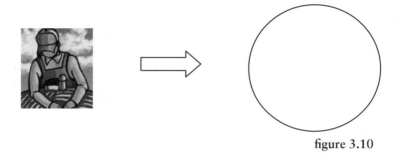

figure 3.10

Two different kinds of pioneering church planters can be distinguished:

- Serial church planters, sometimes known as "apostolic catalysts": those who plant a new church and then move on to repeat the process elsewhere
- Occasional church planters, also described as "founding pastors": those who plant a new church and remain with it, perhaps for a long time, as it develops

Both kinds of church planters have valuable roles, but they have distinctive callings and gifts, which need to be recognized and deployed effectively. Apostolic catalysts need to move on frequently—they are initiators and pioneers rather than consolidators, so staying too long in one place will both frustrate them and begin to damage the church they have planted. Founding pastors may plant only one church, but they are able to make the transition from pioneering to consolidating and provide stable and secure leadership for a young church.

Some church planters are itinerant evangelists who stay long enough in an area to gather new believers into a new church. Others discover Christians in a community who are not connected to any church (as in the spontaneous model) and plant a new church with this group as the initial members. Some church planters share a vision with their own church and gain permission to recruit a planting team from this church. Others join a struggling church that is on the point of closure, or perhaps a failing attempt to plant a church, and replant it (an alternative to the adoption model).

The comparative scarcity of serial church planters in Western societies may be a legacy of the Christendom era, with its focus on pastor-teachers settled in parishes and its antipathy toward itinerant ministry. The recent decision by Anglicans to train and deploy "pioneer ministers," church-planting courses in several training institutions, and growing interest in various circles in the recovery of "apostolic" ministry may all be signs that the missional realities of post-Christendom are at last challenging this maintenance-oriented approach to church leadership. Maybe we will see more church planters equipped and released in the coming years.

Mission Team

Not all, however, are convinced of the wisdom of deploying pioneering church planters as lone operators. Isolation, burnout, and imbalance are familiar problems where a church planter is operating without colleagues. Denominations that have tried to plant churches by sending a church planter alone into a new housing development or a more established but under-churched community have discovered that this is often ineffective and unwise. There are exceptions—some church planters work happily and fruitfully on their own—but these exceptions should not be confused with the rule. A better alternative in many situations is to deploy a mission team to plant a new church (see figure 3.11).

How does a mission team differ from a planting team sent out by a church using one of the earlier models?

- A mission team is deployed by and accountable to a denomination or mission agency, not a church.
- It will normally include team members from a range of churches rather than all coming from one church. Team members may continue to receive support from these churches and periodically report back to them, but they will not be operating under the auspices of their sending church.

- Team formation may involve an interview and selection process, with different expectations on all sides than are normal when volunteers plant a new church out of their own church.
- Team members will often not know each other before the planting process starts.
- More team members may be able to work full-time as church planters than is the case with most planting teams deployed by churches. Team members may raise their own support or be funded by the denomination or mission agency.
- A mission team can be deployed into communities that are beyond the reach of planting churches.
- Once a church is planted, some or all of the team may move on to plant churches elsewhere. Team members may work with an apostolic church planter, traveling from place to place to help form new churches.

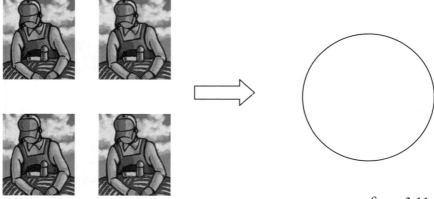

figure 3.11

Some of the advantages of this model are obvious: it enables smaller churches to become involved in church planting, mobilizing one or two people with planting gifts from these churches without unduly weakening them; each team has diverse experiences of church life, enriching it and encouraging it to be creative rather than cloning; teams are mobile and flexible, so strategic decisions can be made more easily about where best to deploy them; if teams move on rather than forming the core of the new church, this encourages the development of indigenous leadership; and teams that move on to plant again benefit from their previous experience.

There are also risks and challenges inherent in this model. First, unless the denomination or mission agency provides ongoing training, pastoral support, and accountability, teams may become isolated, feel overwhelmed, or lose their way. But if it is too closely involved, teams may not develop fully or be very creative. They may be free from the traditions of their own churches, but they may feel under pressure to plant churches approved by the agency or their denomination. Second, the selection and integration of team members is critical. Unlike planting teams drawn from one church, mission teams come from diverse backgrounds, need time to be knit together, and must develop a united vision if their energies are not to be dissipated. Third, teams will not usually know the community into which they are deployed (whereas planting teams from local churches will usually know their area), so they need to research and interpret their context and build relationships in the community. Finally, this can be a financially demanding way of planting churches unless the teams are self-funding.[20]

Another strategy some denominations use is deploying a sizable short-term mission team to engage in evangelistic activities in a community, with the intention of gathering enough people to form the core of a new church. Some members of this team may remain in the community to continue planting the church, or the team may work with a group of Christians in the area who want to form a new church. This strategy is especially popular in Pentecostal denominations, not least in those with black-majority leadership, and may be fruitful in some contexts. However, this high-profile approach and reliance on short-term impact does not fit well with a relational and contextual understanding of church planting; it generally assumes a narrowly evangelistic understanding of mission; and it rarely asks what kind of church is needed.

Cooperative Planting

The final model is a composite approach, both in the sense that more than one planting agency is involved and in the sense that some of the previous models may be adapted or merged. There are situations where a new church is needed but no one church, mission agency or denomination can respond to this challenge alone. This may be the time to explore cooperative planting (see figure 3.12).

The partners in a cooperative venture may comprise a group of local churches from the same denomination working through their regional

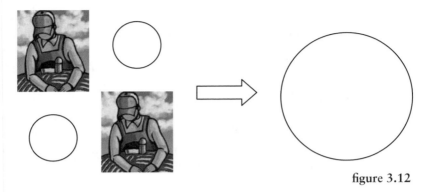

figure 3.12

structure (for example, diocese, area, association, circuit, synod, or division); a group of churches from different denominations working through local or national ecumenical partnership arrangements; a local church working with a mission agency, with each contributing personnel, resources, and expertise; a group of local churches working with an experienced church planter; or a mission team working with a group of churches.

Cooperative planting has several advantages:

- Smaller churches that would be unable to participate in church planting alone are able to contribute to a cooperative strategy.
- A partnership approach can seize opportunities for church planting that would otherwise be missed.
- The planting team can be selected from different places and may bring a wider range of skills and experience than normal (except in the mission team model).
- The complementary strengths of a local church and a mission agency may result in a more balanced strategy that gives proper attention to, for example, visionary leadership and pastoral sensitivity.
- Partnership in church planting may enhance the relationships between the partners and lead to cooperation in other initiatives.
- Planting in partnership with others may reduce any tendency for church planting to be (or be regarded as) competitive or empire-building.
- A cooperative approach may enable the planting of more than one church in an area.

Though an attractive approach in theory, in practice this model is fraught with difficulties and is feasible only if relationships between the planting agencies are strong and if there is a common vision inspiring them. Although there are some exceptions, attempts to plant ecumenical churches (where different denominations cooperate to plant a church that has shared denominational ownership) have rarely been successful, as indicated in the previous chapter. Such attempts have been hampered by denominational bureaucracy, discord over internal issues that matter deeply to those involved in the discussions but are of no interest at all to the community in which a new church is to be planted, the time taken to gain permission and resolve differences, and lack of common vision.

It may well be that informal ecumenical ventures or partnerships between churches of the same denomination have greater potential for church planting than formal ecumenical partnerships. Partnerships between a church (or a group of churches) and a mission team or mission agency may also have more to offer than has yet been widely recognized. And a cooperative and strategic approach to church planting in a city or region would be very valuable, whether this is actually implemented via many independent planting ventures or a cooperative church-planting initiative.[21]

Choosing a Model

As with the motives for planting in the previous chapter, the twelve models described in this chapter are not presented in order of preference. Accidental parenthood may be more common than is often acknowledged, but it is certainly not a highly recommended model. The only grouping of approaches we have suggested is that the first eight models involve a local church in the planting process, whereas the last four are initiated within the wider church (by individuals, mission agencies, denominations, or groups of local churches).

How does a church planter, mission agency, local church, or denomination choose which model to use? As we indicated at the start of this chapter, the determining factors are the context within which a church is to be planted, the available resources and personnel, the motives of those involved, and their expectations. In practice, familiarity with a particular approach, personal preferences, and ecclesial convictions may also be influential. The bottom line for most church planters, as they ponder these various models and factors, is a growing conviction that God's Spirit is showing them the way forward.

● ● ●

Questions for Further Reflection

1. Is it helpful to think in terms of distinct models? How much overlap is there between them? How easy are these different models to identify in a real-life situation?

2. Try to find a recently planted church in your area (preferably one that is between two and four years old), and interview those who planted it. What church-planting model did they use, and why?

3. What are the key criteria for assessing the strengths and weaknesses of the various church-planting models? What factors might encourage you to adopt one (or more) of these models? What is the role of prayer in this discernment process?

4. Are there any biblical examples of the models of church planting we have examined or the motives that inspire them? You might look at Acts 8:1-4; 11:19-26; 13:1-3; 15:36-40; 16:6-10; 18:1-5.

5. Which of the models are more or less likely to result in attractional churches and which in more incarnational forms of mission?

4

PLANTING **CHURCHES: WHERE?**

For many church planters and some planting churches, Where should we plant? is not a question they spend much time considering. This may seem surprising, but the location is very often the first component of a church-planting venture to fall into place. A church adopts a church-planting strategy because it has a specific area in mind, a community for which it has been concerned for some time. Or a church planter feels called to plant a church in a particular neighborhood or network. There are many other questions to ask, but *where* is not one of them. And the more organically a new church emerges, the less location matters.

For other church planters, planting churches, and mission agencies, the location may not be determined until somewhat later. Questions of motivation, strategic considerations, and discussions about the appropriate model may all precede or intersect with conversations about where to plant. Mission agencies and denominations committed to strategic church planting are not restricted to locations near an existing church that supplies the planting team. They can investigate many possibilities before deciding which to prioritize. Some church planters sense a call to pioneering ministry and make themselves available to be sent wherever they can be most effectively deployed. And some planting churches are willing to consider various localities before deciding where to plant.

Ecclesial factors will play some part in discussions about location. Denominations that deploy church planters with only limited consultation about where they should go (for instance, the Salvation Army) will have greater freedom to select locations for strategic reasons. Denominations that place greater emphasis on the personal calling of church planters or decisions taken locally (for instance, the Baptist Union) will have much less influence on where churches are planted. Denominations at each end of this spectrum might learn from each other's experience and embrace a mediating approach.

The practice of planting churches into networks rather than neighborhoods changes the focus of the discussion, but this does not make the question of where to plant redundant. Most networks have some geographical boundaries and places where they often gather, so church planters will think carefully about where best to engage with a network or subculture. Of the models examined in the previous chapter, multiple congregations appears to require least thought about location, since the current premises will be used for fresh expressions of church; but if these new congregations hope to reach particular sectors of the community or social networks, it makes sense to check whether the premises really are a suitable location.

This chapter suggests that it is worth carefully investigating the issue of location, even if we already have a strong conviction about where to plant a new church. There are various reasons for this (some of which were indicated in earlier chapters).

- If church planting is to impact substantially under-churched communities rather than adding more churches to well-churched areas, there are strategic issues to be considered. Church planters and planting churches will need to weigh the competing claims of locations they know and to which they feel drawn and other communities in greater need of new churches.

- The intended location may be less suitable than it first appears. Inadequate research, often the result of overconfident assumptions about how well the area is known, has hindered many church-planting ventures. There may, for example, be developments planned that will dramatically change the constituency of the area.[1]

- There may be other neighborhoods or networks that a planting church or church planter should also consider beyond the one to which they are first drawn. One of these might be a better cultural fit or present a sterner challenge but significant opportunities.

- Consultation with other mission agencies or local churches may reveal that there are already more churches in the intended location than are immediately obvious or that other church-planting initiatives are in process. Discovering this may open up possibilities for cooperative church planting or may suggest somewhere else might be preferable.

- Between national and local perspectives on location, there is also the possibility of regional or citywide consultation to identify locations where new churches might be planted. I was involved briefly in such a process in Leeds in the 1990s, which highlighted priorities and encouraged different denominations to plant in places where they had resources or felt an affinity with the community.

Feasibility and Discernment

Church planting is a demanding, costly, long-term, and risky project, as well as potentially a very exciting and fruitful form of mission, so great care as well as faith is needed before action. Deciding where to plant is a significant issue, which has implications also for the model chosen. It may be helpful at a very early stage in the planning process to consider various models, but final selection of the model should wait until the location is determined. What I am advocating here can be described as either a "feasibility study" or a "discernment process." It means carefully assessing various factors before deciding whether and where to plant.

Referring to this assessment as a discernment process reminds us that the question of paramount importance is whether God is calling us to plant a church in a particular neighborhood or network. It is not enough to present cogent strategic arguments. It is not enough to engage in extensive research and demonstrate that a new church is needed in a community. It is not enough to identify gifted and enthusiastic pioneers and planting team members. Those who commit themselves to church planting need the assurance that they have done all they can to discern the mind of Christ and that they are in step with the Holy Spirit as they move forward.

Referring to this assessment as a feasibility study reminds us that investigation and reflection, analysis and prayer, human responsibility and divine direction need to be held in balance. Investigating a possible location, assessing the resources that will be needed and those that are actually available, examining models that might be suitable, exploring mission options that might be alternatives to planting or other locations that might be worth considering, analyzing the results of the investigations and summarizing various scenarios—these, and many other, aspects of a feasibility study contribute information and perspectives that can inform the discernment process and help us to pray intelligently and act responsibly.

Community Research

One of the significant contributions of Challenge 2000 was its insistence on research as a basis for church planting. Many churches do not regard research as vital when planning evangelistic or community initiatives—sometimes with consequences that would be amusing if they did not represent a waste of time and energy. It is perhaps unremarkable, then, but still worrying, how little research some church planters and planting churches undertake.

As indicated above, this may be due to overconfidence in assuming that all the necessary information is already known, especially if the chosen location is in the vicinity. Reliance on "common knowledge" may be thought sufficient. But, all too often, our "knowledge" is partial and outdated, and it rarely includes likely future developments. Other reasons for skimping on research include determination to plant quickly, fear of what has been called "the paralysis of analysis" (where action is indefinitely postponed in favor of gathering yet more information), and the temperament of pioneers who become irritated by delays and data gathering.

But well-conducted research that leads on to effective analysis and action offers a much more secure foundation for a church-planting initiative. It takes time, but it offers several benefits:

- A more accurate and up-to-date understanding of the community than is otherwise available, including how the community feels about itself and its environment.
- A more realistic appraisal of the personnel and resources needed to plant a church in the location.
- A more considered view of which church-planting model might be best suited to the neighborhood or network.
- A more comprehensive awareness of what other mission agencies and churches are doing in the vicinity and how this might impinge on plans.
- An insight into what God is already doing within the community and how church planters might make connections with this.[2]

Community research is certainly not a process exclusively or even primarily associated with church planting. Community workers, youth workers, pastors, and evangelists have conducted "community surveys" or "community audits" for many different reasons over the years, to say nothing of such research undertaken by other agencies. Consequently, there are many processes and tools available, and considerable experience and expertise, so that church planters and planting churches have a wealth of resources they can adapt for their own purposes.

Churches considering church planting may also discover (if they ask) that some of their own members have expertise in this area and may be willing to design and oversee this community research. Gifts in the areas of research, data collection, and analysis may not be perceived as relevant to church planting, but if community research is understood as part of the process, more people can be involved than those who form the planting team—increasing the ownership of the whole venture in the planting church. This may not be sufficient reason to undertake community research, but it is a very positive by-product.

One limitation of community research tools is that most assume that a geographical area is in view. But churches today are planted into social groupings that may not be defined primarily by geography, but by ethnicity, age, subculture, leisure interests, or many other factors. The same basic principles apply, but the materials need to be adapted for research into networks. Actually, whatever the nature of the community, customization is better than using off-the-shelf tools to discover the information needed in each context. What we require is not just information gathering but research that will inform a decision about whether this is where we might plant a church.

As with all good research, we need to identify the key questions before we begin. Failure to do so usually means we amass lots of irrelevant information and sometimes means we omit important data. Andrew Grinnell, who oversees the Salvation Army's NEO teams, suggests three basic questions for church planters as they research a community:

- What are the mission opportunities?
- Is church planting the best response?
- Are we the best people to plant?

What follows here, then, is not a definitive process but an indication of what community research generally entails.[3] There are two main kinds of information to gather: technical data and soft data. *Technical data* can be collected from various sources (libraries, local government departments, the Internet, and so on) and does not require personal interaction with the community. *Soft data* involves spending time in the community and interacting with those who belong to it. Another distinction between different kinds of data is signaled by the terms *quantitative* and *qualitative* (which do not overlap precisely with the previous terms). We will explore these components in more detail below.

There are five basic components of community research:

- observation
- conversation
- investigation
- interpretation
- application

At the risk of oversimplification or implying that these components comprise five steps that always take place in this order, we will consider them in turn. In practice, researchers weave in and out of these activities and are often involved in more than one at the same time.[4]

Observation

The first element is perhaps the most underrated but provides an essential foundation for the other elements. Simply observing the community—people, buildings, environment, facilities, and activities—provides all kinds of insights into what it is like, how it functions and interacts, what it values, where its centers and boundaries are, what has shaped it, and how it is changing. If the community is a neighborhood, walking (not driving) around the area and taking time to observe carefully will give church planters a "feel" for the area that they cannot gain in any other way.

- Walking around the area with others (in the planting team or from the planting church or mission agency) may be helpful, as different people will notice things that others miss. Observing the community together also gives opportunities for conversation and reflection en route.
- Walking around the area alone may also be important so that, free from the distraction of companions, we can concentrate fully on the sights, sounds, smells, and "buzz" of the community.
- Walking around the area at different times of day and night may also be vital in understanding the neighborhood: in some areas different communities are visible at different times.
- Depending on the nature of the area, pausing to sit quietly in public spaces, parks, or cafés, and watching and listening to the people and activities nearby may offer further insights. Browsing in local shops helps build a picture of the community and its interests.
- Observation can, of course, be combined with praying for the

community. Prayer-walking has been popular in many churches in recent years; this can sharpen the observation process and enable a different kind of listening as we look for signs of God at work in the community and ask what more God wants to do there.

- Taking a camera to record significant places, buildings, people, and activities may enable ongoing reflection on the community and help to communicate with others what we have observed.
- Being attentive to what is known as "spatial symbolism" is important—discerning the historical, cultural, and spiritual messages conveyed by buildings and locations in the community.

This observation process needs to be undertaken sensitively and respectfully, especially in communities that are tight-knit or suspicious of outsiders and soon notice strangers walking around or watching as they drink tea in the local café. It is best to avoid walking around in groups of more than two or three people, to refrain from overt observation, and to be very discreet in the use of cameras. Discretion is not to deceive but to avoid causing unnecessary offense or (in some areas) the risk of being mistaken for undercover police officers or other officials.

It is surprising how much observation can reveal about a community without any further research, especially if several people observe the community on various occasions. Such observation visits and reflection together afterward also offer early opportunities for the planting team to interact together and develop a shared vision for the community. It may also be useful for members of the planting church or mission agency to participate in this observation process, so they gain insights into the context into which they will be deploying the team.

If the community into which a church may be planted is nongeographical, observation of the people and places that are significant for them is equally important. However, it may not be feasible, or advisable, to detach this from the next element in the research process.

Conversation

Observation alone is insufficient. The stories that have shaped the community and the area in which the community lives, works, shops, or relaxes are carried by people as well as by buildings and the environment. Engaging people in conversation, listening to their stories, asking probing but nonintrusive questions, confirming by further conversations what earlier conversations have suggested, and reflecting on the missional implications are crucial if church planters are to penetrate below the surface of the community. Such conversations can also confirm or, if necessary, correct impressions gained through the observation process.

Conversations can reveal perspectives on the community that observation alone cannot and that statistical data is ill equipped to provide. Researchers can discover how people spend their time, what influences their thinking, what hopes and fears they have, what belief systems and value systems are prevalent, and how they make decisions.

This aspect of community research can be undertaken in various ways:

- Inviting people to complete a questionnaire designed to elicit information that will be helpful in assessing the feasibility of church planting there.
- Convening a focus group that brings people together to discuss issues within the community. This may explore what they value in the community as well as needs and concerns.
- Adopting an informal approach that does not prescribe questions or gather groups together but invites story-telling and general comments on the community.
- Interviewing a range of people in the community (old/young, rich/poor, single/married, men/women, working/unemployed, from different ethnic groups, and so on) in order to understand the community from different perspectives.
- Consulting representatives of various statutory services (planning and housing officers, social workers, those who work with the elderly, young people, homeless people, families, and children) and voluntary agencies (tenants' groups, residents' associations, neighborhood groups, support networks for vulnerable members of the community, and local political groups). There may also be a local strategic partnership that provides a forum for many organizations to work together.
- Using the "snowball" approach, whereby initial conversation partners are asked to suggest other significant people whom the researcher might interview.
- Arranging to meet key people in the neighborhood who know many others and have their finger on the pulse of the community. These include community police officers, teachers, shopkeepers, doctors' receptionists, restaurant owners, hairdressers, youth workers, real estate brokers, those who work in the local cafés or post office, local government officials, and the leaders of various faith communities and other churches.

- Engaging in "double listening"—listening to God as well as to the interviewee and making connections between gospel and culture.[5]

In some communities, questionnaires may work well. In others, where they are regarded with suspicion, questionnaires are likely to produce little useful information and will alienate people. If questionnaires are used, researchers should be up-front about their purpose and whether (and how) those they interview can access the information obtained. Questionnaires need to be designed well if they are to extract information that will help researchers rather than producing reams of extraneous material. It may be worth consulting agencies with expertise in this area.[6]

Whatever approach is used, these conversations need to be handled with great care: they have the potential either to build positive relationships that will aid the process of church planting or to alienate the community. Some church planters report that their initial conversation partners became friends and eventually members of the new church. Others have struggled to overcome negative impressions created by poorly conducted research.

In older and more stable neighborhoods there may be individuals who have unofficial but very influential roles in the community. When I moved into East London in the late 1970s, there were still some local "barons" who meted out summary justice to miscreants and mobilized community support for those who needed it. Getting to know one of these "barons" provided invaluable insights into the community (and some challenging pastoral encounters when he joined the church and wondered how to apply his former methods in a Christian community).

Robert Linthicum has identified four significant roles in urban communities.[7] Writing primarily for community organizers, he advises them to discover and get to know the "gatekeepers" (those who decide whether people are accepted in the community), the "caretakers" (those who offer a listening ear and practical support to others in need), the "flak-catchers" (those who pass on news and gossip in the community), and the "brokers" (those who have connections and can get things done). Would-be church planters in older rural and inner-city communities can benefit enormously by discovering and developing good relations with such people.

In newer, more transient, or more affluent communities, such roles may not have emerged or may not exist in a more individualistic culture. But in well-established social networks, these roles often emerge and can be identified by observation and asking questions. In effect, researchers undertake a "power audit" of the community.

Investigation

In many contexts (although less so in relation to networks or new housing developments) a wealth of information is available by way of resources that can be accessed more or less readily through local libraries, council planning departments, various statutory and voluntary agencies, websites, and census data. This aspect of community research is ideal for those who struggle to engage strangers in conversation but are happy to spend hours working through documents, extracting relevant information, and analyzing its meaning in the context of church planting. Information can be gathered on numerous issues that may help to determine whether a planting venture should go ahead and, if so, with what focus: the size of the community, its age range, gender balance, ethnic diversity, class mix, level and types of employment, family dynamics, degree of transience, housing, modes of transport, links with other communities, social needs, and income levels.

Investigation in libraries, in government offices, and via websites is no substitute for what can be discovered only through observation and conversation, but it provides more objective data to set alongside other information and perceptions. While observation and conversation major on "soft" data and qualitative research (although they may also contribute toward quantitative research), investigation majors on technical data and quantitative research. In some cases, researchers may also come across other recent research into the community.

Researchers need to ensure that the data they use is up-to-date and targeted on the area in which they are interested. The 1991 British government census was used extensively by church planters in the 1990s, but some did not appreciate that the data on which they relied was becoming increasingly dated and unreliable as the decade went on. Information from the 2001 British census is readily available online, making access and analysis easier, but those who use it must be aware that the information becomes less reliable each year that passes until the 2011 census data is available.[8] Nor is the available information always related to the precise area they are investigating; quite often different boundaries are used by different agencies and for different purposes. Failing to recognize and adjust for this can diminish the value of the information extracted and distort conclusions based on it.

One helpful source of both technical and soft data is the local newspaper (often also now available online). Although local newspapers are often notorious for factual inaccuracy, reading past and current editions can help researchers identify prevalent and persistent concerns and issues in the community, learn something of its history and achievements it takes pride in, note tension points, and discern the mood of the community. Newspaper reports and stories (and those on local television or radio stations) can confirm or challenge insights gained by observation or in conversations. They can also illustrate or question the validity of data obtained by investigation. And sometimes gatekeepers, caretakers, flak-catchers, and brokers become visible in the articles and letter pages.

An important dimension of investigation is discovering demographic trends and projected developments. When considering planting a church in an area, it is helpful to know if and when the community is likely to grow or shrink, whether there are significant changes planned, where new housing may be located, and how any planned changes will impact the social and ethnic makeup of the community, employment prospects, the provision of community facilities, and various other factors.

Interpretation

Information alone—whether gained through observation, conversation, investigation, or a combination of all three—is not enough. The next stage of the research process is analysis—interpreting the information in order to understand what has been observed, heard, and unearthed. Without this stage, the community research will have produced a mountain of unprocessed information that will gather dust on a shelf (or lie ignored in old computer files). This is a waste of resources and discouraging to those who spent hours gathering information that church planters and mission agencies failed to use to discern whether or how to move forward.

Interpretation includes the following elements:

- Collating the information gathered from different sources, cross-referencing this and making decisions about its relevance and weighting.
- Identifying key questions that the research process is designed to answer. These questions should mostly have been identified at the outset, but further questions usually arise as the research develops.
- Digging beneath the surface of the facts and figures to ascertain not only *what* the community is like but *why* this is so. The history of the community may offer very important insights into why the community functions as it does, why certain needs are apparent, and why some but not other aspirations are present.
- Highlighting information about the community that is of particular

importance for a church-planting venture. This could influence the timing of any initiative, the size and makeup of the planting team, where and when a new church might meet, its ethos, and many other issues.

Interpretation also involves reflecting theologically on the information gathered:

- What messages have we heard from the physical environment or picked up from our conversations?
- Have we discerned points at which the gospel affirms or challenges local cultural norms?
- What will it mean to identify with this community and engage in incarnational mission?
- Are there any indications of how receptive the community may be to the gospel or how it might receive church planters?
- Have we found any "redemptive analogies" (images, figures, historical incidents, physical features, and so on) that might help us contextualize the gospel?
- How, where, and through whom is God already at work in the community?

Reflecting on these issues may help us focus our efforts, clarify our priorities, adjust our language, and avoid giving offense. It may also save us from unrealistic expectations and time lines.

Application

The interpretation stage leads to the final part of the process, where we grapple with the fundamentally important question: So what? How will the information and analysis be used? What recommendations will flow from the interpretation of the data? What will be the implications for the mission agency, planting church, or planting team?

If this community research has been understood as a discernment process as well as a feasibility study, both elements will have been apparent at each stage: prayer-walking during the observation phase, listening to God as well as listening to people, prayerful reflection on the data gathered, and openness to prophetic insight as the information is interpreted. At the application stage, the research informs prayerful discernment of the way forward.

If the research is not perfunctory but plays a significant role in determining whether and where to plant a church, various recommendations may emerge:

- That the community is under-churched and so church planting should be seriously considered here.
- That other approaches to mission rather than church planting would be preferable in this community.
- That the community is undergoing, or will shortly undergo, demographic changes, so this may or may not be the ideal time to plant a new church.
- That there are enough churches already in the community and church planting is unnecessary here.
- That another nearby community is worth investigating further as a more suitable context for church planting.

Recommendations from community research should not be regarded as determinative. If we have a strong conviction that church planting here is in line with the purposes of God, we may choose to go ahead, fully aware that we do so in the face of recommendations to the contrary. But the research process has still been a valuable exercise in helping us to understand the implications of this decision.

Before a final decision is made, however, on whether and where to plant, two further aspects of research and consultation need to be taken into account.

Consultation

During the observation, conversation, and investigation phases of the research, a picture should have emerged of the role of other churches in the community. Churches with their own premises or a visible presence in the community will have been easy to identify and investigate, but churches meeting in homes or in poorly advertised locations are less easy to unearth. There are other churches too that we may need to take into account—churches that meet outside the community but have members or home groups meeting within it and churches further away that may also be considering church planting.

Before deciding where to plant, mission agencies and planting churches should consult with these other churches. A great deal of pain and bitterness has been caused by church planters who fail to do this. Consultation is not only common courtesy but an opportunity to learn more about the community and existing mission activities. There is no knowing how these churches will respond to an agency or church proposing to plant a church near them. Some may feel threatened and discourage this even though they are making little impact in the community; others may welcome this proposal with open arms, grateful for a mission partner in an under-churched community; some may be convinced that church planting would be disruptive and suggest an alternative location; others may offer support and even encourage some of their own members to join the new church. There may even be possibilities of adoption or cooperative church planting.

To be authentic, consultation needs to take place during the research phase and certainly before we make a final decision about whether and where to plant. It is inappropriate to seek permission from existing churches to plant a new church, but conversations that can actually influence the decision are preferable to a cosmetic consultation exercise that amounts to no more than informing existing churches that a new church is imminent. In my experience, and that of Urban Expression as a church-planting agency, consultation with existing churches has been extraordinarily valuable, has influenced decisions about where to plant churches, and has resulted in life-giving partnerships and shared mission initiatives.

One question always worth asking existing churches is whether there have been previous attempts to plant churches in the community that have failed. If our research has revealed that church planting is feasible and needed here, others may have discovered this too and may have tried to respond. Learning from any abortive attempts may help us decide how or whether to proceed.

Resource Audit

The community research process and consultation with other churches may indicate that we have found a suitable location for church planting, but do we have the personnel and resources to seize this opportunity? The final component in determining where to plant a church is an audit of the mission agency or planting church. As with community research, there are resources available from several agencies to help design such an audit.[9]

The audit might include the following components:

- Historical research to tell the story of the planting church or agency and provide a context within which to consider church planting—this is particularly important if church planting has not been on the agenda before, or not for many years.

- A SWOT analysis that investigates our strengths, weaknesses, opportunities, and threats. This helps in assessing our capacity for church planting.
- A gifts identification process that reveals whether there is a viable planting team to be deployed and who might undertake specific tasks in any venture.
- Where the adoption model is being explored, the audit should include the church that might be adopted, since its history, resources, convictions, liabilities, hopes, and fears need to be investigated thoroughly before we decide to proceed with this most sensitive of planting approaches.

When a mission agency is already committed to church planting, a less extensive audit may be necessary, but many issues remain relevant. Is this location within the remit of the mission agency? Are there other locations that should be considered as priorities for various reasons? Will planting another church overextend its resources? Can it recruit a planting team to respond to this opportunity?

On the basis of what we learn from this resource audit, three crucial questions should be considered:

- *Does the agency or church have a vision for church planting?* The audit may reveal that church planting is well understood, high on the agenda for many people, widely owned, and a focus for prayer. Or it may indicate that the vision for church planting is limited to a few enthusiasts, based on unrealistic expectations, locked into inappropriate models, or well below other items on the agenda. It is helpful to know this before proceeding! The latter discovery may not preclude church planting, but it ought at least to delay it while further envisioning takes place or while other pressing issues are addressed (this may be especially pertinent in "accidental parenthood" situations).
- *Does the agency or church have the resources for church planting?* From the audit it will become clear whether there are sufficient people—available and suitably gifted—to plant a new church. Different planting models and different contexts require different numbers and different skills. The audit will also assess the financial resources available; different models and contexts also need different levels of funding. If the audit reveals deficiencies in any

area, one option is to look for partners in a cooperative church-planting venture.

- *Is there a match between the planting agency and the proposed location?* Answering this question will require information from both the community research and the audit. A new church may be needed in the community, and the planting agency may have the resources to plant a church, but this does not necessarily mean that we should proceed. Can the kind of church that is needed be realized? Can any cultural gap between the planting agency and the community be crossed? For any church-planting initiative to be feasible, enough suitable people need to be living in (or be willing to move into) the community. It may be that the planting agency should consider an alternative community with which it is better matched. However, it is important that we do not always choose easier church-planting contexts and neglect the harder cross-cultural challenges.

Decision Time

Some church planters (and some planting churches) may be impatient with the amount of research and consultation suggested in this chapter. In fact, the community research, audit of resources, and consultation with other churches can be carried out alongside each other and need not take that long. Detailing the various components gives the impression that this process is longer and more complex than it actually is. Essentially what we need to know before deciding whether and where to plant is this: Do we have the resources and is this the right location? Mission agencies with a track record of church planting can draw on past experience and present expertise. In some situations community research may have been done recently by others. Such factors will reduce the amount of work and the time involved.

But I have become convinced after many conversations with church planters and planting churches that it is perilous to truncate this research process. Many missed opportunities could have been seized and many failed initiatives, some with very damaging pastoral consequences, could have been avoided if proper research had been carried out. Planting churches too quickly was a serious strategic weakness in the 1990s (driven in part by the time-limited goals set early in the decade); we do not need to repeat this now.

At some point, though, a decision needs to be made. Is this the place to plant a church? Do we have the resources? What do we sense God is saying to us? A related question is, Which approach to church planting would be most appropriate? The research process may also have explored this issue or may lead inexorably to a particular model. This may also be the time to review our motivation: Why are we planting a church, and what are our expectations? We will address further questions—When should we plant? Who should be involved? And what kind of church should be planted?—in the following chapters, but these issues may also be considered at this stage.

Remembering the dual-track approach suggested here of a feasibility study linked with a discernment process, we need to answer two questions. Is church planting feasible here? And is God calling us to plant? Four conclusions are possible:

- It seems feasible to plant a church, and the call of God also seems clear.
- It does not seem feasible to plant a church, but the call of God seems so clear that we will proceed regardless.
- It seems feasible to plant a church, but we do not discern the call of God.
- It does not seem feasible to plant a church, nor do we discern the call of God.

In the last two scenarios, no church planting takes place, at least in the immediate future. These scenarios do not preclude the possibility of planting a church at a later date or in a different community, but they do mean that the current proposal does not proceed. In the first scenario, the way seems clear for church planting to go ahead—with no guarantee of success but with confidence based on prayerful research. In the second scenario, church planting proceeds in full awareness that it will be risky and contrary to normal strategic considerations. It is vital to make room for such scenarios (significant mission advances would not have occurred without them), but we need to acknowledge what we are doing and our dependence on God to lead and provide in unexpected ways.

Community Mapping

Another component of community research that church planters may find very helpful is known as "community mapping." This does not need to be done before deciding whether and where to plant, although the information gathered up to that point will help with the mapping process. Mapping reveals more about the location in which church planting will take place.

Community mapping recognizes that different kinds of maps are needed to represent and interpret a community. The most basic, of course, is a scale representation of the roads, railways, rivers, open spaces, shopping precincts, industrial developments, and major buildings in an area. Anyone interested in a community will make use of such a map and will decide where to locate its boundaries.

But there are also "mental maps," which reflect the image people have of their community and the key locations within it. Inviting people to draw a sketch map of their community can be very revealing. I have done this in several different communities, and each time the exercise has surprised people: often there are very detailed areas surrounded by unknown spaces; familiar routes are marked with confidence, but nearby streets are either ignored or misplaced; invisible barriers and no-go areas become evident; and other boundaries are acknowledged than those the official map indicates.

Different people have different mental maps. Someone who drives around and beyond the area will perceive it differently from someone who walks or catches buses and rarely ventures out of the area. Members of different ethnic groups will define boundaries that do not appear on geographical maps (compare, for example, the mental maps of Catholics and Protestants in Belfast). Subways and pedestrian bridges enable some to cross major roads with ease but dissuade parents with children in strollers or those who are nervous about such places. Mental maps may exaggerate or minimize actual distances between places depending on how familiar these journeys are.

Mental maps can help church planters understand the community more deeply and make informed choices about where to do what. It is valuable to know the community centers, gathering points, and perceived boundaries before deciding where to live, set up projects, start meetings, or simply hang out. Choosing one side of a road or park rather than the other may make a significant difference. If a social network is in view, discovering its mental map will be essential.

There are other forms of community mapping:

- *Mapping neighborhoods.* Although in some areas these may be clearly defined and obvious, especially in urban areas it is often difficult to work out where one neighborhood ends and another starts. But as "turf wars" demonstrate, these are symbolic boundaries that church planters must respect even if they try also to transcend them.
- *Mapping networks or "communities of interest."* Intersecting the

neighborhoods are diverse networks of relationships that emerge around shared characteristics or interests. Church planters may choose to engage deliberately with such networks, rather than working within neighborhoods, but even those who continue to focus on neighborhoods need to be aware of these networks and their role within the community. These networks will have focal points, though not necessarily in the neighborhood where many live. These may be places of worship, sports grounds, shopping centers, cultural centers, clubs, or centers of art, music, or fashion. Such locations may be where church planters choose to concentrate or at least interact.

- *Mapping through time.* Community research usually pays some attention to how a community has grown up and changed over time, especially in the case of older neighborhoods. Learning how an area has taken shape and becoming familiar with significant stories and community memories can enable us to empathize with the community, understand the strength of local reactions on certain issues, and engage more sensitively with our neighbors. In some communities, historical research uncovers deeply rooted trauma or repeating patterns and problems that may stir us to pray for healing and lasting transformation.

Community mapping is a never-ending activity. Neighborhoods expand or shrink, new housing developments appear, networks emerge and disintegrate, and church planters gain fresh insights into how the community functions. Community mapping can also be a form of prayer and an opportunity for ongoing reflection on God's activity in the community and God's intentions for it.

Location, Location, Location

There is a further dimension of the *where* question: Where will the new church meet? Exploring this issue does not presume that starting meetings is the first or most important aspect of church planting. Regular or even occasional meetings may begin much later in the planting process than church planters tended to assume in the 1990s. But if the church is to have any corporate existence, it will eventually need somewhere to gather. This issue may have been addressed during the community research, which might have thrown up various possibilities or pointed in a particular direction. But we may prefer to postpone discussion of meeting places to avoid focusing prematurely on meetings.

In practice the options may be quite limited, especially in new housing developments or in areas with minimal community facilities. But it may be worth considering this question in principle and reflecting on the implications of various choices. Church planters, sooner or later, find themselves in discussions about whether to rent, buy, or even build; whether to start meeting in a small building and move to a larger one as numbers grow or to start in a larger one to avoid the need to move; and whether the priority is a space for the church to gather or a place where the church can connect with the community.

Underlying these practical issues are deeper questions about the nature of the church and its mission, and where it might meet in order to fulfill its calling and express its identity. It has long been recognized (though not in many churches) that buildings profoundly shape communities, limiting their scope and encouraging them to act and relate in certain ways. Familiar and fierce debates about seating arrangements or remodeling reveal a subconscious recognition that where and how we meet affects who we are. With attention and effort, such influences can be minimized or transcended, but church planting offers us an opportunity to choose or create a space that is consistent with the values and vision of the church and its mission.

We may also want to weigh the benefits and drawbacks of meeting in premises used for many other purposes, which are not associated especially with church activities. Such locations may be cheaper and more flexible, but they demand much more of the planting team in terms of setting up, dismantling and storing equipment, and creating the desired ambience. They may be more accessible and less intimidating to some sections of the community, but such buildings may have unhelpful associations for others (such as those who were unhappy at the school in which a church now meets). A multipurpose meeting place may embody our conviction that church is not to be separated from everyday life, but not having a permanent base may convey the message that this church is unlikely to be committed long term to the area.

There are five main options for us to consider, each of which will influence the kind of church that emerges:

- domestic space
- public space
- sacred space
- social space
- virtual space

Domestic Space

Many churches are planted in homes and continue to meet in domestic settings, some by choice and others for lack of alternatives. Not only is there biblical precedent for churches in homes, but there are significant advantages. Among these are the minimal financial costs, an informal atmosphere, the intimacy of a relatively small group, the ease with which we can eat together, accessibility within the community, and opportunities to invite neighbors to join in. The proliferation of home-based churches in recent years—house churches, home churches, cell churches, household churches, base ecclesial communities, table churches, simple churches—is building on insights gained from experience with house groups, cell groups, and home groups in the second half of the twentieth century. Small can be beautiful.

However, there are inbuilt limitations, and contextual factors may discourage the use of homes. An obvious restriction is the number of people who can comfortably fit into most homes, especially in communities where rooms are small. If a growing church wants to continue meeting as a whole group, with or without subdividing into further domestic settings, a different kind of space is needed. Some churches choose not to grow beyond the number who can thrive in a domestic setting, multiplying home-based churches rather than expanding out of homes; others perceive the need for larger gatherings.

Visibility is another factor, which church planters may regard as a help or a hindrance, as churches in homes are more hidden. In some communities, homes are natural environments to invite friends to sample a new church; in others, local culture dictates that only close family are welcome in homes, so invitations to others present cultural barriers. Some homes might present unwanted physical barriers to people with disabilities, and home-based churches that advertise their activities can face legal challenges about the use of homes for public meetings, especially if (as in one situation I know) the neighbors complain.

If churches are planted in domestic settings, they need to embrace that environment and resist incongruent practices. Shared meals within which bread and wine have eucharistic significance, interactive forms of learning, multivoiced worship, and simple structures are typical components of churches in homes. Those who join the church are almost all likely to be friends of existing members and not intimidated by coming into an intimate setting where there is little room to be a spectator.

Some church planters may opt to meet not in their own homes but in the homes of people in the community with whom they build relationships, whether or not they are yet Christians, seeing this as more missional. Some find biblical warrant for this approach in Jesus' instruction to his disciples to find a "person of peace" in whose home they could stay.[10] These homes may be culturally more accessible to others than where the church planter lives.

Public Space

Some churches are planted in public buildings or move to these when they outgrow homes. Public spaces include community centers, schools, colleges, libraries, meeting rooms in hotels or restaurants, town halls, recreation centers, and many other places. The church planted there may have no connection with the owners or other users of such buildings beyond paying rent and negotiating use of the premises. The space is chosen as a neutral venue, accessible to the public, and more visible than meeting in a home. Over time some churches may forge stronger links with those responsible for the building and participate in other activities based there or even end up managing the facilities. In some contexts church planters may choose to purchase a public space rather than renting one, which may be exclusively for church activities (in which case it is no longer public but takes on some of the features of domestic or sacred space) or designated for shared community use.

Public spaces have obvious advantages over homes, including more room, flexibility, and opportunities to develop various community-oriented activities or participate in existing activities in shared buildings. Renting public space requires less initial outlay and allows ease of transition to an alternative space if the needs and priorities of the church change, but storage of equipment and the need to set up and clear this away each time the church meets can become wearisome. Public spaces may also be bland, uninspiring, impersonal, and not very conducive to corporate worship. Some may defy all attempts to beautify or soften them. If a public space is chosen, can it be a building with "soul"?

Sacred Space

Many emerging churches are rediscovering the value of sacred space and devote considerable attention to creating an environment conducive to worship, learning together, and responding to God. Some choose to meet in traditional church buildings, often preferring old sites and sometimes interpreting their presence and activities as "reopening the old wells"[11] or recovering sacred spaces. Others meet in public buildings but transform all or part of these into sacred spaces, creating "holy ground" through the use of installations or developing chapels in community buildings. One church I know meets either in the open air (very unusual in the British climate) or in an ancient chapel no longer used for other purposes, appreciating both the "cathedral of the open skies" and the resonances of an old sacred building. Some churches are planted into buildings owned and used by other churches, sharing their sacred space. This may work well if the new church is distinctive (often such arrangements involve a church serving a particular ethnic community), but can otherwise be confusing.

This preference for sacred space is often interpreted as rejection of the functionality of modernity and sensitivity to the emerging spirituality of a postmodern culture. Those who are searching for spiritual experience, it is suggested, may not associate this with plastic chairs in a secular public space or be attracted to churches that gather in such places. Not all are persuaded: some interpret the notion of sacred space as a return to Christendom or even to pagan notions that designate holy places and fail to integrate spirituality and daily life. It is common to hear members of planting teams yearning for a "proper church building" in place of the rented premises they currently use, but this may owe more to their upbringing than to missional instincts.

Social Space

Another option that has appealed to several emerging churches is to inhabit shared social space, becoming part of an existing community and integrating their own activities into what that community is already doing. Churches may not only use pubs or cafés as their meeting places but participate enthusiastically in other activities and events associated with these venues. The boundaries between church and community are blurred as church members become members of the community and members of the community become involved in the church. A church in Edinburgh, for instance, does not just meet in a health clinic; it is invited by the management to provide opportunities for members of the clinic to engage with issues of spiritual health. The pastor of the church is chaplain to the clinic and its users.

Churches using social spaces of this kind have much lower barriers between themselves and other members of the community and many opportunities to develop friendships and cooperate in ventures that enhance the well-being of the community. "Belonging before believing" characterizes the journey of most people into such churches. These initiatives are examples of incarnational rather than invitational approaches to church planting. They are particularly appropriate when church planters are engaging with social networks rather than neighborhoods. Whether such churches are sustainable over the long haul (and whether this matters), how they help people move from belonging into believing, and how they address the homogeneity that often characterizes them are questions that cannot yet be answered with confidence.

Virtual Space

Some church planters have avoided questions about where the church will meet by planting into cyberspace. Those who plant and join such churches need not meet together physically at all but interact with each other at a distance through the medium of the Internet. From their homes, offices, or Internet cafés, they participate in a translocal or even global community. Some have welcomed this as a contemporary expression of the authentic missionary instinct to incarnate the gospel into all cultures and communities; others have castigated it as stretching the meaning of "incarnating" too far and colluding with cultural trends that diminish authentic community.[12]

Just as the models described in chapter 3 may be stages on a church-planting journey rather than discrete approaches, so church planters may choose different locations at different stages. Some may evolve naturally, as shared public space facilitates growing partnership between users of a building so that a church is now operating in social space. Other spaces may be hybrids from the beginning: a converted barn on a farm may have features of both domestic space and public space; a specially adapted bus operating in various locations as a mission, worship, and community space for young people may blur boundaries between social space and sacred space. And some church planters may use different spaces for different purposes.

Location is not the most important question facing church planters, nor is it necessarily the first issue to be addressed, but whatever choice is made has implications for the kind of church that is planted and its mission in the community.

● ● ●

Questions for Further Reflection

1. To which of the five kinds of spaces identified in this chapter as contexts for church planting are you drawn, and why? Are there any other options?
2. How can a planting agency ensure that neither a feasibility study nor a discernment process swamps the other element?
3. Does it matter in which order church planters address the questions "Where?" "How?" and "Why?" as they embark on church planting?
4. How would you adapt the community research process described in this chapter if you were planting a church into a network rather than a neighborhood?
5. Should church planters always sense a call to a particular community, or can you be called to be a church planter and be willing to go wherever an opportunity arises?

5

PLANTING **CHURCHES: WHEN?**

Very few churches are planted too slowly. It is possible to dither and prevaricate during the planning period, to research and analyze endlessly without reaching a decision, to try so hard to avoid risks or being under-prepared that we lose support and momentum. But more often, church-planting ventures are damaged or jeopardized by precipitate action, rushing ahead without adequate preparation or consultation.

Timing is a crucial issue for effective church planting. The factors that influence when to plant vary according to the nature of the planting agency, the church-planting model used, the makeup of the planting team, and particular contextual issues.

Churches Planting Churches

In eight of the church-planting models we explored in chapter 3, the planting agency is a local church (nine, if the cooperative strategy includes one or more churches). How does a church decide when it should plant a new church?[1] And once it has made this decision, when does the process begin, and how does it prepare to become a planting church?[2]

Deciding When to Plant

The feasibility study and discernment process we worked through in the previous chapter relate not only to whether and where a church might be planted but also to the timing of any venture. A church might conclude that it has the resources needed to plant a church, that it has identified the appropriate area or network, and that God is calling it to this, but there are at least two further questions it should address before deciding that now is the time to start the planting process.

First, how widely owned is the vision to plant a new church? Church planting is a major commitment, not only for those who will comprise the planting team, but for the planting church. The decision to plant will have implications for the whole church for years ahead. There are considerable costs in terms of relationships, time, energy, finance, emotions, structures, and priorities. Some of the planting models are more demanding than others, but all of them place demands on the church, which will not be the same community as it was before.

So it is vital that there is thorough consultation. The vision to plant may have originated in the leadership team, in a home group meeting in the area under consideration, or in the heart of an individual pioneer, but the church needs to own it before the process gets underway. This will take some time and may test the patience of those who are by now fired up and eager to move forward, as it is very easy for them to forget how long they took wrestling with this challenge. But Roger Ellis warns, "Leaders must not expect the rest of the church to apprehend in one evening a vision which has been conceived during months of careful preparation."[3]

There may, of course, be some who do not accept the rationale for planting a new church, do not believe God is calling the church to do this, or feel implacably imposed to join such a risky and costly venture. We need to listen to these people and weigh their convictions carefully, only proceeding if the church as a whole remains convinced that the time is right to do so. More problematic is the tendency in some churches for members to give passive acquiescence to proposals only to raise objections once the vision looks like it might become a reality.

Second, are there other matters within the church that we need to address first? In most churches the demands of planting a new church will preclude or defer other significant initiatives, so it may be helpful to explore whether church members have other dreams, hopes, or visions that cannot be pursued if and while church planting goes ahead. These may or may not be sufficient to delay or rescind the planting plans, but eliciting them and, where possible, affirming their potential may encourage those who express them to set them aside for the time being and support the planting initiative. Sometimes, though, these hopes and dreams may indicate that church planting is not the current priority and that we need to explore other possibilities.

There may also be unresolved internal issues that we should address before embarking on church planting or at least acknowledge as elements in the planting process. Especially in accidental parenthood situations, but not only in these contexts, church planting may be only one component in a complex scenario. These other issues may not preclude church planting, but it is unwise to treat church planting as a way of distracting attention from relational problems, dissent, or other internal struggles.

Consultation to explore these various issues can take place while the community research is underway or the results are being analyzed, so this need not delay unduly our decision about whether to plant. What is uncovered may or may not influence when (or whether) church planting begins. But if and when the planting process starts, we should be able to move forward with greater clarity and confidence.

Preparing the Planting Church

Once the church has made its decision, the planting process can begin. There are three priorities: preparing the church to become a planting church, clarifying expectations, and selecting and equipping the planting team. The time needed to complete these tasks will help determine when a new church is actually planted, and the quality of this preparatory work will have positive or negative consequences for the new church, the planting church, and the relationship between these churches. We will examine each task in turn, although in practice they usually run concurrently.[4]

Depending on which church-planting model is chosen, there are significant differences in the issues that we need to address in preparing a church to become a planting church. A long-distance approach will generally require much more attention to logistical issues and cross-cultural preparation than a mother/daughter initiative. Church planting by adoption introduces complications that are not pertinent to church planting on multiple sites. And there are pastoral and constitutional questions involved in planting by dispersion that do not concern those planting multiple or satellite congregations.

The costs. The planting process has the capacity to engage and transform the planting church as well creating a new church. This is the hoped-for win–win outcome—that the effort expended, risks taken, and costs incurred will result both in a new church emerging *and* in multidimensional growth in the planting church. George Lings comments, "Churches that plant new congregations set in motion a dynamic, both in the sending and the new church, which tends toward further growth and planting."[5]

However, not all planting churches report this experience. Some find the process much more demanding—even traumatic—than they expected and struggle to appreciate the benefits. Even when the church they have planted flourishes, there are questions about the cost to the planting church and sometimes a degree of resentment that this flourishing has been at the expense of the health of the planting church. When the new church fails to thrive, the planting church may carry even more concerns and regrets.

One reason why church planting fell out of favor toward the end of the 1990s was that many planting churches had not anticipated the pain involved in the process. They were unprepared for the consequences and became reticent about commending this practice to other churches. It is, therefore, very important that churches understand the implications of being involved in church planting. Becoming a planting church is a great privilege, but there are significant costs that churches need to recognize if they are not to suffer post-planting trauma. The enthusiasm needed to galvanize a church-planting venture can easily distract attention from possible pastoral consequences and hinder adequate preparation of the planting church for what it may experience.

Church-planting literature has frequently used the analogy of the "life cycle," recognizing parallels between church planting and the human reproductive process.[6] Thus, having a baby (especially a first baby) is a wonderfully joyful experience, but parents face major adjustments. While nothing can fully prepare parents for a baby, if they are not alerted to at least some of the consequences, they may struggle unnecessarily. Furthermore, it is the baby, rather than its parents, that is the center of attention, and this may exacerbate their struggles. Similarly, in a church-planting context, the planting church needs to be alerted to the consequences of what it is doing and prepared as fully as possible. It is dangerous to focus attention exclusively on the planting team or the new church and to neglect the well-being of the planting church. The "prenatal" phase in the church-planting process is the time to explore these issues.

The consequences. There are five consequences of planting that churches need to recognize, some of which require forethought if they are not to cause difficulties.

First, and most obviously, those who comprise the planting team will not be involved in the planting church in the same way as they previously were. In some models (multiple congregations, multiple sites, and satellite congregations), the planting team will remain part of the planting church but their attention will be on the new developments, so their roles and commitments will change. In other models (adoption and mother/daughter), team members may remain nominally part of the planting church and even retain limited responsibilities, but they increasingly become part of a different church and community. In others (accidental parenthood and most long-distance initiatives), they quickly become detached from the planting church, although friendships and some other links may persist.

Second, although the absence, gradual withdrawal, or changed level of involvement of the planting team may be acknowledged as part of the cost of planting, planting churches are often unprepared for the bereavement that settles on the church. Friendships are disrupted, the "church family" has members missing, and there is a grieving process that (using another life-cycle analogy) is similar to that experienced by parents when children leave home. Knowing that this is natural—even rejoicing at the maturity it demonstrates—does not fully offset the sense of loss. Planting churches need to be prepared for these feelings and encouraged to develop coping strategies.

Third, depending on the size and composition of the planting team, the planting church may "feel" different. It is not just that people will be conscious of physical absences but that the spiritual balance or age profile or gift mix of the church may have altered. The planting team is usually not comprised of a cross section of the church but of those with specific gifts needed in the planting process. The resulting changes in the planting church are sometimes obvious and sometimes hard to define or quantify, but they may be deeply felt. Some planting churches have replaced the numbers they have lost quite quickly but have struggled for much longer to adapt to the changed dynamics of the church.

Fourth, there will be "job vacancies" in the planting church, as those who have fulfilled certain roles leave these to concentrate on their responsibilities in the planting team and, in due course, in the new church. In churches with plenty of gifted and willing volunteers, this may be an opportunity for those who are well able to take on new responsibilities but were inhibited in the past by those they regarded as more talented. However, these people will need induction and encouragement in their new roles, and the church may need to take time to adjust to their different ways of doing things. Other planting churches may struggle to fill the vacancies, especially if they have not been identifying and training replacements. Whatever the available resources, this may offer planting churches a useful opportunity to review what they are doing and only continue with roles and activities that are newly judged to be worthwhile.

Fifth, the financial implications of church planting need to be spelled out in detail. There may be both increasing costs and decreasing income. The costs will depend on the church-planting model adopted, whether anyone in the planting team receives a salary, whether houses or other buildings are bought, rented, or repaired, and what additional equipment is needed. Some of the models (though usually not multiple sites, multiple congregations, or satellite congregations) will result in reduced income, as those who comprise the planting team sooner or later divert their financial support from the planting church to the new church. Only in the case of the adoption model is the planting church likely to receive a modest increase in income during the first phase of the process.

Preparing a planting church to face these consequences will not generally prevent them happening, but it does enable the church to think ahead, develop contingency plans, and seize opportunities. It also limits the number of disgruntled reactions in the church once some of these factors become apparent, because the church was warned that these things would probably happen.

Different models. The dispersion model of church planting needs separate attention. Some of the issues we have considered do not apply because the planting church ceases to exist or at least must be handled very differently. There may be feelings of bereavement, perhaps more intense than in other situations, because there is no longer any opportunity to revisit the planting church. The "feel" of the new churches that emerge and the balance within them will be even more different from the planting church than in the other models, but this actually may be less problematic in that everyone is involved in new churches where differences of these kinds are to be expected. And there will be many new roles to be allocated, but again in newly planted churches rather than replacing people in the planting church.

But the dispersion model raises other issues that need to be explored during the prenatal period. Is there a church constitution that must be consulted for guidance on how to wind up the affairs of the planting church? Are there legal and financial implications that need to be discussed with lawyers or accountants? Will one of the new churches inherit trust status from the planting church; will that original trust cover all the emerging churches, or will each need a new trust? If the church has staff, will they be employed by the new churches, serve the network of dispersed churches, or no longer be employed? If the church owns a building, will this be retained for some new purpose or disposed of, and how will any proceeds be disbursed? And beyond these administrative and personnel questions, because the dispersion model is more radical than the others, extra care is needed to ensure that the planning church really understands the implications and is wholeheartedly committed to this.

Other models also involve dynamics that influence the preparation needed in the planting church. The adoption model requires preparatory work in both churches (separately and together) and sensitive decisions about autonomy, buildings, leadership, and finance, as well as the issues we considered earlier in this chapter. Multiple congregations, multiple sites, and satellite congregations cannot be effectively planted without exploring models of leadership, accountability, and networking, the sharing of resources, and how to express both unity and diversity within a multifaceted church. Accidental parenthood may mean the preparation process is fraught and tense, but the quality of the preparatory work done in this period will be crucial for the outcomes in both churches, and any prospect of healthy relationships between them. And a vital issue in preparation for church-planting using the mother/daughter model is discussion about how and when the daughter church might progress toward independence.

Preparation. Whichever model is chosen, how can the planting church be properly prepared? There are various ways, all of which will take time, but this is time worth investing if the church is to be strengthened rather than damaged by the planting process. Some of the preparation activities can take place concurrently with the feasibility study and discernment process.

- *Teaching:* explaining what church planting is and why it is happening here. It is important to establish a biblical and theological basis for church planting, helping the church to perceive church planting as a normal function of a local church and a significant dimension of mission. This is an opportunity also to explore ecclesial and contextual issues, encouraging the church to reflect on its mission context and understand why the new church may be quite different from the planting church.[7]

- *Learning:* listening to stories of other planting churches, visiting other initiatives, receiving visits from church planters or representatives of churches that have been involved in church planting, reading about church planting, and discussing what has been shared and learned. A disturbing number of planting churches have gone ahead without learning from others—and have often made unnecessary mistakes in the process.

- *Envisioning:* encouraging all church members to own the vision, whether or not they will personally be involved in the planting team, and to see the potential of what is happening for the community in which the new church is being planted, for their own growth as a church and for the wider church, which can learn from this venture. The fact that the church is becoming a planting church and is giving away people and resources for the sake of mission is a cause for thanksgiving.

- *Consulting:* the implications of church planting need to be explained clearly and honestly so that the planting church really understands the costs and the benefits. The church then needs time to digest the information and ponder its implications, to raise concerns and objections, to discuss the planting process on which they are embarking, and to offer constructive input. Sensitive leadership will be needed to guide the church through such a consultation process, so that the discussion does not get bogged down but results in genuine ownership of the planting process and helpful insights that shape what happens.

- *Reassuring:* as the time approaches for the planting team to be deployed and the new church to be planted, various concerns and objections may be raised. Some will have been raised before; others may be new. Common concerns include fear that the initiative may fail; worry about the impact of such failure on the planting team and the reputation of the planting church; anxiety about the effects on any children involved in the venture; uncertainty about the financial implications; reluctance to lose friends or church stalwarts to the new church; and concern that dividing into smaller units may result in lower quality of ministry. It is impossible to provide complete reassurance on all the issues that may be raised, but we may be able to anticipate concerns, investigate their underlying assumptions, highlight benefits as well as costs, and explain why not planting is even more problematic.

- *Training:* preparing those who will take up responsibilities in the planting church once members of the planting team lay these down. The prenatal period provides an opportunity for apprenticeship, induction, and handing over the responsibilities without unnecessary disruption. This training process may overlap with or even be integrated into training for the planting team.[8]

These dimensions of the preparation process reinforce each other and should certainly not be artificially separated. Envisioning and reassurance, especially, will need to run through the whole process as concerns are raised and sometimes threaten to swamp the process or obscure the vision. Although these concerns often reveal more about the insecurities and priorities of those who raise them than points that need further consideration, we need to listen carefully and engage with these concerns. Otherwise, rumblings of discontent or submerged resentment may jeopardize future developments. However, some concerns may reveal issues that have not been fully thought through and so can play a constructive role in the process.

Planting churches will be well advised to integrate this preparatory work into all aspects of their program and community life—sermons, home groups, prayer meetings, main gatherings, business meetings, pastoral visiting, and informal conversations. Planting a church is a major undertaking by the whole church, not just the planting team, and has the potential to transform the church for good or ill. Inadequate or halfhearted preparation risks problems further down the road as well as squandering an unusual opportunity to explore missional and ecclesial issues together and to introduce new initiatives within the church.

Beyond the planting process. One further aspect of the preparation period that is important enough to require separate treatment is the development within the planting church of a new vision for its *own* future beyond the planting process. This may only be embryonic at this stage and cannot be developed until the planting process is underway and the planting church has adjusted to the changing dynamics of the post-planting period. But a vision of its own life beyond the process of church planting is crucial so that the church does not invest hope and energy entirely in planting a new church. Otherwise, once the planting team has been deployed and the new church is up and running, the planting church can become lethargic and begin to stagnate.

Depending on the resources available and on the planting model used, it may be helpful if the planting church initiates (or at least starts planning toward) a different venture. This might be a social action project, an evangelistic initiative, a proposal to reshape or renew the church's premises, an overseas mission trip, or something else that is quite different from church planting. This may feel burdensome on top of the demands of preparing to plant a church, but such a venture may energize those who are less interested in church planting and galvanize the church once the planting team has been deployed. The danger of overload needs to be weighed against the danger of stagnation if no new initiatives are taken.

It may even be worth encouraging the planting church to regard itself as a "new" church—which in a sense it is, both because it has a reduced membership (at least for a while) and because it is now a planting church. What we must avoid, if at all possible, is any sense that those who remain in the planting church are the leftovers or that the mission of the church has ended now that it has planted another church. This is no healthier for a church than it is for new parents to lose all sense of their own identity once their baby arrives.

Clarifying Expectations

A second priority during this period is clarifying expectations so that the planting church and the planting team are working from the same brief. It is worth taking time to ensure that all involved have agreed on how to assess the outcomes and how to negotiate changes to the initial plan in light of unforeseen developments, as this may save misunderstandings and disagreements later.

At the heart of this is usually the relationship between the planting church and whatever is planted. The nature of this relationship is, of course, influenced by the planting model chosen. With multiple congregations, satellite congregations, and multiple sites, there is no expectation that what is planted will become independent, although some degree of self-determination is anticipated. But with mother/daughter, accidental parenthood, dispersion, and long-distance planting, we envisage that independent churches will emerge sooner or later. Church planting by adoption is more complicated, so clarifying expectations is even more important.

Different expectations have often been a cause of tension and discord, usually because these were not made explicit and those involved had not agreed on how to monitor and, if necessary, adjust the relationship between the planting church and the emerging church. A common scenario is where a planting church expects the church it plants to be very similar to the planting church, but it begins to develop differently. Another is where a planting church expects the new church to remain much more strongly linked to it and dependent on it than the new church expects. When eventual independence is the agreed-upon outcome, there may still be conflict over how soon this should be achieved. When we anticipate some form of semiautonomy, there may be persistent disputes over which decisions are made by whom.

Drawing on the life-cycle analogy again, the parallel here is with the disappointment of parents whose children turn out differently from their expectations and the struggles of teenagers to negotiate increasing freedom from parental control. Planting churches (like some parents) may need help to accept, value, and celebrate these differences rather than being threatened or disconcerted by them.

What can we do before the planting process begins to address these issues and lay strong foundations for the future? As well as clarifying expectations and agreeing how we will handle disagreements, we can talk through structural, practical, and cultural matters that can undermine relationships.

- To what extent is the planting church prepared for the new church to look and feel different, to have different priorities and practices, to embrace different ecclesial and theological perspectives, and to build links with other churches? Especially when the new church is in a different cultural context from the planting church, such differences may be essential and marks of sensitive mission, but will the planting church celebrate this or feel threatened by these differences?

- What steps, if any, will we take to encourage those who join the new church also to forge links with the planting church? These newcomers have no history in the planting church and may see no reason to connect with it in any way. Their lack of interest in the planting church may stimulate or accelerate the process by which the new church becomes independent. If this is not the outcome we desire, how can we enable them to feel part of the planting church as well?

- How will we handle transfers between the churches or different congregations in the church? There is often a drift in either direction as members of the planting team find the new initiative too demanding and return to the planting church or as others from the planting church find the new church more attractive and decide to join this. While this is natural and may actually strengthen relational links, it may also unsettle the churches and become a distraction.

- What freedom to act will the planting team have, and what status will the leaders of the new church have? Where will decisions be taken, and about what issues? On what matters, if any, will the planting church have a veto?

- Who will pay the bills and any salaries? What equipment and resources will be shared and what will not be? The degree of financial independence or dependence often indicates the reality of a situation and highlights adjustments that may need to be made on either side (just as teenagers may want independence but continue to expect their parents to fund their lifestyle).

Some of these issues will be more or less pertinent to different models of church planting. Long-distance planting will not be affected much by transfer of personnel or forging links between newcomers and the planting church. Churches planting on multiple sites are less likely to struggle with theological or cultural diversity. But the distribution of financial and other resources may be a source of tension in multiple congregations or where the dynamics of accidental parenthood are present. And decision-making processes need to be very clear when planting satellite congregations or using the mother/daughter model.

If our intention is to maintain a strong relationship between the planting church and the new church (which is implicit or explicit in several of the church-planting models), there are some practical steps that we can take before the planting process commences that will enhance the sense of partnership and may avert problems later:

- Involving many people from the planting church in preplanting activities, such as helping with community research, prayer-walking, or distributing publicity.
- Enlisting the help of members of the planting church to train the planting team in particular aspects of mission and ministry.
- Using members of the planting team to train those who will take over their responsibilities in the planting church.
- Establishing a process for the regular exchange of information between the new church and the planting church, and opportunities for continuing discussion.
- Planning ways for the new church to express gratitude to the planting church for its support and to share discoveries, encouragements, and concerns with it.
- Scheduling regular leadership meetings between leaders of the planting church and the new church (or leaders of the various congregations).
- Inviting someone from outside to act as a consultant and facilitator.

Planning the Process

In chapter 7 we will examine the third priority in this preplanting period, the selection and equipping of the planting team. These three tasks—

preparing the planting church, selecting and equipping the planting team, and clarifying expectations—may be relatively straightforward or very demanding, depending on the context and the familiarity of the planting church with the challenges of church planting. Because they are interrelated tasks, some churches have found it helpful to appoint a "church-planting planning group" to guide and coordinate this threefold process.

This group is not the same as the planting team, although some members of the planting team may also be members of this group. Its task is to oversee the church-planting process from the point at which the church has decided to plant to the point at which the planting team is deployed. It is responsible for planning how to prepare the planting church, how the planting team will be chosen and trained, and how expectations will be clarified and agreed-upon. It is this group that may be in the best position to answer the question, When should we plant the new church?

This planning group might also continue to operate after the planting team is deployed, if the church-planting model anticipates close ongoing links between the planting church and the planted church. It effectively evolves into a "church-planting liaison group" with primary responsibility for monitoring and maintaining good relations between the church and the planting team—and, in due course, the new church. This may be appropriate in the case of mother/daughter church planting, accidental parenthood, and church planting by dispersion (in the latter case, acting as a liaison between the dispersed churches). With other models, where longer-term interdependence is anticipated, that role is probably better left in the hands of the church leadership team and those who lead congregations within the church.

Action

This chapter began with the claim that very few churches are planted too slowly and has proceeded to describe a thorough process of preparing the planting church. If a church is determined to plant another church, it is worth doing this well, even if this takes a couple of months longer than we expected.

But some churches never become planting churches because they refuse to move beyond the research and consultation phase and take the risk of acting by planting another church. It is always possible to find reasons for delaying: to commission yet more research, to plan another training course, to initiate a further round of consultation. Nothing in this chapter (or this book) is intended to excuse procrastination or undue caution. The challenges and opportunities are too great for dithering and risk aversion. Preparation is important—but pointless unless it leads to action.

Mission Agencies Planting Churches

Most church planting in Britain in recent years, including fresh expressions of church, has been initiated by local churches rather than mission agencies. Many of the emerging churches owe their existence to the activities of individual pioneers or groups of friends, with or without the support of local churches or mission agencies. But three of the church-planting models that we considered in chapter 3 may involve a mission agency taking a leading or supporting role. Mission agencies may deploy church planters or planting teams or be partners in a cooperative strategy.

Although church planting by local churches and churches emerging without the support of other agencies may continue to be popular approaches, the role of mission agencies is becoming more significant. This trend is likely to continue if the cross-cultural mission context of post-Christendom Western culture is more widely acknowledged and we adopt a more strategic approach to church planting. But there is very little written about church planting by mission agencies in Western societies, so it may be helpful here to identify some of the pertinent issues.

Various agencies can become involved in planting churches:

- An organization that has previously focused on other activities, such as youth ministry, evangelism, cross-cultural mission, or community development, begins to recognize that planting churches is coherent with its core purposes and may be crucial to the success of its other activities. Sometimes groups emerge from these activities that are, in effect, embryonic churches, so the organization may evolve naturally into a church-planting agency.
- A missionary society that is involved in church planting elsewhere in the world, but has not planted churches in its own country (so as not to appear to be competing with churches that support its work overseas), realizes that in an era of global mission it can no longer sustain this anachronistic distinction and that church planting in its own country is a valid aspect of its ministry.
- A denomination that was once committed to strategic church planting but has not recently been involved in this rediscovers this dimension of mission and initiates a church-planting strategy. I have worked with three denominations in Europe in the past

few years that have made this decision and are developing the infrastructure to support this strategy. Few British denominations currently have church-planting strategies or the expertise to deploy church planters. This needs to change.

- A diocese, synod, association, district, circuit, or other regional body realizes that it has responsibilities and opportunities beyond maintaining existing churches. It identifies neighborhoods and networks where church planting is appropriate and deploys church-planting teams, encourages long-distance or cooperative planting, or helps to facilitate planting by adoption.
- A mission agency may be set up specifically to engage in church planting or with church planting as one of its core purposes. This may operate independently or in partnership with a particular denomination.

Agencies with no recent experience of church planting would be advised to think through various issues before they proceed and as they consider when (and also where) to plant churches, including the following:

Strategy and Capacity

- The integration of church planting with other and more familiar purposes of the mission agency: can this be achieved so that church planting is not just bolted on?
- The church-planting models that the mission agency can most effectively use or adapt: which approaches cohere best with its values, priorities, and resources?
- The factors influencing where church planting is attempted: how many areas can be considered and on what basis should decisions be made?
- The short-term and longer-term relationship between the agency and churches that are planted: will the agency oversee them or encourage them to find other support networks once they have been planted?
- The capacity of the agency to capture learning and identify good practice: how will experience be shared so that church planting becomes increasingly effective?

Consultation and Relationships

- The relationship between the mission agency and those who have supported its work in the past: how will they respond to this change of direction?

- The relationship between the mission agency and existing churches in the areas where new churches might be planted: how will this be negotiated?
- The denominational allegiance of the churches that are planted: if a denomination or agency with strong denominational ties plants churches, are they free to opt out of that denomination?
- The expectations of the mission agency and its planting teams: is there clarity and agreement on what success means, what time frame is in view and how outcomes will be evaluated?

Recruitment and Support

- The recruitment, training, and deployment of church planters and church-planting teams: how can suitable people be identified and equipped?
- The allocation of staff and resources: are there people available with the necessary gifts to oversee church-planting initiatives?
- The support and accountability structures that need to be put in place: what level of support and what mode of accountability will be helpful and sustainable?
- The degree of freedom a church planter or planting team can exercise: will the agency set limits on this or predetermine the kind of church that can be planted under its auspices?
- The relationship between church-planting teams that are deployed and supported by the mission agency: should teams be deployed in close proximity so they can be mutually supportive and learn from each other? To what extent should this determine when and where churches are planted?

Mission agencies with experience of church planting elsewhere (missionary societies, for example) will be able to draw on that experience, but they will need to take into account various contextual factors in their country, rather than assuming that principles and practices that apply elsewhere are necessarily transferable. And even mission agencies set up to plant churches in their own country will need to revisit many of these issues and learn from the experience they accumulate.

Working through these issues will take time, which will have an impact on the question of when churches are planted. Church planting need not wait until every issue is resolved, but preparatory work to ensure that the mission agency is equipped as well as possible for the task of church planting may have long-term benefits that will outweigh the frustration of initial delays. After all, local churches may only have the capacity to plant one church in any generation (few plant more often than this), but mission agencies may develop the capacity to plant many churches year after year. So it is worth investing time putting in places strategies, policies, and structures that will enable them to sustain, reflect on, and refine what they do.

When Does a Church Begin?

This chapter is concerned with the question, When should a church be planted? We have advocated consultation to ensure that the decision to plant has widespread support and have then concentrated on the preparatory work we need to do. It is not easy to quantify how long this preparatory period will be, because different factors in each context will shorten or extend it. But in most situations we are looking at a period of several months from the conclusion of the community research and the decision to plant until we deploy the planting team. So the community research and preparatory work is likely to occupy a planting church for at least a year. Experienced planting churches and mission agencies may be able to reduce this period.

Frustrating though it may be to pioneers and activists, this preparatory period is vital if the planting process is to be properly planned and the planting agency is to benefit from what it does, rather than being wounded by it. The term *preplanting*, which we have used to label this preparatory period and will use again in this section, may not be very helpful if it suggests these activities are not integrally connected with the whole planting process. But it does highlight the need for various activities before and beyond starting a new church.

Differentiating "preplanting activities" from "planting a new church," however, raises the questions, What do we mean by church? and, When does a church begin? Specifically, what do we mean by "planting" a new church and how we can ascertain if and when a church has been planted? Depending on our ecclesiology and expectations, there are various points at which we might claim that a church has begun:

- The planting team is the new church as soon as it has been commissioned.

- The planting team is the new church when it begins to meet as a team within the community where it is planting.
- The church has been planted as soon as newcomers join the planting team.
- The church has been planted when it is officially launched (and named).
- The church has been planted when it starts to meet in a public place.
- The church has been planted when it has continued for an agreed-upon period of time.
- The church has been planted when it is formally constituted as a separate entity from the planting church.
- The church has been planted when the core elements of mission, community, and worship are all present (either privately or publicly).

Mission, Community, Worship

The suggestion that mission, community, and worship are the three core constituents of an authentic church has received widespread, although not unanimous, support. Some worry that other constituents (such as discipleship, teaching, the sacraments, or catholicity) are absent; others argue that those are included within these three dimensions. And any one of these elements, it seems, can be the starting point for a new church: mission activities may develop into worshipping communities; fresh expressions of worship may inspire missional communities; and communities may engage in mission and worship together.

Church planting in the 1990s usually assumed that a new worshipping community would be the basis for mission activities. How large this community must be and how regularly it must meet before it could be regarded as a church provoked debate, but most equated church planting with establishing a worshipping community. So a group of friends eating together each week and praying for their neighborhood was not sufficient. Community development work, evangelistic activities, and other forms of mission were valued highly but did not in themselves constitute church. But regular meetings for corporate worship (even if these were initially in a domestic setting) indicated that a new church had been planted.

Prioritizing corporate worship in this way is a legacy of the Christendom era, in which mission and community were often marginalized. Church planting should not be warped by this inherited bias. It is time we reinstated mission and community as equally central constituents of church. This does not mean that we should interpret every mission activity and any gathering of Christians as "church," but it does mean that mission and community are as indicative of a new church emerging as regular corporate worship. So intentionality may be the defining criterion. If a community is forming with the intention of engaging in mission or if missional activities are intended to create a community, we may recognize that a church is emerging, whether or not this community is yet worshipping together.

Nevertheless, however flexible our interpretation of church, we should probably refrain from claiming that we have planted a church until this comprises others than the planting team. If a planting team is quite large, it may organize corporate worship activities very soon and may assume these constitute a new church, but actually this is just the planting team worshipping together. Likewise, community gatherings and mission activities that involve only team members may be essential but should perhaps not yet be designated as church. But when the planting team begins to dissolve into a community that is engaging in mission and learning to worship together, it is probably time to acknowledge that a new church is emerging.[9]

Preplanting Activities

The term "preplanting," then, refers to activities that contribute toward the planting of a new church but take place before the planting team is deployed and before we can claim with any credibility that a church is emerging. Many of these activities continue into the planting phase and eventually become the responsibility of the new church. Members of the mission agency or the planting church can participate in these activities alongside the planting team.

Prayer. The planting team will undoubtedly want to pray together in the months leading up to their deployment. This may be the most significant aspect of the preparatory period as they forge relationships, pray for the neighborhood or network with which they will be engaging, and discover a common vision and purpose. The planting church or mission agency will incorporate prayer for this venture into their regular patterns of prayer and may also arrange special prayer gatherings. Prayer partners and those with intercessory gifts may be invited to pray for the planting team and for the network or neighborhood. Prayer will undergird the discernment process and the decisions about where and when to plant, which model to use, who should be involved in the planting team, and what kind of church is needed. Prayer will accompany the envisioning of the planting church and the training of the planting team. And the planting church or mission agency will commit itself to continue to pray for the team, to pray for the emerging church, and in due course to pray about future developments.

Raising funds. Depending on the planting model chosen and the resources of the planting agency, we may need to raise funds to support one or more of the planting team, provide equipment, rent premises, and cover other planting costs. In some situations the planting team is self-supporting or approaches supporters for financial backing. In other contexts the planting church encourages its members to contribute additional resources to meet the costs of church planting. Occasionally it may be possible to raise support from external sources, such as charitable trusts.[10]

Identifying meeting places. We considered in chapter 4 the kinds of locations where a church might meet for various purposes (including but not only corporate worship). Our community research may already have identified some possibilities, but we may want to do further work on this before the planting team is deployed. In some situations we will be able to draw on the expertise or local knowledge of members of the planting church in assessing the merits of different options. Various factors are worth considering:

- *Location and visibility in relation to neighborhood or network.* In some contexts good visibility is important, but in some a lower profile may be preferable.
- *Accessibility.* The community research will indicate the centers and boundaries of a geographical community, if this is our context. We will also take into account local modes of transportation (including parking so that where we meet is as accessible as possible). A network church will need a building that is culturally accessible.
- *Availability.* If we are renting premises, we need to know at what times and how regularly the meeting place is available, whether availability is assured or might be changed at short notice, how flexible the agreed-upon starting and finishing times are, and whether the space with be available for additional activities.
- *Facilities.* Does the meeting place have suitable chairs (check the size of the chairs in elementary schools!), adequate and available storage, effective heating and lighting, reasonable acoustics, and any other equipment we may need? Bringing in lots of equipment each time the church meets is time-consuming and wearing. Are there enough rooms for the planned activities?
- *Size.* Choosing a large meeting place can be intimidating for a

small group, which may struggle to settle here. Choosing a smaller meeting place is less intimidating, but if the church grows, this may mean moving to a different location, unsettling people and disrupting relationships.

- *Atmosphere and appearance.* Buildings that are physically similar can have a very different "feel": this may be intangible but it makes them more or less welcoming. We need also to consider how suitable their appearance, décor, and state of repair are for our context.
- *Associations.* It is worth checking on the reputation of a potential meeting place and whether it is associated with particular activities, memories, or sections of the community. Its history and ethos may be an asset or a liability (this is particularly important when the adoption model is used).
- *Cost.* This varies enormously and needs to be included within the overall budget for the planting venture. It may or may not be worth paying more for premises that tick many of the above boxes.
- *Publicity.* The planting team may prefer not to publicize their arrival in the community or invite people to public events. Getting to know people and making friends may be their priorities. In other situations, where a higher profile seems appropriate, members of the planting church or mission agency may work alongside the planting team to design and disseminate information about what is planned.

The community research may also have discovered other issues that we could explore in more depth, conversations that we should follow up on, links with community groups that we could strengthen, or social problems that we could investigate. What the community research uncovers is relevant, not just to the decision about whether and where to plant, but to the kinds of preplanting activities that we should prioritize.

Launching a New Church

There is one more issue that pertains to the question of when a church is planted. Church-planting literature often advises that a definite launch— when a new church "goes public" and becomes visible in the community— is important, even crucial. Entire chapters may be devoted to this one event, urging church planters to prepare well for this launch and to maximize its potential. The launch event can happen at various stages and may take the form of the following:

- A commissioning service for the planting team as they are deployed.
- A celebration involving members of the planting church and the planting team.
- An evangelistic event to which local people are invited.
- A community event to which local dignitaries are invited.
- A fun event advertised in the local media and through leaflet distribution.
- An ordinary church meeting with members of the local community who have started meeting with the planting team.

Some planting teams opt for high visibility very early; others prefer to build relationships and meet unobtrusively with members of the community before going public at a launch event once they have gathered enough people. Some launch events will not be repeated; others are designed so that those who attend experience a typical church meeting. Whatever and whenever the event, it should be fully integrated into the planting process: the planting team needs to be clear about why they are doing this, when they have the people and resources for it, and how they will follow it up.

But is a launch event necessary? There may be internal and external expectations that are hard to resist, but there are contexts in which an official launch may not be appropriate:

- In a community that is suspicious of institutions and hype, a public launch may alienate rather than attracting people.
- In a cross-cultural context where members of the community may be very wary of attending public meetings, a public launch may be unhelpful.
- In a community where previous attempts at church planting have failed, it may be detrimental to launch publicly yet again.
- In church-planting ventures that operate relationally rather than through events, a public launch may be superfluous or misleading.

In some situations, apparently successful launch events have had negative consequences. They may have attracted a good crowd, but they have stirred up antagonism in the local community. Or the planting team may feel deflated and discouraged the following week when visitors to the launch event do not return. Church-planting teams would be wise to weigh the advantages and disadvantages carefully before following the advice in older church-planting books about holding such an event.

We noted in chapter 3 that church-planting literature uses various analogies to describe the planting process. In this chapter we have used "life-cycle" imagery at several points. So why switch to the nautical imagery of launching a ship rather than comparing the start of a new church to the birth of a baby? Is it because launching is clear-cut, the triumphant conclusion to a successful process that is publicly celebrated? The birth of a baby may be painful, messy, and take longer than expected. If we used horticultural imagery, we would compare starting a new church to seeds slowly, almost imperceptibly, breaking through the soil and becoming visible. Switching to launch imagery may indicate incoherence and discontinuity in the planting process. In any case, the style and significance of any launch event will indicate what the planting team (and planting agency) understands by "church" and what they envisage emerging from the planting process.

●●●

Questions for Further Reflection

1. What are the advantages and disadvantages of mission agencies rather than churches planting churches?
2. Can we do too much preparation before planting a new church?
3. How can churches emerge relationally and organically if the planting process is very carefully planned and organized?
4. What are the essential elements that must be in place before any community can be designated a church? Who decides this?
5. If you were responsible for planting a church, would you hold a launch event?

6

PLANTING **CHURCHES: WHAT?**

An Emerging Question

Most church planters in the 1990s asked the questions we have considered thus far: why, how, where, and when to plant churches. But many did not think it necessary to spend much time wondering what kind of church to plant. They assumed they knew what church was and concentrated on the planting process. Those who did ask questions about what kind of church to plant were generally interested in making adjustments to familiar models rather than exploring radically different possibilities.

Toward the end of the decade, however, as the frenetic rush to plant as many churches as possible by the year 2000 slowed, questions emerged about the kinds of church that were being planted. Were they truly missional? Were they contextually appropriate? Were they culturally attuned? Were many different kinds of churches needed in a diverse society?

Some church planters responded at a local level, planting churches that took greater account of cultural and contextual factors. Others appropriated models of church that had been effective elsewhere, whose advocates promoted them as suitable for contemporary culture.[1] There were also some denominational responses, not least by the Assemblies of God, which engaged in a process of missiological reflection designed to ensure that future church planting was truly missional.[2] "What" seems to have taken its place alongside "why," "how," "where," and "when" as questions church planters and planting agencies need to address.

But some church planters (who may resist being labeled as such) and others interested in transforming inherited churches want to dig deeper and to address the *what* question at a more philosophical level. They are asking not only, What kind of church? but, What do we mean by church? Alongside more contextual and diverse forms of church planting and fresh expressions of church are various emerging churches that are wrestling with this more fundamental question.

133

So in this chapter we turn our attention to the question of what it is that church planters actually plant. We do this conscious that some church planters are wary of engaging in what they fear are endless and sometimes self-indulgent debates about the meaning of church, whereas some emerging churches question whether most church planters have begun to address this issue at the depth necessary to incarnate the gospel into emerging culture. At one end of this spectrum are church planters who regard these discussions as unwarranted distractions from the urgent task of planting churches that accord with (their understanding of) biblical principles and will "work" in any context. And at the other end of the spectrum are those who wonder if church as a separate entity is worth retaining, let alone multiplying.

My intention in this chapter is not to adjudicate between these positions or to advocate a particular expression of church. My more modest aims are to set out some of the design issues that church planters would be wise to consider early in the planting process and to offer resources for those who want to explore ecclesial questions in a missional context.

Within the question, What are we planting? are other questions we need to consider:

- Who is responsible for asking and answering this question?
- What assumptions and expectations do we bring to the discussion?
- For whose benefit are we asking the question?
- What factors come into play in designing a new church?
- At what point should decisions be made, and how firm should they be?
- How do ecclesial and missional factors interact?
- What are the essential features of church, and what variations are possible?

Planting or Cloning

Before we consider these questions, however, it may be worth revisiting the experience of church planters in the 1990s, many of whom ignored the "what" issue or engaged with it only at a logistical level. There were serious limitations to this approach, which critics dubbed "cloning" or "replication" rather than "planting" or "reproduction." But it had the advantage of allowing church planters to focus on the host community[3] and on missional activities. It saved them countless hours discussing ecclesial issues.

The effort and creativity involved in designing a new church depends on the extent to which it is modeled on the planting church or on a template provided by a planting agency. In all planting ventures *some* thought must be given to what the new church will be like and how it will function, even if we intend to replicate a familiar model. Its location, the mix of people in the planting team, where it meets, and other factors mean the church will have its own unique character. But these variations are incidental, rather than intentional, when we use a cloning approach. Visitors familiar with other churches in our network or denomination will easily recognize the family resemblance in the new church.

In some situations, cloning may seem appropriate, and there may be little incentive to be unduly creative:

- Church planting in communities that appear to be socially and culturally similar to that which the planting church serves.
- Church planting prompted by a church running out of space in its building, where the motivation is to find room to replicate a successful church.
- Church planting where the planting church or agency is convinced that its own ecclesiology is sacrosanct.
- Church planting where the planting team is large and drawn either from the same church or from very similar churches, bringing with them shared assumptions and expectations.
- Church planting where the new church remains closely tied to the planting church or agency, which discourages creativity and regards innovation as disloyalty.

But merely replicating a familiar model of church seems less sensible in the increasing number of contexts where other factors are involved:

- Church planting in communities that are socially and culturally dissimilar to that which the planting church serves.
- Church planting that is cross-cultural, motivated primarily by a concern to reach those who are culturally distant from existing churches.
- Church planting where we want members of the host community to discover an appropriate expression of church for their own context.
- Church planting where the planting team is small or drawn from various churches, bringing with them diverse perspectives and ready to learn from each other and to do things differently.
- Church planting where the planting church or agency encourages

the planter or planting team to experiment within a supportive accountability structure.

Of the twelve models we presented in chapter 3, those where cloning is more likely are mother/daughter, adoption, and multiple sites. Those where cloning is less likely are the dispersion, multiple congregations, cooperative, and spontaneous/emerging models. In an accidental parenthood situation, cloning is theoretically excluded, although sometimes it is surprising how much is unwittingly copied. The other models (satellite congregations, long-distance, church planter, and mission team) may result in either planting or cloning.

In a diverse and changing culture, cloning will be effective in fewer and fewer situations. Most church planters today ask questions about the kind of church they are planting. The consequence is fresh expressions of church, emerging churches, and more creative church planting.

So why revisit cloning? Because there are dangers in the contemporary fascination with the "what" question that comparison with cloning may help us identify.

First, planters can become besotted with imagining and designing a new church and fail to heed the warning to "stop starting with church." Missional and relational priorities can be subverted by intense and lengthy discussions about what the new church will be like. I know of situations where a beautiful, radical, and culturally cool church never got off the drawing board because there was no energy left actually to plant it. Is this really better than cloning an existing model but actually getting to know people in the community?

Second, planters may not appreciate how many assumptions about church they bring with them. Nobody starts from scratch or with a blank sheet of paper. Even where a church is set up in conscious opposition to a known model, familiar dimensions of church will be incorporated into what is planted. They may be reconfigured, renamed, or reorganized, but essential similarities are not difficult to discern. In many planting ventures, supposedly radical changes are cosmetic rather than fundamental. Many "fresh expressions" are really not all that fresh! This is not surprising. There are only so many ways of configuring the community life, mission activities, worship, teaching, financial arrangements, leadership structures, and other aspects of church. But, as I have discovered on several occasions, those involved can be very disappointed once this dawns on them. By contrast, cloning ventures that acknowledge their dependence on known models may gradually evolve into something quite different and result in great excitement. Are unrecognized assumptions more of a hindrance to creative planting than cloning?

Third, planters can be unduly dismissive of inherited church practices and idealistic about new practices. While cloning unthinkingly adopts practices, more creative forms of planting may carelessly abandon existing practices. Sustaining new practices, especially if these require constant creativity, is very demanding. Some new churches, after experimenting with fresh patterns, revert to more traditional forms, with renewed appreciation. After all, inherited forms of church, whatever their perceived weaknesses and need for renewal to connect with a diverse and changing culture, evolved and were tested over a long period and have significant strengths. Traditional*ism* may be problematic, but there are usually good reasons why traditions endure. Is indiscriminate rejection of traditions any more helpful than unthinking captivity to the past?

Cloning is not the answer. But as we wonder, "What do we plant?" we should heed these cautions. The difference between inherited and emerging churches, or between cloning and planting, may not be as marked as we often assume. Insisting that innovation and tradition are never absolute, Leith Anderson comments, "A conservative guess is that 98% of our behavior is rooted in one tradition or another. Those who operate at the 99% level are considered to be the old-fashioned traditionalists, and those who operate at the 97% level are called avant-garde nontraditionalists. It is mostly a matter of degree."[4]

The problem with cloning is not that many features of church continue unchanged, but that the opportunity to assess these and explore alternatives is squandered. Asking radical questions may (and often does) result in reaffirming inherited practices, but this process ensures planters know *why* they are doing what they are doing. A church planter I know was very disappointed when his research indicated that the best time for the new church to gather was at 11:00 a.m. on a Sunday morning. He was willing to meet any time of any day or night, but the results of his research were unequivocal. Wisely, he accepted them, and the church meets at a traditional time—but for missional and contextual reasons.

On the other hand, church planting that arrogantly assumes that inherited patterns are obsolete is equally defective. Dogmatic iconoclasm is no more attractive than dogmatic traditionalism. Church planters need a more nuanced, self-aware, and humble stance, courageously pioneering creative possibilities without denigrating what has gone before or depriving themselves of potent resources. There are encouraging signs that such attitudes are becoming more common.

By Whom and for Whom?

Church planting, then, is an unusual opportunity to reimagine church, experiment with new patterns and practices, integrate missional and ecclesial dimensions, review inherited traditions and assumptions, configure the relationship between gospel and culture in fresh ways, and pioneer on behalf of the wider church. The point is not to introduce changes for the sake of change but to grapple with the ecclesial implications of our changing mission context.

Church planting is also an opportunity to engage sensitively with the many networks and neighborhoods that comprise this mission context. Ecclesial creativity is inadequate and may be harmful if it is not accompanied—indeed inspired and guided—by missional sensitivity. We need church planters who will operate *both* creatively *and* contextually.

But who is responsible for all this? Who will decide the shape and ethos of a new church, and at what stage? For whose benefit is this process?

There are several possible answers:

- The planting church, denomination, or agency is investing heavily in the process and may feel it should play a major role in designing the new church. Especially if the original vision emerged from the planting agency, it may regard designing the church as an integral component in the venture it has initiated.
- Members of the planting team are also investing heavily in the process. They may have made significant life changes to be involved; they are taking the risk of developing something new; and they are doing the practical work of birthing a new church. Furthermore, they are in a better position than the planting agency to discern what kind of church is needed in the host community and are responsible for moving from vision to reality, adapting as they go.
- Christians in the host community who become members of the new church were not involved in the planting process but may be in a better position than even the planting team to determine what is needed. An important question is how fixed the initial design is and how much flexibility there is for the church to evolve as more people get involved.
- Some (though not all) church planters solicit the input of non-

Christian members of the host community. What kind of church do they propose? If communities are suspicious of organizations imposing ready-made institutions or programs, an invitation to help design a new church (if this offer is genuine) may help to offset this and may encourage people to get involved.[5]

- A further factor is whether the church will be generalist or specialized. Will it aim to be accessible to the whole community or be designed for a particular network or subculture? Is it legitimate to tailor a church for a particular section of the community, thereby making others feel excluded? Or is this crucial in order to reach networks and subcultures beyond the orbit of existing churches?

There is probably a balance to be struck between the expectations of these "stakeholders," each of whom may have helpful perspectives. In the various church-planting models, one stakeholder or another may be more influential, but none should be excluded. A balance is especially difficult to achieve in ecumenical ventures, with competing denominational perspectives interacting with the vision of the planting team and with what is culturally appropriate in the host community.

Acknowledging the interests of the various stakeholders also helps us appreciate that the issue is more complex than simply "cloning or planting." Missiologists differentiate three approaches in cross-cultural mission (although different writers advocate different terms): replication, accommodation, and contextualization.[6] In relation to church planting, replication equates to cloning and involves minimal creativity or cultural sensitivity. Accommodation means adapting to local circumstances so that the church has indigenous features. Contextualization implies planting seeds and nurturing what grows in the local soil.[7] As the cross-cultural nature of church planting in Western societies shaped by postmodern and post-Christendom realities becomes more apparent, church planters will need to understand and embrace the dynamics of contextualization. This will mean shifting the balance between the expectations and contributions of the stakeholders.

Nevertheless, in practice, new churches often take on many characteristics of the church planter or planting team (even though they may not realize this until someone points it out to them). However genuine our attempts to design the church in accordance with the expectations of the various stakeholders, new churches tend to have many of the strengths and weaknesses of those who planted them. This is unremarkable but nonetheless sobering, especially if a solo church planter is responsible for shaping a new church. This tendency can be counterbalanced to some extent if planters are determined to empower the church by leaving many questions unanswered until it emerges.

Convictions, Context, and Constraints

The kind of church that eventually emerges depends on the interaction of three factors: the convictions of the stakeholders, the context in which the church is planted, and constraints that impact the planting process. Church planters may be more conscious of some factors than others but, if they recognize their influence, planting teams can reflect on how to balance their (sometimes apparently competing) demands.

Convictions

As indicated above, those who plant churches and those who deploy church planters do not start with a blank sheet of paper, however open they may be to planting a different kind of church from any they are familiar with and however much they want to be responsive to the host community. They bring with them theological convictions that will shape their understanding of what they are called to be and do, guide their approach to mission, and inform their expectations of what kind of church they are planting. Some may bring ecclesial convictions and a clear vision of what the new church can and should become. Some will be attentive to denominational loyalties and distinctives: they may be surprised to discover how rooted they are in a particular tradition when certain principles or practices are questioned. Some will express passionate spiritual convictions, convinced they have heard from God about the nature, priorities, and shape of the new church.

The design process becomes interesting and relationships can be strained when different team members bring different but equally firm convictions or when the convictions of the planting team diverge from those of the planting church or agency. One motivation for planting a new church may be, as we saw in an earlier chapter, a desire to belong to a church where particular theological, ecclesial, and spiritual convictions can be expressed. In some cases, denominational distinctives may be perceived as baggage to offload rather than traditions to honor or resources to value. When team members come from different churches, careful and gracious negotiation may be needed to ensure that all convictions are acknowledged and respected. The team must decide how to work toward an agreed-upon vision that is neither fudging nor imposition.

Convictions are a crucial component in answering the question, What kind of church are we planting? Convictions energize commitment and provide an anchor in a process that can otherwise be prone to being tossed to and fro by various experiences and challenges. But unacknowledged or unstated convictions can be dangerous, like hidden rocks beneath the surface that can hamper ventures that appear to be progressing well. A church planter was telling me recently that he had taken for granted that all the members of his team had common convictions, but a key member of the team acknowledged eighteen months into the venture that he disagreed with some fairly fundamental convictions. He decided to leave, and the team spent many more months recovering from this setback before the planting process could begin again. So it is vital that all involved own their convictions and submit them to the scrutiny of others. It is better to discover early in the process that we have incompatible convictions than to press ahead without realizing this.

But convictions alone are not enough. Furthermore, the planting process has the capacity to challenge our convictions. This can be liberating but also disturbing, especially where we need to rethink how we interpret the Bible, how we understand God's mission, how we integrate pastoral and ethical principles, and how we understand the gospel. Church planting may be a journey of discovery; the process may have as much spiritual impact on the planters as on the host community.

Context

New churches are not planted into a vacuum but into specific contexts. This may be a geographical neighborhood or a social network, but it consists of particular people and places. These people and places have cultural distinctives, their own history, values, needs, and aspirations. They are also set within the wider context of a particular time in history, the political and economic climate of the city or nation in which they live, and the even wider context of social and religious movements, cultural shifts, and geopolitical developments. The term *glocal* has been coined[8] to indicate that global and local factors are hard to separate in the networked world of the twenty-first century.

Church planters may be more or less aware of these contextual factors, but they influence the planting process and the kind of church that emerges. In my experience, most church planters today take local contextual issues more seriously than was the case in the 1990s. Careful research and reflection on the implications of the context for the planting process are becoming standard practice.[9] This is encouraging and should result in more effective mission and new churches more deeply rooted in networks and communities. Whether for lack of time or lack of interest, many are less aware of wider issues. The reverse is true in the "emerging church" scene, where there is much reflection on cultural and global trends but often limited engagement with the local context.

Some church planters emphasize context over convictions, concerned to avoid imposing an alien expression of church. They resist the temptation to decide in advance what the new church should be like and adopt an incarnational approach that watches to see what fruit the seeds of the gospel produce in a community. They have convictions, of course (indeed, their incarnational approach is a conviction), but they hold these lightly so as not to disempower the host community. I mentioned in chapter 2 my encounters with church planters who have planted a church they do not enjoy but which they are convinced is the kind of church needed in its context. This raises again the question we asked earlier, For whose sake is the church being planted?

Others bring strong convictions about the kind of church they want to plant but, sooner or later, realize this is unsuitable and allow their context to soften or revise their convictions. Those who refuse to adapt may struggle to plant any church at all; if they succeed, what they plant may embody their own ecclesial preferences but is likely to be perceived as an imposition on the community. Sadly, not a few emerging churches seem more interested in expressing their ecclesial, cultural, and theological convictions than engaging with their local context.

Convictions and context should be held in creative tension. We need to identify and own both, and expose them to ongoing reflection and inter-action. There will be aspects of our context that are gospel-friendly and that we can affirm, use as redemptive analogies,[10] and celebrate in culturally attuned churches. Other aspects that we perceive as hostile to gospel values, we may challenge or offer a countercultural alternative. Church planters, as we suggested earlier in this chapter, are engaged in contextualization. This involves the interplay of context and convictions, the persistent cross-fertilizing of the "indigenizing principle" and the "pilgrim principle."[11]

Constraints

This third factor is always present in church-planting situations but may not be appreciated in the early stages and so may cause considerable frustration. There are, inevitably, constraints that limit what church planters can achieve and the kind of church they plant. Ignoring these constraints or pretending they do not matter results in strained relationships, disappointed expectations, and sometime bizarre expressions of church. I have visited new churches that have tried desperately to transcend their limitations but have palpably failed to do so. A classic scenario is a church with pretensions to host huge celebration events that has invested in expensive sound technology and operates with a bank of microphones in a small hall that contains fewer than ten people and needs no amplification.

Obvious constraints include the number of people in the planting team and in the church as it emerges; the time and energy they have to invest in the church; their gifts and skills; the limitations of wherever the church gathers; the equipment and financial resources; the mission opportunities and pastoral demands that may restrict ecclesial creativity; and the expectations or requirements of the planting agency (for example, who can officiate at communion in an Anglican church).

As with convictions and contextual factors, church planters need to identify constraints as soon as possible (although others will appear during the planting process) and respond to these creatively, rather than being disabled by them. One of our Urban Expression teams soon discovered that none of them were musical, making sung worship difficult. Rather than struggling on or resenting this constraint, they seized the opportunity to explore other forms of worship—until a guitarist joined them and they were able to integrate songs into a richer and more varied experience of worship than they would otherwise have enjoyed.

Underlying all we have said in this chapter, but have not yet made explicit, is the longing of church planters to discern the mind of Christ for the church they are planting. Context, constraints, and convictions may need to be identified and held in creative tension, but in what ways is God at work in the host community and what kind of church does God want planted? There may be situations where cloning or more creative forms of planting seem appropriate, but what is the Spirit saying? There may be various stakeholders with vested interests in what is planted, but ultimately church planting is for the glory of God and to participate in the divine mission of reconciling all creation to its Creator.

The reason this has not yet been made explicit is that some church planters tend to rely wholly on their intuition as to what God is saying to them, conflate this with their own convictions, ignore contextual factors, and fail to appreciate constraints. A more helpful way forward may be similar to the combined feasibility study and discernment process we advocated in chapter 4. Acknowledging our convictions, recognizing constraints, and respecting the context are not alternatives to seeking God's direction but resources for a prayerful discernment process.

Laying Foundations

Church planting usually involves laying the foundations of a new church (although with multiple sites, multiple congregations, or satellite congregations some foundations already exist), foundations on which others will build in the future.[12] This is a responsibility and a privilege, an opportunity to shape the church, clarify its values, impart a vision, establish patterns and practices, and set a direction. Inadequate foundations jeopardize the stability of what we build on them and place limitations on what we can achieve. Some churches have such shaky foundations that they cannot thrive or even survive. Others are rescued by replanters with the skills to underpin what was badly established.

Every new church is subtly or markedly different, even in situations where cloning rather than planting has occurred, because of the particular combination of convictions, context, constraints, and church planters involved. Those who have been involved in planting other churches can certainly draw on that experience, but we must beware making assumptions or importing inappropriate patterns and practices.

Foundational Issues

There are, however, some foundational issues pertinent to all new churches—and many existing churches where these were not addressed properly when they began. One contribution the practice of church planting can make is to help churches, networks, and denominations reexamine the foundations on which they are building. Church planting can throw into sharp relief critical issues that have not been given proper attention before. It can also embody alternatives that may spark the imagination of existing churches and stimulate reflection and renewal.

If laying the foundations of a church is not already daunting enough, church planters also need to remember that they are pioneering on behalf of others, cross-fertilizing gospel and culture, developing fresh expressions of church, and exploring new ways of being the followers of Jesus together in a changing society. Designing a new church is exciting and energizing, but we carry responsibilities for both the future of the church we are planting and its contribution to the renewal and mission of the wider church. This is not meant to weigh church planters down under an intolerable weight of expectation but as a plea for care and sensitivity for the sake of those who will build on the foundations we lay.

The influence of different traditions may predispose church planters to consider certain issues to be foundational. Some may emphasize the importance of governance structures, whether these be accountability to episcopal oversight, or relationship with an apostolic team so that the church is "built on the foundation of the apostles and prophets,"[13] or the responsibility of the church to be self-governing, or other stipulations. Others may regard as essential a clear doctrinal statement so that members of the new church know what it believes and where it stands on contentious issues. Others again may expect the church to be led by ordained or accredited leaders, with certain functions restricted to such leaders. Church planters in some denominations may be required to plant churches that adhere to a range of doctrinal, ethical, and organizational stipulations.[14]

We cannot here investigate these issues or assess the legitimacy of regarding them as foundational. Church planters operating within networks or denominations that insist such matters are put in place can access these guidelines. Instead, we will examine other issues that are generic and arguably more foundational—the interrelated dimensions of *vision, values, purposes,* and *ethos.* Because these are interrelated, some may be tempted to imagine that it is immaterial which we address first (and in practice they often evolve as they are tested against each other). But churches that prioritize one or another of these foundational issues often develop in quite different ways.

There has been widespread interest, at least in some sections of the evangelical church, in the "purpose-driven" model mediated through the ministry and writings of Rick Warren.[15] I am often asked what I think about this model, to which I respond in various ways. This is a clear and attractive presentation of principles taught within Church Growth circles for many years. Churches can benefit from this and become more purposeful and selective in what they do. But I am wary of some of its theological and cultural assumptions. I resist the idea of churches being "driven" by purposes or anything else. And I am not persuaded that churches should be founded on purposes.

Could it be that prioritizing purposes in this way betrays and enhances the tendency in many evangelical churches to activism and achievement? Church planters do need to ask the foundational question, What is this church (or any church) for? Indeed, the practice of church planting recalls the church to this question and helps prevent it slipping back into maintenance mode and self-absorption. But it is not necessary, and may be unhelpful, to start with a mission statement or a summary of the church's purposes. What might be the impact of starting instead with values, which are about being rather than doing, or with vision, which is about imagination rather than agendas?

First Things First

Values. Many church planters (and others) find it difficult to identify their core values or the values they want the church they are planting to embrace. Some struggle even with the concept of values. I have had several extended conversations or email exchanges with church planters trying to express their values who constantly revert to statements about activities or purposes. Values are about who we are or aspire to be, rather than about what we are doing or intend to do. Values express what matters most to us, our worldview, our deepest convictions and passions, how we want to be known, how we expect to behave, or, as church planter and founder of the Hope Chapel movement Ralph Moore suggests, what we want as our epitaph.[16] Values are rich in theology but are not statements of faith, which contain propositional statements rather than lifestyle commitments. Values express something deeper than intellect assent and inspire people and churches in ways doctrinal statements rarely do. Values undergird relationships and priorities, exclude certain ways of behaving, guard our hearts and consciences, and shape our habits and reflexes.

Urban Expression is a values-based church-planting agency committed to relationship, humility, and creativity (each of which is spelled out in further values statements). Our values are foundational to who we are, what we hope for, how we relate to each other, how we assess opportunities, how we treat others, and the kinds of churches we plant.[17] We also have a mission statement, commitments, strategies, and purposes, but our values are primary. The growing interest in what has been dubbed "new monasticism"[18] points in the same direction with core values and commitments that express who we are rather than what we hope to achieve. A well-known British example is the Northumbria Community, whose rule of life is rooted in the values of availability and vulnerability.[19]

Church planters may be tempted to ignore this dimension of the "what" question and concentrate on seemingly more urgent aspects of designing the new church—especially because identifying values usually takes longer than we expect. But this is a temptation worth resisting. Identifying our values—avoiding statements that are generic and vague, limiting any list to a memorable collection, making sure that these are truly shared by our whole team—enables us to move forward with clarity and confidence.

Vision. Values are about who we are; vision is about what we see. Vision sparks our imagination and energizes our creativity. Vision looks with the eyes of hope and faith at what does not yet exist and starts to pray this into being. Vision inspires commitment and sacrifice in order that our dreams may become reality. Church planting is demanding but can also be exhilarating as we live and work toward a vision.

Vision may be encapsulated in a poignant phrase, a picture, even the name of the church. It may be painted with broad brush strokes or described in minute detail. It may originate in a biblical text or image, in a prophetic word, or in prayer. It may become clearer and more intense as the planting team researches the community, walks around it, and imagines an alternative future for it. Vision may be expressed by imagining what the new church will be like two, five, or ten years from now. But a reality check is also essential: visions can stray into fantasy and confuse faith with wishful thinking.

A challenging question for those interested in missional church planting is whether our vision embraces only the church we hope to plant or the host community. Do we have a church vision or a kingdom vision? A kingdom vision will include the contribution a new church can make to the transformation of the community, but it should not be limited to this. I have introduced many church planters, especially those working in cities, to Doug Gay's poem "The New Glasgow,"[20] in which he imagines his city as the New Jerusalem. He revels in what Glasgow will be like when God's kingdom is fully present there. Some have written similar poems expressing a vision for their community. Church planting is not an end in itself. There is a broader vision—the mission of God, the kingdom of God—which points us beyond merely planting churches to the reconciling of all creation to our Creator.

Purposes. They may not be as fundamental as either vision or values, but clarifying our purposes is important if the church we plant is to be focused, accountable, and effective. If values express who we *are* and vision expresses what we *see*, purposes express what we want to *accomplish*. These will include generic purposes that might characterize any church and purposes specific to this church and its context. A popular way of summarizing purposes is through a mission statement—a succinct and memorable statement of intent. This may be expanded into a longer document (sometimes referred to as a "philosophy of ministry") that expounds in greater detail the components of the mission statement. Further work may then be necessary to crystallize these purposes into objectives and to set goals that provide a means of measuring progress.[21]

How the new church will understand the scope of its mission is especially important. This may mean clarifying the geographical area or social network in which it will operate. It may also mean exploring different aspects of mission (such as community development, social action, evangelism, environmental stewardship, peace-making, working for political and cultural transformation) and agreeing priorities. Many church planters in the 1990s (influenced by Church Growth missiology) prioritized evangelism with a view to adding other dimensions of mission later. Some emerging churches today prioritize other areas of mission and marginalize evangelism. A holistic approach from the beginning may be preferable so that a broad-based understanding of mission is embedded in the church. If elements such as evangelism, social action, and global mission are bolted on later, rather than being integral, the church may struggle to embrace these wholeheartedly.

There is some debate as to whether the time invested in clarifying objectives and agreeing on goals is time well spent. Mission statements, objectives, and goals are familiar to many in the workplace, and governments have set targets in education, healthcare, and many other areas of public life. But there is growing disquiet about whether such targets actually motivate those responsible for meeting them, whether they commodify activities that are not really susceptible to precise measurement, and whether they stymie initiative rather than encouraging efficiency. Underlying these concerns are questions about who is responsible for establishing objectives, goals, and targets, and how they obtain ownership of these.

This can be a cause of tension between church planters and those who deploy them. The expectations of the planting agency may be expressed in terms of measurable outcomes within a specified time frame, but church planters may be uncomfortable with these stipulations, especially if they are generic and not related to the context in which the planters are working. Friends of mine planting in Canada have opted for an incarnational and long-term approach, but their funding is under threat because their mission agency operates with attractional and short-term expectations. My friends could achieve what is expected if they changed their approach, but they are convinced this would be inappropriate for their community and counterproductive in the long run.

Inner-city church planters have often suffered under expectations derived from church planting in suburban or small-town contexts if these are applied without any appreciation of the very different demands of their context. It may also be unwise to apply standard goals and expectations to the different models we surveyed in chapter 3 (especially if the mother/daughter model is regarded as normative).

Reflecting on church planting in the 1990s, George Lings and I concluded that "setting goals for planting does not work,"[22] at least insofar as we expect them to motivate those involved. In British society, goals do not motivate people; in postmodern culture, goals seem modernistic and pretentious; in the cross-cultural planting context that predominates today and means each situation is different, goals often appear arbitrary. Church planters may sometimes find it helpful to agree on objectives or even to aim for particular goals, as long as these are contextually appropriate and accompanied by the necessary resources, but these goals should not become prescriptive or burdensome. Much more important is the identification of purposes for their activities and for the new church. Clear statements of purpose provide guidance on what to do and, even more important, what not to do out of the many things churches can do. They provide a focus for meaningful activity, a basis for internal and external accountability, and a means of ensuring they are not neglecting any of the priorities they have identified.

Ethos. Of the four foundational elements we are discussing, ethos is the hardest to define clearly. Church planters may have vision statements, purpose statements, and values statements, but ethos is not easy to capture in statements. The ethos of a church is the way it feels, both to regular participants and newcomers. More than what the church says it believes or stands for, more than programs and activities, more than structures and policies, ethos defines what kind of church it is and is probably the main reason why people do or do not join. Ethos may be almost indefinable, but it is usually tangible. Church planters may explore this issue by identifying a biblical image of the church that inspires them or describing the spirituality of the church they want to plant. A simple exercise I sometimes use to help a church identify its ethos is to invite people to say which animal or motor vehicle their church resembles. This can be revealing and stimulate a very interesting discussion.

If a church has a building of its own or can adapt another space in the way it wants, this may reveal its ethos. When my wife and I visit church buildings, we often ask each other, What kind of community worships here? or What kind of God do they worship here? We may or may not be correct in our conclusions, but different church buildings feel very different and seem to be pervaded by a distinct ethos. Visitors to church events also seem to detect the ethos of a church very quickly, often before a word is spoken or a song is sung. Ethos is reflected in how people describe the church to those who are unfamiliar with it. Examples include a family church, a preaching center, a celebration, a church for the unchurched, a serving church, a peace church, or a church in the community.

● ● ●

These foundational issues are not, of course, as easy to distinguish in practice as they are in this chapter. They all impact each other, and different aspects will be more visible and require greater attention at different stages. Ethos, in particular, emerges from the vision and the values and from the relationships between those who are incarnating the values and pursuing the vision. But church planters and those who deploy them will do well to address these foundational issues carefully, in the preplanting period and as the new church emerges. It is on these issues that planting teams need to be united. There may be divergent views on many other things, but on these issues heartfelt unity is vital.

How can our values, vision, purposes, and ethos be identified? Often these become clear through a combination of focused discussion, prayer, biblical reflection, exercises that stimulate our imagination, attempts to draft summary statements, revisions, arguments, and growing consensus. Different people may contribute different components. Some may be better at refining ideas, others at stimulating the conversation. Some think aloud or in pictures; others process ideas as they write or pray. Some are methodical; others leap from idea to idea. Discerning these foundational issues is an ideal opportunity for developing as a team and for involving many different people in the planting process. It is essential that many voices are heard so that values, vision, purposes, and ethos are truly owned and not imposed.

Laying foundations is the responsibility of the church planter or planting team, who will themselves normally be accountable to a planting church or agency. But we recall again at the end of this section that there are various stakeholders involved, not least those who will be members of the new church and who will bring their own vision, values, purposes, and ethos into what is emerging. Just as convictions interact with context and constraints, so church planters will find their own vision and values both shaping and being shaped by those who become part of the church. This does not mean abdicating responsibility for laying foundations, but it does mean accepting a measure of provisionality for the sake of seeing an indigenous church emerging rather than imposing something on a community.

What Is Church?

We noted earlier in this chapter that some emerging churches are asking not only, "What kind of church?" but "What do we mean by church?" or "What is church?" We cannot delve deeply here into the emerging church conversation, but many church planters today are aware of this conversation and are thinking more carefully about what they are planting. We also suggested in the previous chapter that church happens at the intersection of mission, community, and worship. Consequently, church planting may proceed along any of these three trajectories rather than prioritizing gatherings for worship.

The varied ways in which churches are emerging make church planting more interesting, but probing questions about the nature of church raise issues that might once have been taken for granted. Church planters and planting agencies may need to identify what room for maneuver they have and where their boundaries are. What theological convictions, church patterns, ethical stances, or approaches to mission can be reexamined and what are not up for debate? These conversations will overlap with the discussion about values, ethos, vision, and purposes, but it is important not to assume everyone agrees what is and is not essential about church.

An exercise I have used with many church planters invites them to decide whether certain aspects of church are *negotiable* or *nonnegotiable*. There are twenty-three features in all, including praying together, adopting a church name, welcoming all ages, behaving with ecological responsibility, having a statement of faith, sharing bread and wine, preaching regularly, becoming financially self-sufficient, and appointing recognized church leaders. I have not yet encountered even a small group from the same background in which there was complete agreement, and often there is considerable and passionate debate. This often surprises participants, who tend to assume they all agree on the ecclesial minimum, even if they differ on nonessentials. Some are also intrigued by encountering items on my list that they have never thought about, let alone regard as essential, but which on reflection they decide are nonnegotiable!

Asking "What is church?" tends in my experience to elicit a minimalist answer, rejecting many familiar aspects of church as optional rather than essential. This may be helpful for church planters, saving them from constructing an overcomplicated institution. Limiting the nonnegotiables of church may also encourage church planters to pay more attention to their context: if there are fewer essentials, there is more energy and space to incorporate features that may be negotiable in theory but seem nonnegotiable in practice. Thus, few church planters identify another item on my list—eating together—as nonnegotiable in a classroom exercise, but I know church planters who regard this as essential in their local context and never meet without eating together.

Our increasingly multicultural context also brings up other questions—not only about what is essential but about what is unacceptable. What aspects of which cultures can be incorporated into church life and which must be excluded? What constitutes syncretism, and where is the dividing line between ethical and cultural issues? These questions have been debated in cross-cultural mission circles for many years, and they are now familiar within the emerging church conversation and among church planters in Western societies working in cross-cultural contexts.

A well-known example is the discussion about the contextualization of gospel and church in Muslim contexts, using the C1-C6 rubric to delineate positions on a spectrum.[23] At one extreme is the expectation that Muslim converts will reject their culture and join churches rooted in another culture, bringing little if anything with them. At the other extreme is the belief that they can become "Muslims for Jesus" rather than self-identifying as Christians, and that the emerging "messianic mosques" are as legitimate as messianic synagogues for Jewish believers. Missionaries endorse various points along this spectrum. A similar (but more theoretical) discussion is beginning among missionaries working in Hindu contexts.

Church planters in plural Western contexts where members of other faith communities are becoming followers of Jesus face similar challenges. For example, some of the teams working under the auspices of Urban Expression avoid the terms *church* or *Christian* because of their cultural overtones, opting instead for "communities of those who follow Jesus."[24] Cross-cultural church planters wrestle not only with identifying the essentials of church but with discerning what elements can be incorporated from other cultures and other faith traditions without compromise. Similar issues arise when we plant churches into neighborhoods or subcultures with practices that some may regard as incompatible with gospel values (for example, churches among Goths or in neighborhoods where most couples cohabit).

However, in this discussion about contextualization, we must beware thinking that middle-class Western churches are normative and that any deviations must justify themselves. More likely we have become so familiar with the compromises involved in this "normal" form of church that we do not recognize that syncretism is also present in churches comprised mainly of stockbrokers, teachers, and health professionals. As church planters pioneer fresh and contextual expressions of church, what emerges may challenge us to review our own assumptions.

Some are willing to address more fundamental questions than others. For some church planters and a surprisingly high number of emerging church leaders, the question "What is church?" is legitimate but "What is the gospel?" is not. Whether these questions can really be separated is a moot point, but this stance may indicate how unaware many still are of the impact of Christendom, which made normative a specific historical contextualization of the gospel. Evangelical church planters, especially, are very reluctant to recognize that their understanding of the gospel is culturally conditioned or to allow their cross-cultural mission experience to challenge their convictions and reveal new facets of the gospel. But authentic church planting is a two-way process, reevangelizing the church planter as well as evangelizing others.

Asking the question "What is church?" also gives church planters an opportunity to reject the sacred/secular dualism common in many churches and to eschew phrases like "going to church." Few church planters today identify "church" with a building, but some identify it primarily with meeting for worship. Such meetings may be a vital expression of church and necessary to sustain its spirituality, but church exists in dispersed as well as gathered mode: its community and mission dimensions are at least as important and may develop earlier than the worship dimension. Planting a church is a chance to clarify these issues, to use language that expresses these convictions, and to model a holistic understanding of church.

Structures and Processes

Besides laying foundations, church planters also need to put in place the structures and processes required to support a new church. We may draw on the experience of churches we know and on the expertise of people who know how churches operate. However, we may also want to seize the opportunity to rethink patterns and practices, introduce new processes, and adapt familiar structures.

If the essential aspects of church are mission, community, and worship, we need to reflect on how the church will interpret and express each of these elements. What will the church include within its concept of mission, and what will its priorities be? Will it be interested mainly in supporting individuals in their own mission or will it undertake shared mission initiatives? What rhythm of life will be needed to sustain community and nurture growth in discipleship? What approach to corporate worship will the church adopt, and how will this relate to personal spiritual practices?

Responses to these questions need to be congruent with the foundational values, vision, ethos, and purposes we have already agreed on. They must also take into account the interrelationship of convictions, context, and constraints. Some patterns and practices may flow naturally out of the initial community research: any proposals certainly need to be cross-checked with what that research revealed. Decisions also need to be provisional, open to revision in light of experience. Structures and processes that look wonderful on paper may prove quite unworkable in practice.

Examining these issues in detail would make this chapter unduly complicated, and in any case, many will vary according to denominational requirements,[25] the planting model used, and contextual factors. But a list of typical questions may be helpful:

Mission

- In what forms of mission, if any, will the church engage corporately?
- How will the church support individuals in their dispersed mission activities?
- With whom will the church develop partnerships in mission locally and further afield?
- How will the church exercise hospitality toward neighbors and strangers?
- How can new people join the church and be inducted into its values and vision?
- How will the church interpret the relationship between belonging, believing, and behaving?
- How will the church understand and work out the balance between incarnational and attractional approaches to mission?

Worship

- What will be the components of corporate worship and who will be responsible for these?
- How will the church learn together and grow in faith and discipleship?
- How will the church pray together?

- What will be the role of music and the arts in the church?
- How will the church handle responsibly the exercise of spiritual gifts and prayer for individuals?
- What policies and practices will the church adopt in relation to ceremonies such as christenings, dedications, baptisms, communion, weddings, and funerals?
- Will the church have a written statement of faith (or adopt an existing statement of faith)?
- How will the church ensure that its worship shapes the character of its members and its community life?

Community

- When, where, and how often will the church meet as a community and for what purposes?[26]
- In what other ways will members of the church meet each other?
- Will the church operate as a "bounded set" or "centered set" community?[27]
- Will membership in the church be formal or informal, or will there be other ways of expressing commitment to the church?
- What process operates when people want to transfer from another church?
- How will regular pastoral care be exercised, and how will pastoral crises be addressed?
- What will be the status and role of children in the church, and how will they be nurtured?
- What issues need to be considered in relation to people with disabilities?
- How will the church share news and information internally and with the host community?
- Will the church have a written statement of practice, setting out how members will act and behave?

Leadership

- What forms of internal and external accountability will the church put in place?
- What leadership structure will be developed, and how will leaders be chosen?
- Who will be responsible for guarding the values and maintaining the vision of the church?

- How will decisions be made and reviewed, and how will progress be monitored?

Administration

- Who will be responsible for administration, and what regular practical tasks need someone to accept responsibility for organizing?
- What policies (such as child protection, protection of vulnerable adults, insurance, health and safety, risk assessment, ecological responsibility, and fair trade) need to be developed and implemented?[28]
- What financial systems will be established,[29] how will church members contribute financially, and how will the church demonstrate that it is behaving with propriety (questionable financial practices have caused problems in some new churches)?
- What equipment and resources will the church need for its various activities?
- What legal or constitutional documents need to be produced? Depending on what kinds of activities the church may become involved in and whether it intends to take advantage of tax benefits, should it become a non-profit or other type of organization?[30]

Some church planters may already be impatient with this list (and perhaps with much else in this book), champing at the bit to get on with the task of planting a new church. Others may be committed to a "simple church" approach, in which the ecclesial minimum is very minimal, or expect the church to emerge organically and dislike this talk of structures and processes. There is certainly a danger of becoming bogged down. But addressing these issues at an early stage, even if we make only provisional decisions, can save difficulties later. We will need to address most of these questions sooner or later (even in simple or organic churches), so it is better to anticipate them rather than waiting for problems to arise. Church planting by design is generally preferable to church planting by default.

It is also worth noting that very often practical issues, rather than apparently foundational matters, cause conflict. In this, church planting is no different from the rest of church life, where the amount of time spent discussing an issue is usually in inverse proportion to its importance. But practical issues sometimes point to theological or pastoral concerns: we need to listen carefully to questions about apparently mundane issues if we are to identify these underlying concerns and distinguish them from personal preferences and fears.

Discussions and disagreements about practical issues can cause conflict, as of course can debates about theological, ethical, and strategic issues. There is no way that all such issues can be resolved, or even identified, in advance. But we can put in place agreed-upon processes that may enable conflict to be handled well and so be creative rather than destructive. The above suggestion of a "statement of practice" relates to this. I was deeply impressed when I saw on the wall of one church Matthew 18:15-17 written out in full with a commitment that this was the process church members would use when they quarrel with each other.

Two guidelines might have saved many church planters from unnecessary grief. First, do not start too many activities too soon. Rather than wearing out a new church, keep things simple and sustainable. The amount of emotional, mental, and physical energy needed at this stage should not be underestimated. Second, build into all decisions and initiatives a review process so that nothing is set in stone. It is easier to start activities than stop them once vested interests are involved. Many churches are much too busy but have no agreed-upon review process to assess whether their activities should cease or continue.

One further issue that may appear unimportant but can be contentious is the name of the new church.[31] There are several options (which are not mutually exclusive):

- A denominational name that identifies the church with a particular network of churches or theological distinctives.
- A geographical name that identifies the church with a particular neighborhood, street, meeting place, or wider area.
- A name expressing the founding vision or focus of the church.
- A name expressing the intended ethos or style of the church.
- A name that conveys an image but does not use the term *church*.

We need to consider why any proposed name is thought appropriate, what this conveys to the planting team and the host community, for whose benefit the name is chosen and if there are any drawbacks.

"Community church," "Christian Fellowship," or a name that does not include *church* at all may avoid negative connotations in some contexts, but it may also invite accusations that the new church is a "cult." A name indicating denominational allegiance may provide respectability (although this is less and less relevant in a post-Christendom culture), but this may preclude the church's freedom to establish its own wider links. A geographical name needs to be carefully chosen if it is not to alienate some in the host community; and if the church decides to meet elsewhere or the street or area is renamed, the name will be obsolete and misleading. A name expressing our values or hopes for the future may seem quirky, affected, or pretentious to others.

Or we can wait for a name to emerge as the church develops, rather than imposing one at the outset. Naming implies ownership, so this may be important if the church is to be truly indigenous. Some church planters are confident that God has revealed the church's name to them, but my experience of some such supposedly divinely inspired names is that this conviction needs to be open to scrutiny.

Christology, Missiology, and Ecclesiology

However fascinating many find the question "What is church?" and however important it is for church planters to reflect on what they are planting, ecclesial issues are not primary. More important are the missional questions, How is God at work in the neighborhood or network, and how can we get involved? How might the host community be transformed by the values of God's kingdom? Then comes the ecclesial question, What kind of church can participate creatively and effectively in this mission? We will not be satisfied with a popular shortcut answer—"a church with missional DNA"—but will address this question contextually. What kind of church can participate in the mission of God in the particular community in which a new church is being planted?

Some argue that even missional questions are secondary and that the primary questions relate to Christology, Who is the Jesus church planters represent and proclaim? What is the gospel in relation to the culture, needs, and aspirations of the host community? Others find such fundamental questions threatening and unnecessary, believing that the gospel is unchanging, beyond context, and nonnegotiable. But church planting is an opportunity, not only to explore fresh expressions of mission and church, but also to discover new depths in the multifaceted gospel that the New Testament proclaims and to find contemporary images through which to communicate this gospel. It might even be an opportunity for church planters to encounter anew the Christ they proclaim.

● ● ●

Questions for Further Reflection

1. Reviewing again the twelve church-planting models (described in chapter 3), how does the chosen model affect the balance between the various stakeholders interested in what kind of church emerges?
2. What do *you* regard as the nonnegotiable elements of church? Are there other aspects of your own church or the church you want to plant that you regard as essential in your own context?
3. Which temptation will you find harder to resist—devoting so much time to creating a new church that you marginalize mission, or rushing ahead without thinking through the ecclesial issues and ending up with a clone?
4. Do you agree that it is worth spending time on a mission statement and a summary of core values? Or are such documents likely simply to gather dust on a shelf?
5. Are there any practical issues missing from this chapter that you regard as important for church planters to consider?

7

PLANTING **CHURCHES: WHO?**

It will be evident by now that the questions in this book cannot be addressed in isolation and need not be answered in any particular order. Each has implications for others, and so any conclusions will be tentative until a full picture emerges. In some situations, location (where) is crucial; in others motivation (why) is the starting point; elsewhere the kind of church to be planted (what) energizes us. Realizing that there are different models (how) may open up fresh possibilities, or timing (when) may be the critical factor. Whatever the point of origin, planting churches is a multifaceted process that is not reducible to a step-by-step guide.

Sooner or later, however, we must address the question of who should be involved. This may or may not be the first question. Sometimes church planters take the initiative or at least urge their church or mission agency to act; in other instances a church or mission agency identifies or recruits church planters and planting teams.

In previous chapters, the terms "church planter" and "church-planting team" have appeared frequently but without much definition. "Church planter" has occasionally implied a lone pioneer but has usually meant someone leading a planting team. It is time to define these terms more carefully and address the *who* question.

Church Planters

What does a church planter look like? Some denominations and networks have used the term "breakthrough person" to describe a church planter. But what qualities, personality traits, skills, spiritual maturity, gifts, and experience do church planters need? How can a church discern if it has a "breakthrough person" or needs to find someone else to lead its planting venture? How will an emerging church know whether anyone involved has the capacity to guide its development? How do mission agencies select church planters? How can those who sense a call to church planting assess their potential?

Recognizing who should be involved in church planting is crucial but not straightforward. Most churches have no recent experience of planting and so may be unsure what kind of person they are looking for. Most denominations (though not all) have some experience of planting, but few have agreed-upon criteria for recognizing and accrediting church planters. Mission agencies may or may not be more experienced.

Standard selection procedures in denominations, training institutions, and churches, which are designed to affirm pastor/teachers or possibly evangelists, may be inadequate or even misleading. Gifted evangelists or pastors may not be effective church planters. And gifted church planters may not tick all the boxes required in other forms of ministry. As director of a church-planting course at a theological college, I encountered this issue repeatedly, as applicants were disconcerted by well-meaning colleagues asking the wrong questions and applying inappropriate criteria.

The popularity of church planting in the 1990s, and the pressure to plant many churches quickly, coupled with inadequate screening of church planters, produced many weak and failing churches. We have learned from this, but those who deploy church planters must heed the warnings if problems are not to recur. Encouraging people who are not properly equipped to plant churches is dangerous: these ventures struggle or fail, those involved are discouraged, the witness of the church suffers, and the practice of church planting is discredited. On the other hand, if we fail to recognize those God has called and gifted as church planters, we will frustrate and demoralize them and not benefit as we might from their pioneering skills.

Learning from Research

There are various ways of trying to identify the gifts and skills of church planters. One approach is field research to discover characteristics that effective practitioners have in common. Analytical studies of this kind help us penetrate beneath the surface of stories that we may otherwise celebrate but not properly interpret. A complementary approach, requiring great sensitivity, investigates unsuccessful planting ventures to find recurring deficiencies. Those who have been wounded by such experiences may be understandably reluctant to participate in such research, but their insights can be very helpful.[1]

If this research is done responsibly and factors out idiosyncratic and nontransferable elements, it may be feasible to construct a "church planter profile" and criteria to assess potential church planters. Characteristics identified from field research include visionary leadership, willingness to take responsibility, tenacity and perseverance, effectiveness at planning and evaluating, having an indigenous support system, hard working, problem-solving ability, and the capacity to mobilize people and resources.[2] We should at least be able to build up experience and share this with each other. One result of the popularity of church planting in the 1990s—and of the very mixed results—is that we now have much greater experience of church planting and church planters. We can pool our accumulated wisdom and invite practitioners to participate in the selection process.

However, we must place some caveats on any list of characteristics expected of church planters:

- Be wary of allowing preconceived ideas about what is involved in church planting to determine the qualities of a church planter. For instance, if we interpret church planting as an evangelistic enterprise, we will require a planter with evangelistic gifts. Church planting that involves community development, rethinking church patterns, or cross-cultural mission will demand different kinds of gifts.

- Be wary of cultural bias in determining the characteristics of church planters. The profiles developed in North America relate to a different cultural setting from that in Europe, where different skills may be needed. Similarly, this book derives from its British context, so its contents cannot be transferred without adjustment into an African or Asian context.

- Be wary of assuming that an effective practitioner in one context will be effective elsewhere. Church planting in suburban neighborhoods is different from planting in rural or inner-city communities. Church planting across cultures or into social networks requires different skills than planting within a familiar culture.

- Be wary of failing to differentiate "apostolic catalysts," who plant many churches but move on quickly, and "founding pastors," who may plant only once but remain much longer in the new church. Both are church planters, but they have different personalities, gifts, and areas of expertise.

- Be wary of planter profiles that exclude people for theological or cultural reasons (especially when these are not openly acknowledged). Some profiles assume that church planters are male, for instance, even though few mission agencies actually restrict planters in this way.

- Be wary of emphasizing spirituality, character, competence, or experience to the virtual exclusion of other dimensions, and so failing to produce a rounded profile. Some traditions value formal education highly; in others passionate prayerfulness is much more important.
- Be wary of setting the standard so high that hardly anyone can qualify as a church planter. Some profiles I have seen may be based on research, but they amount to a person specification that would have disqualified the apostle Paul.

Learning from the New Testament

Another approach is to propose a biblical definition of a church planter. Although this is popular in some circles, there are inherent difficulties. The New Testament records many instances of church planting and introduces us to several church planters, but how much common ground is there between church planting in first-century Judea, Samaria, Asia Minor, or Southern Europe and church planting in twenty-first-century Britain? There is also no gift or ministry of "church planter" named or discussed in the New Testament, so any biblical resources must be extrapolated with care.

We can gather from the New Testament information about church planters we encounter there and derive a profile from this. But we cannot know how typical these pioneers, whose exploits are recorded for posterity, are of the hundreds of first-century church planters. We certainly know much more about Paul than any other church planter and have some access not only to what he did but how he perceived his role. In this respect 1 Corinthians is especially revealing as Paul opens his heart to a church that is questioning his credentials and explains what church planting means to him.[3] This may not provide a complete profile, but there are perspectives and priorities here that we can learn from.

If there is no explicit gift of "church planter" in the New Testament, can we equate church planting with another ministry? Given the recent popularity of the "fivefold ministry"[4] list in Ephesians 4:11, it is not surprising that some suggest one of these relates especially to church planting, or that planters exhibit some combination of these gifts. An exercise I use in training courses invites one group of students to compare the role of church planter with that of pastor and another group to compare evangelists and church planters. Cross-pollinating the conclusions leads into an interesting discussion about essential features of these three ministries and how church planting relates to evangelism and pastoral care.

But church planters, though they will likely be involved in both evangelism and pastoral ministry, may be more akin to other ministries listed in Ephesians 4. Some have argued that many church planters exercise apostolic ministry or that apostolic ministry should be interpreted as church planting. Many of the apostles named in the New Testament were involved in church planting, and several dimensions of apostolic ministry fit well with the tasks involved in church planting: pioneering, envisioning, breaking new ground, team leadership, and cross-cultural missionary activity. And as we have seen, some writers use the term "apostolic catalyst" to describe certain church planters.

This restricted application of the term may be preferable. Apostolic ministry should not be collapsed into church planting when it probably embraces other forms of pioneering; and not all church planting is truly groundbreaking. Some of the approaches described in chapter 3 fit the apostolic mold better than others. Cloning does not represent apostolic ministry, nor do other approaches that offer little new to ongoing missional and ecclesial renewal. But cross-cultural planting in increasingly unchurched communities or networks and exploring new ways of incarnating the gospel in a changing culture may legitimately be designated apostolic.

Or we might regard church planting as an expression of prophetic ministry. Researching a community, discerning signs of God at work, identifying needs and redemptive analogies, envisioning a team, interpreting the gospel in a changing culture, and helping people see new possibilities for church and community might all be perceived as prophetic ministry. If church planting involves becoming a voice for the voiceless and challenging injustice, as it often does in poor communities, prophetic ministry is an even more apt designation.

Providing we resist the temptation to define too narrowly the role of a church planter and accept that very different personalities, gifts, and skills may characterize different planters in different contexts, we may be able to recognize apostolic, prophetic, and evangelistic planters, as well as those who are pastors and teachers operating in pioneering situations.

Criteria and Characteristics

Church planting, we have insisted, covers a wide range of activities. Those involved in planting by adoption need different gifts from those involved in spontaneous/emerging planting. Long-distance planting, especially in cross-cultural contexts, requires different skills from planting on multiple sites or the mother/daughter approach. Pioneers operate differently from church planters leading teams. This is another reason why we should not assume that an effective practitioner in one context will necessarily be suitable elsewhere.

Introducing this degree of complexity may help those who recruit and deploy planters to avoid simplistic judgments, but it may also mean that they sidestep the issue altogether. Some dismiss the idea that there is such a gift as "church planter" and concentrate instead on discerning spiritual maturity, character, and skills. Maybe there are too many variables of culture, context, personality, and planting models to be more specific? Perhaps we do better to establish base criteria applicable to all forms of Christian ministry?

My experience of church planters over the past thirty years is that they are very diverse, so I sympathize with the proposal that we should not be unduly prescriptive about what characteristics are essential. However, I remain convinced that some attempt to identify typical features, beyond generic qualifications for Christian ministry, is crucial if we are to sift out those who are ill-suited for this role and endorse those who have what it takes to plant a new church.

So, having explored with potential church planters generic issues of character, gifts and skills, spirituality, theological acuity, relational ability, leadership capacity, experience of mission and ministry, motivation, and vocation, what else should we be looking for?

One quality most, if not all, church planters need is a pioneering spirit, so perhaps we can assess would-be church planters in relation to features that mark out pioneers in other spheres of life. Four, in particular, stand out: pioneers are dissatisfied, visionary, hopeful risk-takers. They are *dissatisfied,* not in the sense of merely grumbling about things, but because they want to bring about change for the better. They are *visionary,* because they look beyond what already is and see what could be, and their faith and imagination are infectious. They are *hopeful,* because they believe change is possible and that their vision can become reality, and they inspire similar hopes in others. They are *risk-takers,* because they are willing to act on their convictions and move beyond the comfort zone into open-ended situations of insecurity.

The new category of "ordained pioneer ministry" in the Church of England has provoked an attempt to define the characteristics of pioneers: vision for planting fresh expressions of church within contemporary culture;

an authentic, integrated understanding of the particular ministry envisaged; the capacity to innovate and initiate; a mature and well-developed devotional life; well-developed abilities to initiate change and enable others to face it in a flexible, balanced, and creative way; demonstrable maturity and robustness to face the demands of pioneering mission and ministry; self-motivation; well-developed understanding of the interaction between gospel and culture; clear vision of the place of their envisaged ministry within the wider church's response to God's mission to the world; the ability and desire to work in a team and collaboratively; and commitment to reshaping the church for mission. This list may be helpful in assessing church planters.[5]

The following qualities would appear on any profile I would design:

- *Self-awareness.* Church planters need to know their strengths and weaknesses, be alert to issues that cause them stress, have a healthy self-image and good sense of humor, and be committed to practices that sustain and renew them.
- *Creativity.* Church planters need to be open to fresh insights, not constrained by traditional patterns but willing to think outside the box, eager to experiment and explore new possibilities, and amenable to input from others.
- *Flexibility.* Church planters need to be responsive to their environment, willing to adapt to unexpected developments, able to cope with and manage uncertainty and change without undue stress, sensitive to cross-cultural perspectives, and capable of integrating convictions, context, and constraints.
- *Perseverance.* Church planters need to be resilient in the face of difficulties, self-disciplined and emotionally stable, sufficiently motivated to keep going without close supervision, open to criticism but not deflected from their strategy without good cause, willing to confront issues rather than avoid them, and able to see beyond immediate concerns.
- *Team building.* Church planters need to be able to inspire and envision others, recognize their capacities, delegate responsibility, manage conflict effectively, and hold together the dimension of "team, task and individual."[6]

But I am not suggesting these qualities should comprise a checklist. They simply indicate issues I think should be part of any conversation with potential church planters. Some of these qualities we may regard as essential; others as highly desirable. We should at least be able to look for evidence of such qualities in potential church planters.

Pioneering Women

None of the above characteristics indicate that church planting should be a male preserve; indeed, many women score higher than many men on most of these characteristics. Furthermore, women are very actively involved in the actual work of planting churches in many contemporary situations, as they were in New Testament times and throughout the history of the church, especially in cross-cultural contexts.

But church planting often appears to be even more male-dominated than other spheres of church life. Almost all books on church planting are written by men,[7] and men dominate church-planting conferences and consultations to the extent that even "token women" may be absent. Noninclusive language mars some now rather dated books on church planting, and patriarchal—and frankly sexist—attitudes are still surprisingly evident among those who plan and organize church-planting events. Female colleagues from Urban Expression with whom I have participated in church-planting consultations have often been the only women present (except for administrative support staff); they and I have been disturbed, and occasionally appalled, by assumptions and attitudes displayed there.

Some have wondered if the language and imagery of "church planting" is unappealing to pioneering women, or if the discussions about strategy, objectives, and goals in some church planting circles are more congenial to men. But even in emerging church circles, where such language and concepts are unpopular and where there is often explicit commitment to gender equality, the male leadership syndrome persists. Is this because blogging is the preferred means of communication in the emerging church and women do not blog as much as men? Or have emerging churches not yet recognized how deeply entrenched male domination is in the church and that more is needed than nodding assent to gender equality?[8]

This is surely not an issue on which church planters and those who deploy them should be lagging behind. Although one or two networks place restrictions on what women can do in line with their interpretation of Scripture, most are open in principle to recognizing women as church planters. If church planting is an opportunity to challenge assumptions, explore new possibilities, contextualize the gospel into contemporary culture, and release gifted people into ministry, this should be a milieu in which pioneering women flourish and are encouraged to flourish.[9]

Recognition and Calling

Whatever weight we place on the various approaches to recognizing church planters we have examined in this chapter and the characteristics we are looking for, the underlying question is whether God is calling someone to be a church planter. Gifts and skills are not enough without a conviction—in the would-be church planter and others—that God is beckoning someone into this pioneering role.

In church planting, as in all areas of Christian ministry, there are personal and corporate aspects to vocation. Either may precede the other. Someone may sense a personal call to church planting and test this out by asking trusted friends, consulting with other church planters, pursuing training opportunities, joining a mission agency, or offering to lead a church-planting venture. Alternatively, a planting church or mission agency may invite someone they consider suitable to respond to the call of the Christian community and take on this responsibility. Whether the personal or corporate dimension comes first, we should consider both carefully and not allow either to override the other.

Nor should calling and gifting be either disconnected or confused. We may expect God to call as church planters those with the necessary gifts and skills, and so we may be wary of affirming the call of someone who seems palpably unsuited to this role. But we must not assume that someone with appropriate gifts and skills is necessarily called to be a church planter. Giftedness may be an indicator of calling, but it is not enough by itself, and there is always the possibility of God calling someone who does not fit our criteria.[10]

Recognition and Funding

Recognizing and calling someone to be a church planter does not necessarily imply that person will be fully or even partly funded. A planting church may have identified a planting opportunity and someone with the skills to lead a planting team but not have the financial resources to support this person. A mission agency may have a policy of recruiting self-funding teams rather than providing financial support for them. And emerging churches may value those who give leadership but regard paid ministry as unhelpful to them and to the church.

There are, of course, advantages to being fully funded: not only financial security, but the freedom to concentrate on planting a church rather than worrying about earning a living or raising support. There is more time to spend in the host community, receive training, and interact with other church planters. There is less danger of burnout through trying to do two jobs at once or of neglecting the family. But this is a very expensive way to plant churches. Relying on a strategy that requires fully funded church planters will mean very few churches are planted, especially if denominational and other resources are stretched in many directions.

There are alternatives: some church planters receive partial support from their church or mission agency and work part-time to bring this up to the income they need; some earn all the money they need and devote what time they have left to church planting; some work in teams that together earn enough to supply at least some of their financial needs; and some choose to "live by faith"—a term that usually means asking friends for support but occasionally means praying for funds and asking nobody except God.

Some advocate bivocational church planting—not just because there is little prospect of denominations with shrinking resources fully funding church planters or even because the scale of church planting needed requires many more planters than could realistically be funded, but because bivocational planting has inherent advantages. These include credibility in the host community as someone who is not paid to plant a church and who understands what it is like to "go to work" each day; protection against becoming cut off from contemporary culture and totally immersed in "church culture"; the opportunity to enjoy a different job and develop other skills; the option of earning a reasonable income ("fully funded" planters are not usually well paid); and the challenge of planting a church that is mutually supportive rather than dependent on a paid member of staff. Incarnational church planting usually requires bivocational planters.

Planters and Teams

One final point (which leads neatly into the second part of this chapter): unless they are working alone, assessment of church planters should take into account the planting team. Some areas of weakness may be offset by strengths in the team. In some situations church planter and team will emerge together; elsewhere one will be in place first. In either case, decisions about the composition of the team and the identity of its leader should not be finalized in isolation.

Church-Planting Teams

Just as "church planter" can mean either a lone pioneer or the leader of a planting team (or, more loosely, anyone involved in a church-planting venture), so "church-planting team" is used in various ways. It can mean the core group of a new church deployed by a planting church or a smaller team sent out to gather such a core group. It can describe a group of Christians living in a neighborhood who decide to plant a church together or a group of friends meeting together out of whose relationships a church emerges. It can indicate an evangelistic team that plants churches in several places, or a mission team recruited from various churches to plant a church in a particular community.

Understanding Teams

We dare not take it for granted that church planters, members of planting teams, planting churches, denominations, or mission agencies understand the dynamics of team ministry. Although the concept of teamwork will be familiar, and many will have had experience of working in teams in other contexts, team ministry in church life is often undeveloped or poorly implemented. In fact, church planting often helps churches see the potential of team ministry, as the close relationships and team dynamics evident among those who are planting a new church stir within the planting church a yearning for a more collaborative and mutually supportive way of operating. This is another issue on which church planting can offer resources for ecclesial renewal.

Where team ministry is unfamiliar or underdeveloped, the planting team and others may need to clarify their thinking and expectations. Some may want to start with biblical and theological perspectives: reflecting on the trinitarian nature of God as the foundation for human teamwork; investigating the ministry of Jesus and his team of disciples; learning from New Testament teaching on multigifted church communities; or gathering evidence from Paul's ministry of how he worked with others in mission teams.

It may be helpful to rehearse the benefits of working in teams. David Shenk and Ervin Stutzman[11] offer a concise summary of what teams offer in a planting context:

- The team is a church: it models Christian community life, demonstrating what it proclaims.
- The team is diverse: a multicultural environment calls for a representative team.
- The team shares power: it provides a model and means of sharing authority and responsibility, discouraging excesses.

- The team shares giftings: it offers a range of gifts and perspectives to tackle the work.
- The team produces synergy, providing for a greater total effect than individuals working independently.
- The team provides mutual support and encouragement.

There are also exercises that can help team members discover their roles and discern how they can work together effectively. Some planting agencies use the diagnostic material developed by Meredith Belbin,[12] which identifies eight team roles and offers perspectives on how these interrelate. Others use gift identification resources, such as Willow Creek's Network course,[13] to help team members discover their spiritual gifts and how these relate to the planting task. Some use a psychometric tool, such as the Myers-Briggs personality profile, to help team members understand themselves and others better.[14] Behavioral assessment analyses, used primarily in the business community, may also be helpful as long as the different context is taken into account.[15] Simply understanding the phases that teams typically go through—"forming, storming, norming and performing"[16] is a popular description—can prevent difficulties and encourage perseverance.

And it does no harm to recall that not all New Testament teams worked harmoniously all the time.[17] Naïve and unrealistic expectations are unhelpful. Where team members do not know each other before joining the team, considerable time and care is needed to ensure relationships are forged and team dynamics are healthy.

Recruiting Teams

In some situations teams simply emerge rather than being chosen or recruited. This can work well, but such teams may be unbalanced and unprepared for what follows. In other contexts team members are recruited via a selection process that involves an application form, references, psychological profile, and interview. Often recruitment involves formal and informal procedures. When all team members belong to the same planting church (as in most of models outlined in chapter 3), they will normally be well known to those who recruit them. But this will not normally be so if team members are recruited from various churches. And sometimes church planters recruit teams from the host community.

Two significant issues for those recruiting teams are *size* and *composition*. What kinds of people should be on the team, and how large should it be?

The size of the planting team will depend on the interaction of several factors. If the team is drawn from one church, these include the size of the church and how many members it is willing to deploy; the number of suitable people who respond to this challenge; which planting model is adopted; the size and nature of the host community; expectations about the growth rate of the new church; and whether the new church will be allowed to emerge from the community rather than being imposed on it. If a mission agency, denomination, church planter, or group of churches is recruiting the team, many of these factors will still apply, but the size of the team will also depend on how effectively team members can be recruited from various places and how many can be integrated into a functioning team.

Although the divisions are somewhat arbitrary, the following schema highlights certain dynamics in teams of different sizes:

- The smallest possible team consists of two people, either a married couple or two colleagues. Planter profiles emphasize what Americans call "spousal cooperation," but this need not mean that both husband and wife are team members. I have met effective church planters whose spouses were not Christians but were supportive of their partner. One of the main tasks of a team of two is to gather a core group around which to build a new church.

- Slightly larger is a team of three to maybe twelve people. This team may also see one of its main priorities as gathering others into a core group, though some teams of this size perceive themselves as a church before anyone else joins them.

- A team of perhaps thirteen to twenty people is more likely to perceive itself as a church as soon as they start doing anything together. They may see their role not as gathering a core group but as encouraging others to join their emerging church.

- A team of twenty to thirty-five people can be described as a proto-congregation or emerging church. This is already larger than many well-established churches, but team members may have come from much larger churches, so what is emerging may not yet feel like a fully formed church. Their aim will be to draw new people into this church.

- A team of thirty-five or more people is effectively a transplant congregation and is likely to function as a church from early in the planting process. There may be expectations of rapid and substantial growth, but the church already exists.

Many assume that larger teams are more likely to succeed. Some still quote the American rubric that planting should not be initiated with fewer than fifty people. Others insist this figure refers to the number required for a public launch and to sustain regular meetings. Smaller teams can engage in other ways with the host community while they gather these fifty people. But this discussion ascribes to the launch event and public meetings priority and significance that many church planters no longer accept. It also begs questions about what "success" means in different contexts.

There are undoubtedly advantages to planting with larger teams: the venture is less likely to fail through lack of numbers; the team will usually have a wider range of skills; there are more people to carry responsibilities and share the workload; there will probably be a stronger financial support base; if it wishes, the team can operate as a church from early in the planting process; and the new church may grow more quickly, perhaps reaching a position quite soon where it can become a planting church itself.

But there are also advantages to planting with smaller teams: the venture is less likely to fail through disunity or unclear vision; the depth of relationships is often greater in small teams, and the level of commitment may be higher if there is no room for passengers; the team is less able to import old ways, so the danger of cloning is reduced and there is more scope for creativity; members of the host community can help to shape the church, rather than simply joining whatever a larger team has already designed; and the planting church may be able to deploy several small teams in different contexts instead of one large team.

If "success" implies numerical growth, planting with a large team is probably better, but if it means empowering the host community, ecclesial creativity, and contextual sensitivity, smaller teams have much going for them. If our strategy is to plant churches that plant churches, larger teams are preferable; but smaller teams allow planting churches to seed several communities at the same time. A large team is feasible when planting into nearby communities that are socially similar. Small teams can plant churches cross-culturally, at greater distances, and in contexts where large teams will be resented. Since most contexts in plural Western societies now have cross-cultural dimensions, small teams may become the norm.

Whatever size of team we recruit, there are questions about its composition. What kinds of people do we include or exclude? On what basis, and by whom, is this decision made? How much of the above discussion about recognizing church planters applies to members of teams?

And how do we integrate personal conviction and corporate discernment when these point in different directions? There are many issues to consider:

- Churches that recruit teams internally must decide whether to approach those they hope will join and discourage others from becoming involved, or invite volunteers to put their names forward. If participation is by invitation only, this can provoke resentment and may also unwittingly exclude some with a strong sense of call and appropriate gifts. But if volunteering is the main mechanism, some may volunteer who are unsuitable, others we want to recruit may not, and we may end up with an unbalanced team. A combined strategy is probably better—identifying key people and inviting them to become team members, and encouraging others who want to join to participate in a selection process. Alternatively we can appoint a core team and invite others to play a supportive role.

- Mission agencies and denominations may be assessing some candidates they have invited to apply and others who have approached them. But they will want to take all applicants (funded or volunteers) through a discernment process, following up references, and satisfying themselves that those they recruit share their vision and values. Many attributes expected of team leaders pertain to team members too. If someone is applying to join a specific team, the team leader should be involved in the selection process.

- Most team members will not be funded but will need to earn their own living and offer what time they can to the planting venture. Depending on the planting model and the circumstances, they may remain in their current jobs or they may need, or choose, to find new jobs. Some may be able to reduce their work commitments to release time for team activities; others may look for a job in the host community. Although some may be able to give only limited time, we can still regard them as team members and treat them accordingly in relation to the selection, training, and support processes.

- Church planting in geographical communities requires team members to live in the area ("commuter planting" is inauthentic and ineffective). Some may already live there; others will need to buy or rent homes there.[18] But if a planting church has members already living in the host community, it should not assume they will all become team members. Some may want this but are quite unsuitable; others may want to remain members of the planting church and resist being co-opted as team members. Geographical proximity is relevant but is not the determinative factor.

- One benefit of teams Shenk and Stutzman note is diversity. The size of the team and available personnel will limit this diversity, but in many situations it is helpful if teams exhibit diversity in relation to gender, age, cultural background, ethnicity, marital status, and spiritual maturity. A diverse team will need to worker harder at internal relationships, but it can engage with a wider range of people. Some communities are quite homogeneous, so diverse teams may be less essential there, but homogeneous teams will struggle to relate to diverse communities. In a cross-cultural context, it is very helpful to have team members from the host community or who can bridge the culture gap between team and community.

- Another benefit of teams is a mixture of gifts. We may be tempted to overload the team with evangelists (if evangelism is our main priority) or creative thinkers (if we envisage a fresh expression of church), but this may not produce a balanced or viable team. It may also denude the planting church of such people. It is advisable to include some team members who relate easily to the host community and some who know how churches work and can help develop things internally. Within the limitations of team size and available personnel, a mix of gifts is good—pastors, administrators, intercessors, evangelists, prophets, teachers, managers, youth and community workers, and so on.

- Some identify particular leadership roles as essential minimum requirements. One proposal outlines eight crucial roles (not necessarily eight different people): team leader/coordinator, worship leader, evangelist/nurturer, community networker, teacher/trainer, prayer coordinator, pastor, and administrator/financial controller.[19] Such lists helpfully identify roles that emerge in many churches, but these may not be roles team members need to play, especially if regular church meetings are less prominent than they were in the 1990s or only begin once members of the host community are ready to assume such roles.

- Some of our conclusions about team selection may be different when planting into networks, especially if we hope to plant a church that incarnates the gospel into a community with distinctive characteristics. In these contexts a more homogeneous team may be necessary, a different set of gifts may be required, and where team members live may be less relevant.

- Particular planting models may also raise additional questions, for example, how many of the original church should be team members in an adoption venture, or how many team members in a satellite congregation can combine this with other roles in the wider church?

Whatever decisions we reach about the size and composition of a planting team, there are two expectations we should underline to potential team members.

First, team members must be committed to common values and a shared vision. This does not preclude a measure of diversity in many other areas, including theological, ecclesial, missional, ethical, or strategic issues (as long as the diversity is not too extreme and those with different viewpoints accept and respect each other). But dissension over values and vision will seriously handicap a team. This issue especially affects teams recruited from various places by mission agencies or where the cooperative planting model is used in an ecumenical venture. But even when the team is drawn from one church, shared vision and values should not be assumed. Teams need to talk openly about their vision and values. A fundamental requirement (which we dare not take for granted but need to test carefully in the recruitment process) is a missional perspective: team members are there for the sake of others, not for their own fulfillment.

Second, all team members need to commit themselves to the team for a minimum period. Planting teams are normally comprised primarily of volunteers, of course, so we cannot insist on this (and circumstances can change, requiring team members to withdraw). But a clear understanding of expectations may hold a team together through periods of struggle and difficulty. We have learned from recent experience that this minimum period may be longer than we previously thought. Three years is realistic in many situations, but some contexts may need much longer, even if this stipulation discourages some from joining a team.

Training Teams

The amount of training teams receive varies widely—from almost nothing to extensive courses and processes. Even those who lead planting teams, especially when these teams emerge spontaneously, may receive little or no training. Among the options available are in-house courses run by mission agencies or planting churches, mentoring and coaching schemes, modules in theological colleges, open learning and online resources, on-the-job apprenticeship, locally delivered accredited courses and specialist programs for particular kinds of church planting.[20] Teams can also gain a wider perspective by reading books on church planting, visiting other planting teams, and identifying problems other teams have encountered.[21] Leaders in emerging churches often look for training once the church has begun, rather than during the preparatory period. Some networks prefer their teams to receive in-house training to ensure they plant churches that embody particular ecclesial convictions; but those who train alongside others from different traditions can reflect more deeply on what they are planting and may resist the tendency to clone.

The potential curriculum is almost endless. Training courses may include single sessions or whole modules on such topics as church-planting motives, models, and methods; team formation and team dynamics; community development, evangelism and nurturing new Christians; spirituality and the spiritual disciplines; hermeneutics and contextualization; cultural exegesis; leading small groups, prayer, and worship; ethical and pastoral issues; and action/reflection approaches to doing theology. The context may also require more specialized training in cross-cultural communication, urban or rural ministry, engaging with other faith communities, youth ministry, disabilities, working with families, or other subjects. Depending on team members' prior knowledge, a broad framework of theology, missiology, and ecclesiology might also be vital.

Team leaders may also need additional training, especially if they have no experience of leading teams. Leading a church-planting team involves the following:

- Establishing and safeguarding the values that will undergird and shape everything the team does.
- Communicating a vision of what the team can achieve and inspiring commitment and confidence.
- Empowering and encouraging team members to discover their gifts and contribute effectively to team tasks.
- Enabling team members to understand how their contributions relate to those of other team members and their common task.
- Delegating responsibilities and holding team members accountable for tasks they have undertaken.
- Providing support, encouragement, recognition, and opportunities for feedback and development.

- Developing effective communication processes to ensure all team members know what is happening.
- Discouraging the formation of cliques and ensuring that tensions and conflicts are handled creatively and resolved well.
- Helping team members sustain their vision, morale, and motivation, especially in times of discouragement.
- Noticing when team members are overworking and encouraging the team to set a realistic pace.
- Identifying leadership potential in others and helping them develop as leaders.
- Maintaining a healthy balance between the task to be accomplished, the needs of individual team members, and the operation and development of the team.

Identifying Tasks

Whether or not we provide training for the planting team, we will need to identify tasks and allocate responsibilities. Tasks are not the same as either gifts or team roles, although hopefully there will be some correlation between these three elements. Tasks are simply things that need to be done and that need someone to do them. Identifying and allocating specific tasks may provoke requests for further and more focused training.

The number of tasks and their nature will vary, depending on the planting model we use and the kind of church we are planting. We will probably also discover additional tasks as the venture develops. Ensuring that we share these tasks sensibly helps avoid burnout and frustration. Some tasks relate to internal team dynamics, others to our engagement with the host community, and others again to how the team interacts with the church that emerges. Maintaining links with the planting church or mission agency may also involve tasks and responsibilities.

Tasks may include processing the community research carried out during the preparation period and ensuring that its conclusions inform our activities and priorities; maintaining and developing links with local churches and other agencies; taking responsibility for internal and external communication; hospitality; journaling on behalf of the team; recording and implementing decisions taken at team meetings; organizing team or community events; developing an evangelistic strategy; initiating community projects; finding somewhere for the new church to meet; working with the caretaker if premises are rented; obtaining and maintaining team equipment; handling team finances; and much more.

Some tasks pertain only to the period before a new church emerges, but others continue into the early months or years of the new church. There may be obvious candidates or volunteers to undertake some of the necessary tasks (gift identification and team role exercises may help with this), but others simply need to be done by someone. One of the joys of church planting is when we can stop doing things that were necessary but were unrelated to our gifts and passions—either because these tasks are no longer necessary or because someone who has joined the new church is able, even enthusiastic, to take them on.

Building Relationships

But team-building is not just about training and allocating tasks. Building relationships that go way beyond the superficial is crucial for authenticity, sustainability, and mission effectiveness. Team members need to get to know each other (especially if they are not from the same church), trust each other, and build relationships that go beyond how they function together. This means investing time in shared activities, eating together, playing together, relaxing together, and becoming friends as well as colleagues. Planting teams can become overly serious and find it hard to unwind unless they invest in ostensibly "time-wasting" activities. When they face pressures and problems, fractured relationships can result if they have not established a firm basis of friendship and trust.

Relationships must not be rushed or forced, but we need to resist the temptation to relate to one another only as team members. Inevitably some relationships will be easier and deeper than others, but we need to ensure that no team member is marginalized or excluded. Humor is vital but dangerous, so team members should exercise great care, especially while relationships are still forming.

Teams also need to learn how to relate to God together. Especially when team members arrive from different places, they will bring various expectations, practices, and spiritual experiences; but even if everyone is from the same church, they may have quite different approaches to prayer, worship, and spirituality. We need not regard this as a problem but as an opportunity for growth, an initial expression of the kind of creativity and sensitivity needed to plant a new church. But we may need to learn to value various ways in which team members pray and worship, and weave these practices into an authentic corporate spirituality. Furthermore, some team members may struggle if the spiritual resources of their church are no longer available to them and they have not yet learned to draw on the resources of the team. This is a crucial adjustment process.

But if the team-building process goes well, the relationships that develop can be rich and deep. Some church-planting team members report an experience of community they have not encountered anywhere else. The term *communitas* is sometimes used to describe this. Drawing on the research of anthropologist Victor Turner, Alan Hirsch and Michael Frost have written at length about communitas, identifying as its key features a context of liminality (being on the threshold or in transition), a pioneering community, a shared task or mission, and risk-taking.[22] Participating in a church-planting team that reaches this level of community can have a profound impact on team members.

Who Else?

Identifying, recruiting, and preparing church planters and planting teams has necessarily occupied us for most of this chapter, but we need to consider some other people who may be involved in a planting venture.

First, there are any children of team members who may or may not be consulted about the changes they will also experience as a result of their parents' involvement. They may have to move, make new friends, change schools, and in other ways adapt to a new context. Their experience of church may also be quite different, especially if they were used to a large church with many other children and an extensive program of activities. Although their parents will be primarily responsible for helping them make the necessary adjustments, it may be helpful for someone else (perhaps in the planting church) to keep an eye on these children and monitor developments. Some planting models involve less disruption than others, and in some situations the children may continue to participate in activities in the planting church.

Second, other Christians may discover that a new church is being planted and decide they want to become involved. Some may live in the host community but are not connected to any church—either because they have recently moved there or because they dropped out of previous church involvement. They may perceive this as an opportunity to connect or reconnect with church or to recommit themselves to follow Christ. Others may belong to another church nearby but opt to transfer to the emerging church. Such people may be a godsend to the planting team, strengthening and encouraging them and opening up many new links into the community. Proposed transfers from other churches, however, need to be handled with care and sensitivity.

But other Christians may also be a huge liability and can seriously hinder or even derail a church-planting venture. Some may be disgruntled and bring lots of baggage from their previous church experiences; others may have massive pastoral needs and be inordinately demanding, distracting the team from its mission; others again may have expectations of influence and leadership in the new church but do not share the vision and values of the team and want to import into the new church elements the planting team was eager to abandon. Some planting teams have been so glad to welcome local Christians into their new church that they have failed to recognize the telltale signs of these difficulties and have been sucked into very painful experiences. We must deal graciously with those who want to become involved, whatever their motives or issues, but we must also act wisely, which may mean discouraging involvement or making very clear what the parameters of pastoral care or opportunities for influence will be.

Third, extra personnel may be available to work alongside the planting team, either for specific periods or as required. The planting church might release other members to offer help with evangelism, community projects, children's activities, music, or in other ways. This can be very helpful if there are key skills, gifts, or areas of experience missing from the team. A denominational mission team might join the planting team for a limited period, or an internship or student placement might be organized. Additional personnel can be very helpful, as long as this does not place too much strain on the planting team, although we need to ensure they understand and share the team's vision and values. But too many short-term helpers can distract the planting team, create unhealthy dependency on external resources, and disempower members of the host community.

Fourth, there are those who in various ways will support the planting team. These may be members of the planting church or staff of the mission agency or denomination deploying the team, or they may be external people. They may include the following:

- Mentors who can help team members develop their skills, use their gifts, discover their roles, and reflect on their experiences.
- Spiritual directors who can encourage team members to grow spiritually through the process of church planting and discern where God is in the experience.
- Coaches who can work with individuals or the whole team, encouraging them to develop as a team and helping them operate more effectively.

- Accompaniers who journey with the team as critical friends, visiting periodically and asking good questions.[23]
- Accountability groups to whom team members make themselves accountable on issues of lifestyle, time and money, family life, and relationships.
- Advisory groups to whom the team reports on developments and with whom it discusses issues and setbacks.
- Prayer partners and supporters beyond the local context, to whom individual team members can turn for support and encouragement.
- Other church-planting teams with whom experiences and learning can be shared through regular or occasional meetings.[24]
- Resource people and consultants on whose expertise teams can draw as and when necessary.
- Friends with whom they can relax and *not* talk about church planting.

Church planting is demanding. Burnout is common, especially where adequate support structures are not in place. Working in teams rather than in isolation is preferable in most situations, but we should not to assume that even the best team can supply all of a church planter's needs. And there have been too many incidents of marriage breakdown among church planters (which may be exacerbated by close and supportive relationships in the planting team). External support structures and people are vital.[25]

Some emerging churches and mission agencies are also drawing on monastic traditions in their search for rules of life, rhythms, and resources that can sustain faith, spirituality, and discipleship. Dubbed "new monasticism" by some, this flows out of recognition that in an increasingly unsupportive post-Christendom culture, followers of Jesus—especially but not exclusively in pioneering situations—need richer and deeper spiritual practices if they are to survive and thrive. A number of "mission orders" are emerging, especially in urban contexts, which use the language of "covenant" rather than "team membership" and which give much greater attention to "formation" than a typical training process.[26] This may be an increasingly common—and crucial—characteristic of church-planting ventures in the years ahead.

● ● ●

Questions for Further Reflection

1. How many church planters have you met? What characteristics, if any, do they have in common?
2. Do you have what it takes to be involved in church planting? If you sensed God might be calling you into church planting, how would you check this out?
3. What kind of church planters are likely to be effective in adoption planting? What skills would they need that might not be associated with planters using other models?
4. What elements are missing from the training curriculum outlined in this chapter?
5. If you were planting a church, what spiritual and relational resources would you need to sustain you? How would you go about finding or developing these?

8
PLANTING **CHURCHES: WHAT NEXT?**

A common feature of church-planting books in the 1990s was where they ended. Having explored at length the dynamics of selecting a planting model, researching a community, preparing the planting church, and recruiting a team, they tended to leave the team to its own devices once the ubiquitous launch event had occurred. One offered a final chapter entitled "The week after the Sunday before"[1] with brief remarks on caring for newcomers and coping with changes; others offered less. Church-planting conferences and training courses also tended to concentrate on the planting process and gave scant attention to what happens once a church begins to emerge.

Perhaps this deficiency was inevitable in a period when there were relatively few church planters with experience of this second phase. It was undoubtedly exacerbated by the rush to plant churches quickly, which focused energies on the initial phase of the process. But the struggle, decline, and closure of many newly planted churches in that decade indicates that more needed to be said and done. George Lings and I concluded from our research into the experience of various denominations that "starting churches is not enough."[2] We should measure the vitality and effectiveness of a church-planting movement not by how many new churches are planted, but by how many thrive.

There is no way of guaranteeing that new churches will thrive or even survive, especially where we experiment with fresh expressions of church or plant churches into challenging contexts. But greater understanding of the processes by which a church matures may help to reduce the failure rate. Preventable failure represents a waste of resources, results in disillusionment and discouragement, squanders mission opportunities, and gives church planting a bad reputation.[3]

Another reason for neglecting the ongoing development of a newly planted church may be uncertainty as to when this becomes simply "a church." There are numerous resources available on all aspects of church life; perhaps new churches should draw on these rather than looking for specialized material. Some new churches seem reluctant to move beyond the designation "church plant" (another reason to drop this noun from our vocabulary): I have on several occasions been invited to do some consultancy with a "church plant" that was over ten years old and on one occasion with one that was over eighty years old! So we may want to encourage young churches to grow up and learn from general resources on spiritual maturity, corporate worship, making disciples, evangelism, social engagement, leadership development, and many other topics.

But there are dynamics and challenges in the early months and years of a new church that require special attention, which justify this substantial final chapter on what happens next in a church-planting situation. There are also significant questions that planting teams and the churches or agencies that deploy them need to ask at this stage.

What Next for the Planting Team?

If a new church is publicly launched or starts to meet regularly for corporate worship, it is tempting to identify this as the point when it is actually planted, even if this moment was preceded by months or years of patiently building relationships in the host community or gathering a core group that already functions as a church in many other ways. Church planters who reject this perception on principle struggle to counter this within and beyond the church. But this perception is worth challenging if the new church is not to slip into ways of thinking that may damage its mission and community life. Churches that emerge more organically may not encounter the same perception, or at least not at such an early stage, but we should not underestimate the power of ecclesial tradition to reassert this default understanding of church.

But, whether or not there is a definable moment at which the new church is planted, there is a gradual evolution in the activities of a planting team. Reprising the past few chapters, and depending on whether they adopt a more incarnational or more attractional approach, church planters and planting teams may have been involved in the following:

- Demographic research, cultural exegesis, and prayerful reflection. This may have begun before the team was formed and continued during the planting process.
- Building relationships with individuals and community groups,

slowly becoming members of the host community and participants in its shared life.

- Identifying "people of peace," learning about the host community from them and developing friendships with them.
- Engaging in social action or community development as an expression of concern to see the community transformed, rather than just planting a church.
- Organizing and hosting social events or participating in community events run by others.
- Discerning ways in which God is already at work in the community and potential redemptive analogies.
- Publicizing the intention of the team to plant a new church and inviting others to become involved in this venture.
- Direct evangelism with the intention of encouraging people to explore the claims of Christ on their lives and to become his followers.
- Gathering people from the community into informal or more organized groups in the expectation that these will cohere as church.
- Becoming more deeply embedded in the community and finding the core of a new church emerging from this incarnational ministry.
- Encountering other Christians who want to become part of this emerging church and working out how to respond to them.
- Laying foundations and erecting the necessary scaffolding for the new church in light of agreed-upon values, vision, ethos, and purposes.

As the church emerges, gradually or suddenly, many of these activities will continue. But three new factors will impact what the team does and how it allocates its time. First, if the church is to be indigenous and members of the host community are to be empowered and released, these activities will increasingly be shared responsibilities involving team and church members together. Second, as gifts in the emerging church become apparent, team members can hand over responsibility for tasks they had done because they needed doing but for which they are not especially gifted. Third, team members will increasingly be involved in pastoral care and other community-building activities. They will need to monitor and adjust the balance between mission and maintenance as the church develops.

While there is no way a planting team can anticipate all the issues they may encounter in the first year or two of a newly planted church, experience suggests that there are several challenges teams frequently face and priorities to which they need to give attention. We will look first at situations where the church develops well before addressing issues that arise when it struggles.

If Things Go Well

In thriving new churches there are some areas in which the team may begin to experience a sense of loss. These feelings will surprise them and be hard to acknowledge. Outwardly everything is progressing well, but there is a sense of disquiet and even disorientation. As they reflect on these feelings (and a wise team leader will encourage this), several losses may be identified:

- Loss of control, as decisions previously made by the team are now shared with or devolved to members of the growing church.
- Loss of focus, as the streamlined activities of a planting team are subsumed into the more disparate requirements of church life.
- Loss of intimacy, as tight-knit and supportive team relationships are sacrificed in order to build relationships with new people joining the church.
- Loss of passion, as the vision toward which the team has been working becomes a reality (although never quite the reality they envisioned).

These feelings of loss are very real and need to be explored; ignoring them, feeling guilty about them, or pushing them away can cause personal stress and relational difficulties. We mentioned in chapter 7 four stages many teams experience ("forming, storming, norming and performing"). Bruce Tuckman, who developed this model, later updated it to include a fifth stage, "adjourning" (others propose "mourning"). This entails the dissolution or at least the transformation of the team, the completion of its main tasks, and the reduction of others' dependency on it.

As team members discuss how they are feeling, they may recognize that some losses are inevitable and simply need to be accepted (and celebrated) as signs that the new church is maturing. Others may prompt the team to reassess their role and priorities, and the extent to which they have imparted their vision to the emerging church. Others again may need compensating strategies to ensure that both the team and the church can thrive.

There is a delicate balance to be struck here. Team relationships are important and need to be nurtured while the team continues to function as a team, but not at the expense of neglecting other relationships in the church or creating a clique that excludes others. The more varied activities of the church are necessary to create a sustainable community, but the team has a watching brief to ensure the church does not lose its missional edge. There is a danger that the original vision might be lost or even hijacked,[4] but the team must also endorse the church's freedom to cast its own vision if it is to be indigenous rather than dependent. And the team dare not evaluate what emerges only by their (often unrealistic) expectations as they designed a new church on the drawing board. While the team still exercises responsibility for the church, it will need to tread carefully in all these areas.

Authentic, rather than mechanistic, church planting has the capacity to surprise the team. Sometimes the outcome differs markedly from what they were anticipating but exceeds their expectations, although I have also met church planters who did not feel at home in the churches they planted. Some have been deeply disappointed, but others have realized that the context demanded the kind of church that emerged and that members of the host community feel at home there. Unexpected but contextually relevant outcomes are a good indication that a team has been guided by incarnational and missional instincts.

But for how long does the planting team have responsibility for the new church? For how long does it continue to function as a team? The answers to these questions depend on the planting model and the meaning of "team" in different contexts. If the team is perceived as the core group of the new church, there is no expectation that it will withdraw at any stage and hand over responsibility to others. If it is commissioned to plant a church and move on, when and how "phase out" occurs is of critical importance. In practice, it is not unusual for some members of a mission team to remain with the new church, and some of the core group of a new church may return to the planting church. Initial expectations are not always fulfilled. But the transition from "core group" or "team" to "new church" is a vital stage and we need to take several factors into account:

- If the planting team or core group retains control too long, the new church can be disempowered and become dependent on those who planted it. But if control is shared or handed over prematurely, the church can struggle. Gradual transition and planned rather than abrupt changes are usually preferable, but the team must be alert to the possibility that they are dragging their heels because of reluctance about this transition.

- It is important to be clear from the outset whether the church planter or leader of the planting team is expected to become the pastor of the emerging church. Some church planters are clear that this is their calling; others may be equally clear that it is not. It is also perfectly acceptable for this to be an open question. What is not helpful is for there to be unspoken assumptions. Nor should we assume that other team members who remain will exercise leadership roles indefinitely.

- If some or all of the planting team remain in the church, at some stage they need to forgo team status and become church members like everyone else; otherwise the church will have an inner circle, which will feel exclusive to others and will hinder its development. Strong team relationships were important in the planting phase but need now to be subsumed into the wider church community. Including others in team activities or blurring the team/nonteam distinction should happen sooner rather than later, probably while the new church is still embryonic.

- If some or all of the planting team move on, this transition needs to be carefully handled so that their responsibilities are passed on to others who have the ability to carry these. Before they leave, team members may be able to train apprentices in various aspects of church life. Some experienced church planters suggest that planning "phase out" should begin very early in the planting process, long before a new church is actually planted.[5]

If Things Go Badly

Thus far we have assumed that the new church is progressing well and that the team can either become fully integrated into it or move on. But there is no guarantee that all church-planting ventures will succeed. Sooner or later we may have to face the possibility that the church we have planted is not going to survive. There are several reasons why church-planting ventures fail:

- Sometimes unexpected demographic changes occur (such as a major employer moving or a government housing project being shut down), which means a church is no longer viable in the area where it was being planted. This situation confronted a couple working with Urban Expression. When a local authority reneged on plans to regenerate their housing project, Urban Expression's planting plans were squashed through no fault of their own.

- Sometimes the planting team lacks the skills, character, or perseverance to plant a new church. An inappropriate person may have been chosen to lead the team, or it may not have gelled or shared a common vision.

- Sometimes a new church fails to achieve "critical mass"—the point at which there is sufficient momentum for it to sustain itself and develop a life of its own beyond the life of the planting team or core group. The numbers required vary depending on the context, and sometimes a new church approaches this point several times but repeatedly falls back (especially in transient communities).

- Sometimes the team is swamped by people with pastoral needs or distracted by Christians transferring from other churches and bringing all kinds of baggage with them.

- Sometimes the planting team makes mistakes that cause the initiative to founder: inadequate research, inappropriate meeting place, going public too early, giving offense in the community, or imposing an alien expression of church.

- Sometimes team members lose heart when progress is slower than expected or as they realize what hard work church planting involves. Some drift back to the planting church or decide to leave the team, which may result in discouragement and imbalance and ultimately incapacitate the remaining team members.

- Sometimes other missional priorities take precedence. A church planter working with Urban Expression has chosen to concentrate on developing a community for people with mental health needs, although she hopes a new church will emerge from this community in due course.

What are the options for a church-planting team once it becomes clear that an initiative is not going to succeed? Once again, the planting model will affect the decisions we make. With mother/daughter, multiple sites, satellite congregations, adoption, and multiple congregations, the team can be drawn back into the planting church. This is not an easy decision, but it is better than encouraging the team to persist when we judge the prospect of planting a new church or congregation to be remote. Other models present different challenges: dispersion, accidental parenthood, and long-distance planting all have features that make it difficult, practically or emotionally, to return to the planting church, though this may occasionally be possible. Where there is no planting church, the core group of an emerging church or a planting team will need to be disbanded or possibly redeployed.

Whatever the circumstances, struggling and abortive initiatives require mission agencies and planting churches to exercise caring responsibility toward those they have deployed. We will consider these responsibilities as we ask what's next for planting agencies once the team has been deployed.

What Next for the Planting Agency?

Planting Agency and Planting Team

In most situations the planting agency (church, denomination, or mission agency) has an ongoing relationship with and some measure of responsibility toward the planting team it deploys. We suggested in chapter 5 that it is important to think through *before* the team is deployed how this relationship will be sustained. Although we cannot anticipate every eventuality, if the ground rules are agreed on and expectations clarified, this can save serious problems later.

It may be helpful at this stage to summarize the roles of planting agencies in the planting process:

- Recruit, assess, and deploy church planters and planting teams.
- Provide initial training, orientation, and ongoing opportunities for learning.
- Participate in decisions about where and when a church should be planted.
- Provide funding for the venture itself or for some of the team.
- Encourage others to offer short-term support and assistance.
- Set up pastoral support and accountability systems for the team.
- Establish criteria for assessing the progress of the planting venture.
- Develop processes to enable them to learn from the experience of the planting team.

Conversations with church planters indicate that planting agencies vary considerably in their ability and readiness to follow through on what they initially offer. Some church planters cannot speak too highly of the support and encouragement they have received. Sometimes, however, expectations have not been clarified or agreed on, which can cause misunderstanding and pain. Sometimes circumstances or priorities change (especially if there is a change of leadership in the planting church) and the team feels marginalized or abandoned. Sometimes a church develops in ways the planting agency is unhappy about: a planting church may be offended or feel threatened if the new church adopts different practices. Sometimes a mission agency fails to ask probing questions or to spot problems before they cause serious difficulties.

So it is worth setting out some of the issues with which planting agencies may need to grapple in the months and years after the team has been deployed.

First, the planting agency needs to be a sounding board for the planting team, offering an external viewpoint that helps them gain a better sense of perspective. Church planting can become all-consuming and very intense; minor concerns can feel like major setbacks; the team can fail to notice things that are obvious to outsiders; and the sheer commitment of team members can mask unhealthy developments. We need to avoid stifling supervision and respect the freedom of the planting team to be creative, but this does not preclude proper accountability.

Second, the planting agency needs to be careful not to confuse support and assessment. It is likely that both are needed, but it is often preferable for different people to be involved in these activities. Indeed, it may sometimes be helpful for someone outside the planting agency to fulfill one of these roles. If support and assessment are conflated, this introduces problematic dynamics into the relationship.

Third, the planting agency needs to celebrate progress and help the team recognize what they are accomplishing. Some teams have such high expectations that they struggle to celebrate anything less than full-scale revival. The planting agency should also monitor the health and energy of the team, especially once the initial adrenaline surge wears off. It needs to be alert to signs that team members are approaching burnout and help them take preventative measures.

Fourth, the planting agency needs to monitor the way things are developing and help the team decide when to persevere and when to call a halt. We suggested in chapter 1 that the criteria for "success" are not just numerical but involve asking who is involved and why, whether the new church is strategically located, how it is impacting the host community, what kind of church has been planted, whether indigenous leadership is emerging, and what the planting team has learned. This is where agreed-upon expectations, assessment criteria, and time frame are so important but, even if these are all in place, the planting team and planting agency may still interpret what is happening in different ways. Planting agencies need to give teams permission to stop. They also need to recognize that church planting in post-Christendom takes longer than it once did, and exercise patience over many years, rather than writing off a venture too soon.

Fifth, if a team accepts that a new church is not going to emerge, the planting agency has a crucial pastoral role with team members, helping them process their feelings and learn from their experiences. For some church planters "failure" has been devastating, deterring them from taking further risks, challenging their faith, and causing them to question God's call on their lives. Perhaps they did not receive the pastoral support that might have helped them integrate their experiences into ongoing discipleship.

Sixth, planting agencies need to debrief team members who leave the team at any stage, whether their experiences have been positive or negative. "Exit interviews" are now standard practice in most missionary societies; planting team members need opportunities to reflect on what they have been doing and learning. They may also have insights that will help planting agencies improve their own performance. Not all team members find it easy to settle back into "normal" church life, especially if they have experienced the kind of communitas described in chapter 7.

We suggested in chapter 6 that authentic church planting is a two-way learning process in which the planting team is transformed by its experience as it participates in the mission of God in a community. As team members move on into new contexts, they may need to explore and process new understandings of God, discipleship, church, mission, the gospel, and themselves.

Planting Agency and Planted Church

Does the planting agency have ongoing responsibilities toward the church that has been planted? The answer to this question varies depending on the planting model and the kind of planting agency involved, but this can be a contentious issue, so it is worth discussing at the outset.

- If the planting agency is a church, the mother/daughter, long-distance, accidental parenthood, dispersion, and adoption models normally assume that the new church will, sooner or later, be independent of the planting church. However, the "sooner or later" dimension may be the point of contention, with either the planting church or the new church wanting independence sooner. With satellite congregations, multiple sites, and multiple congregations, the planting church has responsibility for what emerges and continues to oversee its development.

- If the planting agency is a denomination, the expectation is generally that the new church becomes a member of this denomination and assumes the privileges and responsibilities of this relationship (although theoretically denominations that emphasize the autonomy of the local church should encourage new churches to make their own decisions about this).

- If the planting agency is a mission organization, it faces a choice. Either it accepts pastoral responsibility for the churches it plants and becomes, in effect, a small denomination; or it limits its mandate to planting churches and encourages those churches into relationship with existing networks. Urban Expression has chosen the second option so that we are not distracted from our primary calling.

- If the planting agency is an individual or an emerging group, there is no external agency to take responsibility for what emerges. Independent existence may be an option for a while, but links with other churches are likely to be important for the church's ongoing development.

An underlying issue is, as indicated at the beginning of this chapter, when we claim that a church has actually been planted. Planting agencies have diverse views on this. Some are reluctant to accord a new church full ecclesial status until it has been meeting publicly for a certain period; has an authorized leadership team, a constitution, and a minimum number of members; and is well on the way to financial self-sufficiency. Others are ready to declare the church planted once the planting team, together with any others who may have joined them, has a separate identity from the planting agency. Once again, clarifying definitions and expectations before deploying the team helps avoid confusion and conflict at a later stage.

Planting Agency and the Wider Church

In addition to their responsibilities toward the planting team, planting agencies have other responsibilities. If, as chapter 2 insisted, church planting is not just about planting a new church but about missional and ecclesial pioneering on behalf of the wider church, it is important that planting agencies capture and share the learning from these initiatives. It is a missed opportunity if church-planting ventures, whether or not they are "successful," do not offer others the chance to reflect on what has happened and learn from it.

Some denominations and other planting agencies are much better at this than others. For several years, the Salvation Army has run a two-stage training event for church planters: the first part is for new or potential planters to learn the basics; the second is for planters already in situ to reflect together and continue their training. These two stages overlap so that the two groups can interact. The Cutting Edge initiative of the Diocese of Oxford, which we referred to in an earlier chapter, not only offered support and accountability to several emerging church leaders, but hosted retreats and consultations where they could learn from one another. This project is being written up so others can learn from it. The Anglican Church Planting Initiatives' website[6] has a range of helpful resources derived from many years of supporting church planters. And the Share website[7] will be updated as practitioners reflect on their experiences and offer perspectives on good practice.

It is worth noting that insights from church-planting initiatives may also assist those who are attempting to replant or reenvision struggling churches. Although the contexts may be quite different, some principles are transferable and some processes can be adapted. There are thousands of churches that need to be replanted or revitalized. Some argue that this should be our priority, not planting churches. But this is a false dichotomy: through church planting, denominations can gain experience and test out ways forward that may help to restore declining churches.

Planting agencies that may plant again will also want to incorporate lessons from each venture into their systems and processes. There may have been mistakes and deficiencies that we can remedy, as well as examples of good practice from which others can learn. According to research I have recently carried out, most denominations are supportive of church planting in principle, but few have a church-planting strategy or any guidelines that offer church planters or planting churches a framework for action. Most denominational websites, for example, do little more than mention church planting. Some of those that do have guidelines have not updated them for several years. But the Assemblies of God has worked hard on this issue,[8] the Baptist Union of Holland has done some creative thinking about the "ecclesial minimum," and the Methodist Church hopes to have a church-planting framework in place by the end of 2008. Increased cross-fertilization to share experiences and resources would be very beneficial.

When the planting agency is a church, especially a church that has not previously planted another church, those involved may be focused on their own initiative and unaware of the importance of capturing and sharing what they have learned. Denominations that rely on local planting initiatives need processes to disseminate this learning. Planting churches should also be encouraged to reflect on their understanding of mission and church in light of their planting experience and allow this experience to renew and reshape them.

Planting churches may also consider the possibility of planting another church. The more successful their first venture, the more ready they will be to explore this. Some churches have planted several churches over a period of years, although usually only quite large churches in areas with transient populations can sustain such strategies. There is much to commend this approach, not least that the experience gained through one planting venture is invested in another. Some hoped that such serial planting might galvanize a sustainable church-planting momentum in the 1990s. But this did not happen, and some churches that attempted to plant several times encountered serious difficulties. So while many planting churches should at least consider planting again, there are several issues to think through:

- Church planting is not the only option. A mission-oriented church might consider other forms of mission rather than assuming that further planting is necessarily the way ahead.
- One successful venture does not guarantee a second success. Over-confidence and unwarranted assumptions can blight further initiatives.
- If a church does decide to plant again, it can draw on its recent experience but dare not take shortcuts in research, team selection, or preparation. Nor should it assume that the same planting model will be appropriate.
- Some churches that have planted two or three churches in a relatively short period have experienced "planting fatigue." The new churches may have flourished, but the planting church has struggled to recover. Planting again too soon or too often risks causing lasting damage to the planting church.
- It may be better for the new church to plant again, perhaps with support from the original planting church. At some point, "mother churches" may need to become "grandmother churches."

This final point redirects our attention to the new church. While the planting team and the church or agency that deployed it are wrestling with these transitional issues, the emerging church is also facing challenges and experiencing changes. The planting team or planting church may or may not, as we have seen, continue to assume responsibility for the church it has planted, but whoever is guiding this new community would be well advised to think through the issues highlighted in the next section.

What Next for the Emerging Church?

In chapter 5 we used the life-cycle analogy to reflect on aspects of the early stages of a church-planting venture. This analogy also illuminates the later stages with which we are now concerned. The full life cycle consists of the following stages:

- *Conception:* the point at which a discernment process and feasibility study has led to the decision to plant a church.
- *Pregnancy:* plans are gradually becoming realities, early signs of life are evident, and preparation is underway for the birth of a new church.
- *Birth:* the beginning of a new church, involving some form of separation from the planting agency (though this will vary depending on the planting model).
- *Childhood:* an exciting but vulnerable time, when the new church is discovering its own identity, when rapid growth is feasible, but there is much to learn.
- *Adolescence:* the new church grows in confidence, develops its own vision, and may push for increasing independence (again depending on the planting model).
- *Maturity:* the new church has become a community with its own rhythm of life; it may now also be self-supporting and capable of reproducing, thus starting the life cycle again.

Childhood

A newly planted church can be an exciting community to be involved in. New churches, unless they have brought unnecessary baggage with them from the planting church, tend to be uncluttered, flexible, and focused. Their vision, enthusiasm, energy, commitment, and expectation can engender the same kind of communitas that effective planting teams experience. This can make them highly attractive and may result in rapid growth.

However, young churches are also prone to instability and unrealistic expectations—and rapid growth can exacerbate these problems. Churches that experience substantial growth in the first few months may seem to be thriving, but growth may bring serious challenges. Existing Christians joining the church may have different values from the planting team and founding members. Strong personalities can sway the church because it does not yet have the maturity to test what they propose and exercise discernment. Members of the host community who join the church may have complex pastoral needs that demand more than a young church can offer. Numbers may fluctuate wildly, raising and dashing hopes and making planning difficult. Energy and commitment may be channeled into activism and result in exhaustion rather than effective ministry.

New churches with relatively small numbers or which do not grow as rapidly as expected may struggle to accept their limitations and ape larger churches. I have frequently visited new churches meeting in surroundings much too large for them, or attempting to create a celebration-style event with cell-sized groups, or equipped with impressive but entirely superfluous amplification equipment, or implying through their advertising that their meetings attract hundreds rather than a handful. Sometimes these efforts are defended on the grounds of "vision" and "faith for the future," but they generally make the church look ridiculous and are not conducive to growth.

Other new churches with small numbers may struggle to sustain the level of activity they regard as essential for their community life and mission. They may resist the temptations of going public too soon or proliferating meetings, but still find this hard. They find it especially discouraging when visitors choose not to become involved because the church cannot offer them what they are looking for. Each person who joins or leaves a new and small church seems more significant than in a larger and longer-established church.

Wise leadership. New churches in the "childhood" phase, whether they grow rapidly or struggle to grow at all for some time, need plenty of encouragement if the enthusiasm, energy, and flexibility are to be fully harnessed. But they also need wise leadership if these assets are not to be dissipated. Most of the New Testament letters are examples of such leadership. Written mainly to young churches, these letters contain warnings about doctrinal error and ethical compromise, and advice on missional and pastoral matters, but they are full of gratitude for these churches and encourage them to press on toward maturity. New churches can be damaged by criticism as easily as they can be distracted by deviant ideas or deflected from their primary calling.

Wise leadership in the "childhood" stage of a church will include the following:

- Keeping the church on an even keel so that it is not "tossed back and forth by the waves,"[9] neither carried away by early success nor disheartened by slow progress or erratic growth.
- Rehearsing the core values, vision, ethos, and priorities of the church, so that those who join are inducted into these foundational commitments.
- Investing much time in welcoming new people into the church and helping them become disciples, so that "belonging" leads to "believing" and on to a deeper level of "belonging."
- Encouraging those who join the church to participate in shaping it but to respect the journey the church is on and not attempt to hijack its vision.
- Maintaining momentum once the initial enthusiasm has dissipated, but guarding against excessive activity and keeping all aspects of church life under review, so that only what is both sustaining and sustainable persists.
- Ensuring that mission remains the priority, but developing maintenance processes to nurture the emerging church.
- Developing an effective and sustainable pastoral care system: without this the new church will not thrive, but overemphasis on pastoral care will endanger the mission focus.
- Finding a balance between stability and flexibility: many new churches enjoy the dangerous freedom of being able to introduce changes more frequently than in older churches. But this can become unsettling and very tiring.
- Developing the necessary organizational and administrative systems the church will need as it develops (although in some planting models, where the church is not independent, these may already be in place).
- Identifying church members with particular gifts and passions, and enabling them to take responsibilities in and beyond the church, wherever possible identifying more than one person for each role to facilitate further growth.
- Building links with other local churches and with a denomination or network of churches so that the new church finds its place in the wider Christian community.

- Strengthening relationships with other local community groups so that the church can take its place in the community and form effective partnerships.

Health issues. Just as adults can be profoundly shaped, for good or ill, by childhood experiences, so the experiences of a young church can have huge consequences for its ongoing development. The aim of all church planters and leaders of new churches is surely to nurture churches that are healthy and sustainable. The emphasis on church growth that undergirded church planting in the 1990s has gradually given way to concern for church health.[10] Hopefully this will result in healthier churches being planted—as long as church planters give attention to this issue.[11]

Young churches, if they are to remain healthy, require a measure of protection from what might harm them. As well as attending to the priorities suggested above, wise leaders will also watch out for those who may damage the emerging church. We noted in the previous chapter that planting teams need to be careful when other Christians want to get involved, and the need for discernment continues as the church emerges. New churches attract a disproportionate number of "problem people"— Christians and others—with complex and demanding needs, who stretch the resources of a young church. Others may have specific agendas and try to impose these on the church.

This is not an easy issue to address. If the church's ethos is missional and welcoming, it will attract people. Some "problem people" may, through the love of the community and by the grace of God, experience healing and become a blessing to the church. Others may, through their brokenness, be important signs to the church of its dependence on God. But too many damaged and demanding people can be unsustainable: the pastoral care system is swamped, meetings become chaotic, leaders are distracted from other priorities, and the church gets a reputation that discourages others from joining. And people with their own agendas and designs on leadership can be divisive and destructive.

Wise leaders will help the church to be alert to this issue and deal wisely and graciously with such people. This may mean encouraging some people to join other churches with more pastoral resources; refusing to lurch from crisis to crisis with those whose needs are always presented as emergencies; limiting the amount of attention and pastoral care given to any individual; or resisting those who want to impose their views on the church. But it will not mean dealing brusquely with anyone, writing people off, welcoming only those who appear to be "sorted" or (as far as possible) jeopardizing the church's reputation as a loving community.

Another health-related issue is discouraging dependency. New churches can invest great expectations in their leaders, especially if these leaders are gifted community builders and communicators. And leaders can easily succumb to the temptation to attempt to fulfill these expectations rather than devolving responsibility, encouraging mutual pastoral care and multivoiced church life. But this does not nurture healthy or maturing churches. One safeguard may be for leaders to invest much of their time on the fringes of the church and in mission, rather than at the center of the church. Not only does this model the priority of mission, but it encourages the church not to look to leaders to meet all its internal needs or expectations. Some of the great leaders of the early churches were catechists who spent much of their time teaching and discipling new believers.

Adolescence

As in human families, the transition from "childhood" to "adolescence" in new churches is gradual rather than sudden, so many issues encountered in the former stage continue to be relevant. But there are also issues that are distinctive of the adolescent phase, on which we will concentrate here.

Where to meet. Where the church meets may need to be reviewed at this time (or even earlier). The initial location may for various reasons no longer be satisfactory: the church may be outgrowing the facilities; the building may not be as ideal as it first appeared; the meeting place may not be suitable for the ways in which the church is now developing; another location may have become available that is better positioned or appointed; or the rental cost may have become onerous or even prohibitive. The church may also want to revisit the discussion about whether domestic, social, public, or sacred space is most appropriate.

This may be when the church considers obtaining its own building rather than continuing to share or rent facilities. This decision needs careful and prayerful discernment: it could be a major distraction for the church or a launching pad for the next stage of its mission and ministry. There may be significant contextual factors, such as the availability of a suitable building at a reasonable cost or the exorbitant cost of renting alternatives. There may be cultural factors, such as the message conveyed by a church owning a building and making this available for community use in a neighborhood with few facilities. There may be ecclesial factors, such as the impact a dedicated building would have on the self-understanding of the church and its communal life. And there may be missional factors, as the church weighs what it can and cannot do with and without its own buildings and whether a major building project at this stage would enhance or inhibit its mission.

Wise leadership will encourage the church to identify and challenge presuppositions and assumptions, explore all options before making a decision, weigh the costs in terms of time and finance, and refuse to prioritize building issues over its primary mission. In many situations, frequently changing where the church meets is unsettling, but occasionally a nomadic existence may suit the church's ethos. Sharing, renting, building, or purchasing premises can all be decisions motivated by mission and appropriate for the church and its context. But what is God saying to the church? Once more, feasibility and discernment go hand in hand.

Relating to others. Adolescence is when issues of independence tend to arise—whether the planting model prescribes independence, semiautonomy, or continuing dependence. Sometimes a new church wants independence against the wishes of the planting church; sometimes they agree on the eventual outcome but disagree on the timescale. Just as teenagers yearn to be independent (although most are happy to continue receiving financial support), so many adolescent churches, especially those planted by the mother/daughter model, push for independent status before the planting church thinks this is wise.

The pressure to become independent may be increased by ecclesial assumptions (Baptist churches are especially eager to become independent), by differences in ethos or vision between the planting church and the new church, or by rapid growth that means that only a minority of the new church now have any relational link with or sense of obligation to the planting church.

We recommended in an earlier chapter that this issue should be discussed in advance, but such discussions do not always enable resolution at this stage. In fact, this issue provokes resentment on both sides if it is not well handled. There is much to be said for inviting someone external but trusted by both sides to facilitate further discussion and to help the two churches agree on how to proceed.

Another issue that may need fresh attention at this stage is the church's relationship with other local churches. However much consultation took place before the church was planted, relations with other churches may deteriorate when the new church becomes a reality, especially if any members of those churches decide to transfer to the new church or if the new church grows rapidly and other churches feel threatened by this.

Discoveries. An encouraging feature of a church moving from childhood to adolescence is that people with diverse gifts and skills emerge to lead different aspects of its mission and ministry. In the early months everyone pitched in to accomplish what needed to be done, but there is room now for greater specialization. Identifying the gifts in the church and equipping people to use these should have been underway since the church began, but it takes time for the benefits to be realized. It also requires grace on the part of founding members to make room for those who have joined more recently. One important caveat needs to be sounded: if the church is to be mission-oriented in the adolescent period and beyond, it is vital that gifted people are released for ministry beyond the church as well as within it. Expecting people to use their gifts in the church rather than in the wider community is a significant factor in churches losing their missional edge.

One feature of the adolescent stage that may be less encouraging is the discovery that the new church is not as different from the planting church or other churches as its founding members had anticipated. Another is people leaving to join other churches. Especially if the planting team rejected cloning and thought creatively about what they were planting, those who remain with the church into the adolescent stage may find very disconcerting the realization that the church is less radical than they expected. Where this realization is accompanied by church members opting to return to the planting church or join another church, there may be a deep sense of disappointment and confusion about what has been accomplished. In situations where the accidental parenthood model was operative, these reactions are even stronger and harder to process.[12]

These discoveries and experiences may reveal defects in the planting process or failure to pass on the values and vision of the planting team to the emerging church. They may also indicate how strong the default model of church is and how difficult it is to resist the pull of this. However, there are alternative interpretations. It may be that older churches are changing through their interaction with newer churches, so that the renewing influence of church planting has been effective. And it may be that the radical vision of the planting team was vital to bring the new church to birth but needs to evolve if the church is to be sustainable. Adolescent rebellion against parental norms is often a healthy precursor to an adult synthesis of parental values and the values of the emerging generation.

Wise leadership. Wise leadership in the adolescent phase helps the emerging church to work through these issues, to hold on to what is of value from the planting process, to resist compromise but embrace necessary maturation, and to accept that wherever different churches exist there will be transfers in all directions. A degree of institutionalization and greater stability is appropriate as the church settles into rhythms and patterns of life that will sustain it over the years, but we must not allow this to become ossification or to preclude flexibility and responsiveness to fresh opportunities. It is worrying how soon many new churches settle into a rut rather than a rhythm.

We have mentioned leadership repeatedly in this section, but we should not assume that this is fixed throughout the childhood and adolescent phases. Those who plant the church or who lead it initially may not continue to lead the church as it matures. Pioneers often make poor consolidators, so leadership changes may be essential if the church is to thrive and if the pioneers are to be released to continue pioneering. Some pioneers may struggle to accept that they need to hand on the baton, but it may be crucial for the church and for their own well-being. If leaders move on and pioneer elsewhere, this encourages churches to think beyond their own boundaries.

Other pioneers will be able to transition into a different role as the church matures. There are advantages to stable leadership throughout the planting process and for several years as the church develops (and serious problems have been encountered when leadership changes are imposed from outside), but much depends on the gifts and calling of those involved. The adolescent stage is when leadership changes need to be considered, even if no changes ensue.

In some situations it may be appropriate and necessary to import leaders from outside the church, as is normal in older churches and in most denominations; but the fact that this is normal does not mean that it is always advisable. The alternative is to raise up indigenous leaders from within the church and create training and accreditation processes that enable them to remain within their own community. In some contexts, especially in urban areas, we desperately need churches led by indigenous leaders rather than incomers. Elsewhere, imported leaders can bring new perspectives and different skills to enable the church to move from adolescence to maturity; but they can also fail to embrace the founding vision and lead the church back toward a default ecclesiology and a less missional stance.

Maturity

Members of the planting team may or may not still be involved at this stage, but their vision was surely that the church should reach maturity.

Childhood and adolescence are good and necessary developmental stages, but it is unhealthy for churches to remain in these stages too long. Maturity is the goal. But what does maturity mean?

- Maturity may or may not mean independence, depending on initial expectations and ongoing assessment of what is contextually appropriate. An interdependent network of satellite congregations may be a mature expression of church.
- Maturity may or may not mean financial self-sufficiency. For many emerging churches, this is a legitimate aim, but some may be serving communities where financial self-sufficiency is highly unlikely (for example, youth churches or churches among homeless people).
- Maturity may or may not mean an indefinite lifespan. The assumption in most churches and among many church planters is that churches should persist until the end of time. But churches have come and gone over the centuries, serving communities for longer or shorter periods before closing and giving way to new expressions of church. In a transient and rapidly changing culture, it is likely that many churches planted today will have a limited lifespan, pioneering missional initiatives that bring renewal to the church and incarnate the gospel into diverse communities but superseded by new churches with fresh insights and a missional cutting-edge appropriate to other communities.

Maturity in biblical perspective is daunting and glorious: "attaining to the whole measure of the fullness of Christ."[13] I know of no church that has attained maturity in this sense—and I know many churches that have been around for years that are less mature than some recently planted churches. Maturity and age do not always coincide. But the passage from which this description of maturity comes (Ephesians 4) highlights some of the marks of a maturing church. A maturing church is discerning and stable and not easily distracted or deceived (v. 14). A maturing church speaks truth lovingly and deals well with conflict so that unity is maintained (v. 15). A maturing church benefits from different gifts (v. 11) and values the contributions of all its members (v. 16). A maturing church equips its members for "works of service" as the missionary people of God (v. 12).

Returning once more to the "life-cycle" analogy, we might also interpret maturity as the capacity to reproduce so that the cycle begins again. While not all mature human beings reproduce (some because they cannot, others choosing not to for various reasons), enough do for reproduction to be regarded as normal. But reproduction—planting another church—is not yet widely regarded as normal for churches. During the 1990s a practice that had been regarded as abnormal, exceptional, or illegitimate was accepted by many churches and denominations as respectable, even desirable. The next step is for denominations and churches to regard reproduction as normal and to embed this perception in their ecclesial and missional thinking and practice.

There may be situations where churches cannot reproduce or choose not to, but these may be regarded as exceptional if church planting is seen as a normal, even reflexive, activity of healthy churches. Some churches may be in contexts where there is no need for more churches or fresh expressions of church, though there are few such contexts today. Some may be fully engaged in other aspects of mission and reluctant to be distracted. Some may have already planted new churches and now perceive their role as supporting other planting churches (adopting a grandparent role). Most other reasons for not reproducing have less justification once we regard church planting as normal rather than exceptional.

One of the tasks of church-planting teams, then, is to plant churches that expect in due course to reproduce. They may not be mature enough to do so for some years, although in some situations reproduction may be feasible quite soon; but they perceive themselves as "planting churches" as well as "planted churches." Reproduction is embedded in the core values and vision of the new church, so that church planting is understood as an ongoing process that participates in the mission of God and brings ecclesial renewal. Even where there are valid reasons for not reproducing themselves, such churches will look for ways to support other planting churches—by releasing gifted people, offering financial support, sharing their premises, and in other ways.

While defining maturity may be difficult, this is the outcome everyone involved in church planting longs for. Too many churches planted in the 1990s failed to reach this stage and either struggled on through a protracted period of adolescence, blew themselves apart, or quietly faded away. The responsibility of church planters today is to plant churches that will "in all things grow up into him who is the Head, that is, Christ"[14]— healthy churches that are self-aware, creative, flexible, persevering, and committed to releasing the gifts of all their members. (If this list of characteristics sounds familiar, look back at the list of desirable features for church planters in chapter 7.)

What Next for Church Planting?

Throughout this book we have urged church planters to look beyond their immediate context and consider how what they are doing might have wider missional and ecclesial significance. Church planting, we have insisted, means pioneering on behalf of the whole church as well as planting a new church in a particular community. There appears to be renewed interest in church planting today, after the lull toward the end of the 1990s, and increasing momentum as emerging churches, fresh expressions of church, and church-planting initiatives spring up in many places. But to what might this lead?

It might lead to the emergence of new denominations. This has often been the outcome of church planting in the past and across the globe, either intentionally and accidentally. The vibrant church-planting initiatives of New Frontiers and Vineyard, for example, are recent expressions of the same impulse to reproduce that in previous generations resulted in the formation of the Baptist Union, the Moravians, the Congregational Union, the Plymouth Brethren, the Salvation Army, Elim, and the Assemblies of God (to name but a few). Most denominations started as church-planting movements, even if some forgot this heritage and allowed church planting to become exceptional rather than normal after a couple of generations. As new denominations emerge, perhaps some older denominations might be jolted into recovering their own planting instincts and developing new planting strategies.

It might lead to the emergence of a strategic coalition, like Challenge 2000 in the 1990s, which carries out research and shares resources in order to encourage church planting on a wider scale. That coalition failed, for several reasons, to deliver on expectations it had raised, but this should not preclude the emergence of a new coalition that learns from past mistakes and operates more effectively. Denominational strategies are not enough. It is vital that we forge partnerships that will enable us to identify where new churches are needed, who can respond to these opportunities, how different partners can contribute to these initiatives, and how learning can be shared. Research is needed at regional and city-wide levels to discover the neighborhoods and networks into which churches should be planted. Multiagency approaches are essential to release people and resources to plant new churches strategically into areas beyond the reach of entrepreneurial local churches in the suburbs—especially in inner-city, rural, and cross-cultural contexts.

It might lead to the emergence of a new church-planting movement.

Some hoped this was gathering pace in the 1990s, but the momentum stalled by mid-decade. Some wonder if a new movement might be developing in this decade as new kinds of churches emerge in many places, often spontaneously, and as simpler forms of church reproduce themselves. Much of this is happening beyond the boundaries of the older (and newer) denominations and without the involvement of mission agencies. Church-planting movements have been observed in several non-Western nations, catalyzing explosive church growth and bringing social transformation,[15] so it is not surprising that many long for something similar in the West. But this yearning must be accompanied by a realistic assessment of the potential of an aging, declining, and demoralized Western church. Neither faithless pessimism nor unwarranted optimism will serve us well. If a church-planting movement is emerging or imminent, this is great news, but progress is likely to be steady rather than dramatic.

There are, of course, other possible scenarios. The combined impact of fresh expressions of church, emerging churches, and church-planting initiatives may not be significant, and such developments may not be sustained. Denominations may be preoccupied with other matters or shy away from the challenge of planting new churches. Churches may decide to invest in growth rather than reproduction or try to retain the security of what is familiar rather than taking risks. Coalitions may founder on disagreement over doctrinal niceties or ecclesial preferences. And church planters may be so besotted with their own ventures that they fail to inspire others or share what they are learning.

The purpose of this book has been to provide a framework for practitioners and for those who deploy and support them, to encourage all those involved to think through a range of issues and learn from the often hard-won experience of other church planters. My hope is that it will stimulate more planting and more effective planting, more creative planting and more responsible planting, initiatives that are better researched and contextualized, and new churches that are healthier and more sustainable. But I hope too that it will help those with strategic responsibilities to perceive the significance of church planting for the network or denomination they serve, for the wider church, and for the mission of God.

What Next for You?

And so, finally, the questions become personal. What is your response to what you have read? How is God calling you to be involved in planting churches?

- Could you lead a church-planting team?
- Could you join a church-planting team?
- Could you help with research?
- Could your church plant a new church?
- Could you encourage your church leaders to consider this?
- Could you be involved in an emerging church?
- Could you join a new church rather than a more established church?
- Could you help to support a church planter?
- Could your theological college train church planters?
- Could your denomination develop a church-planting strategy?
- Could your mission agency plant churches?
- Could you help to form a church-planting coalition?
- Could you become involved in church-planting again?
- Could you plant differently next time?
- Could you plant cross-culturally and beyond your comfort zone?
- Could you share what you have learned with others?

I am not suggesting that every Christian should be a church planter, but church planting is crucial for the health and future of the church and our participation in God's mission. It is too important to be left to a few enthusiasts. Directly or indirectly, strategically or locally, full-time or part-time, in planting teams or in support roles, hundreds of thousands of us could become involved. And that might just galvanize a movement after all.

Appendix

SELECT BIBLIOGRAPHY AND RESOURCES

My intention in this appendix is to indicate books, websites, and training courses that may be of particular help to church planters and those who recruit and deploy them.

This is a highly selective list of resources (almost all published since 2000) and reflects my own judgment as to which may be most helpful. It also deliberately draws on writers from different Christian traditions.

Books on Church Planting, Fresh Expressions, and Emerging Churches

Frost, Michael, and Alan Hirsch. *The Shaping of Things to Come.* Peabody: Hendrickson, 2004.

Gibbs, Eddie, and Ryan Bolger. *Emerging Churches.* Grand Rapids: Baker, 2005.

Lings, George. *Encounters on the Edge.* Sheffield: The Sheffield Centre, quarterly.

Lings, George, and Stuart Murray. *Church Planting: Past, Present and Future.* Cambridge: Grove, 2003.

Mission-shaped Church. London: Church House, 2004.

Moynagh, Michael. *emergingchurch.intro.* Oxford: Monarch, 2004.

Murray, Stuart. *Church Planting: Laying Foundations.* Carlisle: Paternoster, 1998.

Robinson, Martin. *Planting Mission-Shaped Churches Today.* Crowborough: Monarch, 2006.

Stetzer, Ed. *Planting Missional Churches.* Nashville: Broadman & Holman, 2006.

Taylor, Steve. *The Out of Bounds Church?* Grand Rapids: Zondervan, 2005.

Books on Community Research and Community Development

Andrews, Dave. *Compassionate Community Work*. Carlisle: Piquant, 2006.

Ballard, Paul, and Lesley Husselbee. *Community and Ministry: An Introduction to Community Work in a Christian Context*. London: SPCK, 2007.

Chalke, Steve. *Faithworks Unpacked*. Eastbourne: Kingsway, 2002.

Croft, Steven, Freddy Hedley, and Bob Hopkins. *Listening for Mission: Mission Audit for Fresh Expressions*. London: Church House, 2006.

Hawtin, Murray, and Janie Percy-Smith. *Community Profiling: A Practical Guide*. Milton Keynes: Open University Press, 2007.

Sider, Ronald, and Philip Olsen. *Churches that Make a Difference: Reaching Your Community with Good News and Good Works*. Grand Rapids: Baker, 2002.

Books on Evangelism and Discipleship

Augsburger, David. *Dissident Discipleship*. Grand Rapids: Brazos, 2006.

Croft, Steven, et al. *Evangelism in a Spiritual Age*. London: Church House, 2005.

Finney, John. *Emerging Evangelism*. London: Darton, Longman & Todd, 2004.

Hammett, Edward. *Reframing Spiritual Formation: Discipleship in an Unchurched Culture*. Macon: Smyth & Helwys, 2002.

McLaren, Brian. *More Ready than You Realize: Evangelism as Dance in the Postmodern Matrix*. Grand Rapids: Zondervan, 2002.

Morisy, Ann. *Journeying Out*. London: Morehouse, 2004.

Rolheiser, Ronald. *Secularity and the Gospel*. New York: Crossroad, 2006.

Tomlin, Graham. *The Provocative Church*. London: SPCK, 2002.

Books on Mission and Contemporary Culture

Drane, John. *The McDonaldization of the Church*. London: Darton, Longman & Todd, 2000.

Frost, Michael. *Exiles: Living Missionally in a Post-Christian Culture*. Peabody: Hendrickson, 2006.

Jamieson, Alan. *A Churchless Faith*. London: SPCK, 2002.

Lyon, David. *Jesus in Disneyland: Religion in Postmodern Times*. Cambridge: Polity, 2000.

Murray, Stuart. *Church after Christendom*. Milton Keynes: Paternoster, 2005.

Roxburgh, Alan. *The Missionary Congregation, Leadership and Liminality*. Harrisburg: Trinity Press, 1997.

Sine, Tom. *The New Conspirators*. Milton Keynes: Paternoster, 2008.

Smith, David. *Crying in the Wilderness: Evangelism and Mission in Today's Culture*. Carlisle: Paternoster, 2000.

Sudworth, Richard. *Distinctly Welcoming: Christian Presence in a Multi-faith Society*. Bletchley: Scripture Union, 2007.

Websites

www.emergingchurch.info
www.encountersontheedge.org.uk
www.urbanexpression.org.uk
www.acpi.org.uk
www.incarnate-network.eu
www.freshexpressions.org.uk
www.sharetheguide.org
www.togetherinmission.co.uk

Training Courses

Crucible: www.cruciblecourse.org.uk
ReSource: www.resourcechurchplanting.com
Mission-shaped Ministry: www.freshexpressions.org.uk
Urban Mission Toolkit: www.catalysttrust.org
Workshop: www.workshop.org.uk
Missional Leadership: www.togetherinmission.co.uk
Invest: www.investscotland.org

Notes

Introduction

1. See www.ubranexpression.org.uk

Chapter 1: Planting Churches Today

1. Stuart Murray, *Church Planting: Laying Foundations* (Carlisle: Paternoster, 1998), 1.

2. C. Peter Wagner's claim—perhaps the most widely quoted phrase in church-planting circles during the 1990s.

3. Murray, *Church Planting*, 297-98.

4. A helpful summary, based on Bob Hopkins's experience, can be found at www.acpi.org.uk/articles/PlantersProblems.pdf.

5. For a summary of such lessons, drawing on a consultation in December 2001, see George Lings and Stuart Murray, *Church Planting: Past, Present and Future* (Cambridge: Grove, 2003).

6. See www.willowcreek.com and www.purposedriven.co.uk.

7. See www.celluk.org.uk.

8. See www.alpha.org.

9. See www.freshexpressions.org.uk and www.emergingchurch.info.

10. One exception is Martin Robinson, *Planting Mission-Shaped Churches Today* (Crowborough: Monarch, 2006).

11. One recent and popular publication is Ed Stetzer, *Planting Missional Churches* (Nashville: Broadman & Holman, 2006).

12. Such as the Baptist network, Incarnate, www.incarnate-network.eu, founded in 2006.

13. Mission 21, organized by the Group for Evangelization and Together in Mission.

14. The course in Melbourne had this agenda, as does the Crucible course run in Birmingham each year; see www.cruciblecourse.net.

15. For an explanation of the term *post-Christendom* as used throughout this book, see Stuart Murray, *Post-Christendom: Church and Mission in a Strange New World* (Carlisle: Paternoster, 2004).

16. Lings and Murray, *Church Planting*, 26.

17. *Mission-shaped Church* (London: Church House, 2004), 34.

18. Despite the widespread interest, Peter Brierley estimates that there are only about 17,000 people involved in emerging churches—not yet statistically significant. This figure is quoted in Tom Sine, *The New Conspirators* (Downers Grove: IVP, 2008), 127.

19. *Mission-shaped Church*, 32.

20. The first British conference on church planting in recent years was held in 1983 under the auspices of the British Church Growth Association. Church planters drew extensively on the writings of church-growth consultant C. Peter Wagner, whose involvement in the 1992 congress embodied the link between church-growth thinking and church planting.

21. An influential contribution to this conversation is Michael Frost and Alan Hirsch, *The Shaping of Things to Come* (Peabody: Hendrickson, 2003), 33-46.

22. We cannot pursue here the question of whether it is legitimate to apply the term *incarnational* to the church in a way that parallels the incarnation of God in Christ.

23. Compare Isaiah 2:2-5 with Matthew 28:18-20.

24. Andrew Walls, *The Missionary Movement in Christian History* (Edinburgh: T. & T. Clark, 1996), 7-9.

25. Bryan Stone, *Evangelism after Christendom: The Theology and Practice of Christian Witness* (Grand Rapids: Brazos, 2007), 48.

26. Lesslie Newbigin, *The Gospel in a Pluralist Society* (London: SPCK, 1989), 227. See also Graham Tomlin, *The Provocative Church* (London: SPCK, 2004).

27. See www.sharetheguide.org. "Fresh Expressions" is an initiative of the Archbishop of Canterbury, funded by the Lambeth Partners, to encourage and resource fresh expressions of church. Anglicans and Methodists are the formal partners, and the Congregational Federation also has a representative on the team. There are useful church-planting resources on several websites, including www.encountersontheedge.org.uk, www.acpi.org.uk, and www.urbanexpression.org.uk, but it is surprising that there is no generic UK-based church-planting website.

28. A small selection of such resources can be found in the appendix.

Chapter 2: Planting Churches: Why?

1. We will return to mental maps in chapter 4.

2. Bob Hopkins, ed., *Planting New Churches* (Guildford: Eagle, 1991), 161-78.

3. DAWN is an acronym for "disciple a whole nation." See further www.dawnministries.org. In the 1990s *Challenge 2000* (now defunct) introduced DAWN principles into Britain.

4. See www.ruralexpression.org.uk.

5. For the Salvation Army's NEO initiative, see www1.salvationarmy. org.uk/alove. For Eden, see www.message.org.uk. Andrew Grinnell, who leads the NEO initiative, has recently carried out some research into what he calls "The Forgotten 5," identifying from government statistics the "super output areas" ("data zones" in Scotland) that experience the highest levels of multiple deprivation. These areas are subdivisions of wards and represent roughly four hundred homes. This information could be used to guide church planters toward the priority areas for planting new churches.

6. Websites are the best means of keeping up to speed with developments in this emerging scene. Good places to start are www.emergingchurch.info and www.opensourcetheology.net. There are also numerous American sites, but the emerging church scene there is very different from that in Britain.

7. On these groupings, see www.pioneer.org.uk, www.newfrontiers.xtn.org, www.saltlight.org, www.vineyardchurchesuk.com, www.jesus.org.uk, and www. peacechurch.org.uk.

8. We will explore this process further in chapter 6.

9. See further Stuart Murray, *Changing Mission: Learning from the Newer Churches* (London: CTBI, 2006).

10. These developments have stimulated lengthy and passionate debate in mission journals and among cross-cultural missionaries.

11. Language tends to be an exception, as many recognize the need for churches operating in other languages.

12. Ephesians 2:14-18.

13. These questions will be very familiar to those who have engaged in the debate around the "homogeneous unit principle" proposed by Church Growth missiologists. The classic text is still Donald McGavren, *Understanding Church Growth* (Grand Rapids: Eerdmans, 1970).

14. For further discussion of customization in society and church planting, see Michael Moynagh, *Changing World, Changing Church* (London: Monarch, 2001), especially chaps. 2 and 8.

15. George Lings, *Encounters on the Edge* (The Sheffield Centre quarterly). The range of fresh expressions is also apparent in *Mission-shaped Church* (London: Church House Publishing, 2004), especially chap. 4.

16. Martin Robinson, *Planting Mission-Shaped Churches Today* (Crowborough: Monarch, 2006), 34-6.

17. See, for example, Derek Allan, *Planted to Grow* (Didcot: Baptist Union, 1994).

18. Some emerging-church pioneers react negatively to the language of "experimenting," which they feel does not do justice to their passion and marginalizes them in relation to the inherited church. But experimenting can be a passionate endeavor, and in time what is marginal may become mainstream.

19. See further www.oxford.anglican.org/freshexpressions.

20. Martin Robinson and Stuart Christine, *Planting Tomorrow's Churches Today* (Crowborough: Monarch, 1992), 54.

21. Alternatively, the two better pianists might join the new church, opening up fresh opportunities for the third best pianist in the larger church. Church planting creates gaps in the planting church.

22. The 80-percent rule (to which there are exceptions) is often quoted in this context: if the building is regularly 80-percent full for the main corporate gathering of the church, further growth is likely to be slow or nonexistent.

23. Teaching on mutual admonition, sharing financial resources, multi-voiced worship, every-member ministry, interactive learning, and so on.

Chapter 3: Planting Churches: How?

1. Interestingly, this model is far less common in America, where some mission strategists are encouraging churches to consider it.

2. For example, Martin Robinson and Stuart Christine, *Planting Tomorrow's Churches Today* (Crowborough: Monarch, 1992), 100-21, and Martin Robinson and David Spriggs: *Church Planting—the Training Manual* (Oxford: Lynx, 1995), 39-46. Bob Hopkins, *Church Planting: Models for Mission in the Church of England* (Nottingham: Grove Booklets 4 and 8, 1988-89), and Harry Weatherley, *Gaining the Ground* (Didcot: Baptist Union, 1994) identify and explore models used in Anglican and Baptist circles respectively. See also *Breaking New Ground* (London: Church House, 1994), especially 43-49.

3. A recent contribution is *Mission-shaped Church* (London: Church House, 2004), chap. 6.

4. We will explore these demands in more detail in chapter 5.

5. An exception to some of these drawbacks is where a small team is deployed with greater freedom to be creative and less support from the planting church. The outcome may have more in common with the "mission team" model considered later in this chapter.

6. See further Stuart Murray, *Church Planting: Laying Foundations* (Carlisle: Paternoster, 1998), 260-66.

7. Or a "well-managed divorce" (a term suggested by George Lings).

8. Church-planting books in the 1990s used the term *colonization* to describe this model of church planting, but this is not helpful in a postcolonial era and implies the imposition of an alien church culture. Another term, "helicopter" church planting, conjures up images of an invasion by paratroopers. "Long-distance" is less colorful but also less problematic.

9. Fans of *The Simpsons* may recall Homer Simpson praying desperately to Jebus to save him from disaster.

10. More crudely put, "changing the bait to catch more fish."

11. The "satellite" imagery has drawbacks. I gather that Anglican church planters have largely abandoned this because it seems to imply living in an artificial environment, disconnected from the real world, dependent on mission control, and ultimately having no future but crashing back to earth or burning up on reentry.

12. This would be true especially of New Church movements such as Pioneer and Ichthus, from which Roger Ellis and Roger Mitchell wrote *Radical Church Planting* (Cambridge: Crossway, 1992), which advocates this model.

13. Cell UK encouraged progress toward this approach in 2007; see www.celluk.org.uk.

14. The subtitle of Bob Hopkins and Mike Breen, *Clusters: Creative Mid-sized Missional Communities* (3DM Publications, 2007).

15. Ecclesial tradition also plays a part in this. Baptist churches, with their heritage of independent churches, struggle to maintain a satellite congregations model for any period of time.

16. The term "emergent church," used widely in North America and to a lesser extent in Britain, seems close to identifying a coherent movement, or even a brand. The term currently still indicates something more organic but with many shared interests, values, and reference points.

17. See further Eddie Gibbs and Ryan Bolger, *Emerging Churches* (Grand Rapids: Baker, 2005); Michael Frost and Alan Hirsch, *The Shaping of Things to Come* (Peabody: Hendrickson, 2003), and Stuart Murray, *Changing Mission: Learning from the Newer Churches* (London: CTBI, 2006).

18. See Felicity Dale, *Simply Church* (Dallas: Karis Publishing, 2002), www.simplechurch.org.uk, and www.dickscoggins.com/books/networks.php. The term "organic church" refers to a similar approach; see Neil Cole, *Organic Church* (San Francisco: Jossey-Bass Wiley, 2005).

19. Here and elsewhere in this book the term "church planter" is used primarily to designate pioneers or those who lead church-planting teams. It can, of course, be extended to include anyone involved in a planting team or even those involved in deploying such teams.

20. A helpful resource for planting via mission teams is Tom Steffen, *Passing the Baton* (La Habra: Center for Organizational Ministry Development, 1993).

21. On cooperative planting, see further Murray, *Church Planting*, 285-92.

Chapter 4: Planting Churches: Where?

1. Urban Expression failed on one occasion adequately to research a location, relying on the confidence of a church planter that it was suitable, only to discover three years later that the housing project was being depopulated and could not sustain a planting initiative.

2. Some church planters still seem to assume they will bring God with them into a community, but many more now operate with a *missio Dei* approach that recognizes God is there before them and invites them to join in.

3. A recent resource aimed at those involved in starting fresh expressions of church is Steven Croft, Freddy Hedley, and Bob Hopkins, *Listening for Mission: Mission Audit for Fresh Expressions* (London: Church House, 2006). For more extensive resources and a very clear overview of community research, see Murray Hawtin, et al., *Community Profiling* (Milton Keynes: Open University Press, 1994). Some denominational websites offer resources, as do www.astoncharities.org.uk, www.faithworks.info, www.shaftesburysociety.org, and in Scotland, www.transformationteam.org.

4. Another popular way of describing this research process uses the acronym TSAR: technical data, soft data, analysis, and recommendations.

5. The term "double listening" appears in the *Mission-shaped Church* report, but other writers have also used this to refer to other processes.

6. Such as Christian Research: www.christian-research.org.uk.

7. See Robert Linthicum, *Empowering the Poor* (Monrovia, Calif.: MARC, 1991), 48.

8. See www.neighbourhood.statistics.gov.uk for England and Wales, www.scrol.gov.uk for Scotland, and www.nicensus2001.gov.uk for Northern Ireland. Some of the data on these websites is updated more often than every ten years.

9. For example, www.faithworks.info.

10. See Luke 10:5-7. There are some interesting examples of such "people of peace" in Martin Robinson, *Planting Mission-Shaped Churches Today* (Crowborough: Monarch, 2006), 78-83.

11. With reference to Genesis 26:18.

12. For a discussion of the missional and ecclesial issues involved in virtual churches, see Mark Howe, *Online Church? First Steps towards Virtual Incarnation* (Cambridge: Grove, 2007).

Chapter 5: Planting Churches: When?

1. We will not consider separately in this chapter the models (spontaneous/emerging and independent church planter) that have no planting agency. Some of the material here is relevant in those situations, but issues of timing when there is no planting agency relate mainly to contextual factors and the judgment of the church planter or the emerging church.

2. In this chapter and elsewhere, "planting churches" is used as a noun to describe local churches that initiate church-planting ventures. The title of the book uses the same term as a verb to describe the whole process of church planting. Some prefer the noun "sending churches," but this language does not suit all the planting models.

3. Roger Ellis and Roger Mitchell, *Radical Church Planting* (Cambridge: Crossway, 1992), 128.

4. The first two will be examined in this chapter, team selection and equipping in chapter 7.

5. Quoted in Martin Robinson and Stuart Christine, *Planting Tomorrow's Churches Today* (Crowborough: Monarch, 1992), 145.

6. Bob Logan first suggested this imagery, which we mentioned in chapter 3. We will use this further in chapter 8. Other analogies can be found at www.acpi.org.uk/planningframeworks.htm.

7. See further Stuart Murray, *Church Planting: Laying Foundations* (Carlisle: Paternoster, 1998).

8. We will address this issue in chapter 7.

9. We will investigate further in chapter 8 the relationship between the planting team and the emerging church.

10. We will return to the subject of finance for church planters in chapter 7.

Chapter 6: Planting Churches: What?

1. Popular examples were seeker-sensitive churches inspired by the Willowcreek Community Church in Chicago, cell churches commended by Korean and North American advocates and, a little later, purpose-driven churches modeled on Saddleback Community Church in California. Few questions were asked at this stage about the transferability of such models into very different cultural contexts.

2. See www.x-pansion.net. Other denominations could learn much from this process.

3. We will use the term "host community" in this chapter and elsewhere to describe the neighborhood or network in which a church is planted. This term is preferable to "target community" and indicates that the community is the (sometimes unwitting) host and that church planters are (usually uninvited) guests. This language picks up the spirit of Jesus' instructions to his disciples in Luke 10:5-9. It also reminds us that we need to honor and respect the host community, behave well, and receive as well as give.

4. Leith Anderson, *A Church for the 21st Century* (Grand Rapids: Bethany House, 1992), 146.

5. There are some resources on this issue at www.sharetheguide.org/section2/deeper/possibilities/create.

6. See, for example, Louis Luzbetak, *The Church and Cultures: New Perspectives in Missiological Anthropology* (Maryknoll: Orbis, 1988); Gerald Arbuckle, *Earthing the Gospel* (Eugene: Wipf & Stock, 2002); and Charles Kraft, *Christianity in Culture* (Maryknoll: Orbis, 2005).

7. Texts on cross-cultural church planting include David Hesselgrave,

Planting Churches Cross-Culturally (Grand Rapids: Baker, 1980); Greg Livingstone, *Planting Churches in Muslim Cities* (Grand Rapids: Baker, 1993); and Paul Hiebert and Eloise Hiebert Meneses, *Incarnational Ministry: Planting Churches in Band, Tribal, Peasant and Urban Societies* (Grand Rapids: Baker, 1996).

8. Attributed to various independent sources in the 1980s and 1990s.

9. The question "What kind of church?" may be addressed in the initial community research (see chapter 4). If contextual issues interact with convictions at this stage, before hard-and-fast decisions are made, it will be easier to develop this process later.

10. A term used by cross-cultural missionaries searching for ways to present the gospel in particular cultures. Redemptive analogies may be objects, stories, historical events, cultural practices, or other familiar aspects of a society that help people understand and connect with the gospel.

11. See chapter 1.

12. See the classic biblical statement in 1 Corinthians 3:9-11.

13. Ephesians 2:20.

14. Seventh-Day Adventist church planters, for instance, are required to plant churches that embrace the twenty-eight fundamentals of their church (see www.adventist.org).

15. See Rick Warren, *The Purpose-driven Church* (Grand Rapids: Zondervan, 1995). For a UK perspective, see David Beer, *Releasing your Church to Grow* (Eastbourne: Kingsway, 2004).

16. Ralph Moore, *Starting a New Church* (Ventura: Regal, 2002), 67.

17. See www.urbanexpression.org.uk/convictions/values.

18. See www.newmonasticism.org.

19. See www.northumbriacommunity.org.

20. This is included in Jonny Baker and Doug Gay (with Jenny Brown), *Alternative Worship* (London: SPCK, 2003), 94-5.

21. This has been standard fare in church-planting ventures influenced by the Church Growth movement, which drew on business management models and advocated goals that were SMART (specific, measurable, attainable, realistic, and timed).

22. George Lings and Stuart Murray, *Church Planting: Past, Present and Future* (Cambridge: Grove, 2003), 20.

23. See the articles by Phil Parshall, "Going too far?" and John Travis, "Must all Muslims leave Islam to follow Jesus?" in *Evangelical Missions Quarterly* 34:3 (October 1998). The application of this discussion to emerging churches in Western culture appears in Michael Frost and Alan Hirsch, *The Shaping of Things to Come* (Peabody: Hendrickson, 2003), 91-93.

24. It is interesting to note too how many emerging churches avoid the term *church* in their name, perhaps recognizing that this term is just as unhelpful in emerging postmodern Western culture.

25. Church planters working within a denominational framework might check to see if there is any guidance or a checklist of requirements. If not, it might be worth suggesting this.

26. Churches tend naturally to work with weekly rhythms when planning patterns of activities, but monthly or seasonal rhythms may be more creative and less liable to multiply meetings.

27. On these concepts and their application to church planting, see David Shenk and Ervin Stutzman, *Creating Communities of the Kingdom* (Scottdale: Herald Press, 1988), 103-4; and Stuart Murray, *Church Planting: Laying Foundations* (Carlisle: Paternoster, 1998), 180-82.

28. On child protection policies, see the Churches' Child Protection Advisory Agency (www.ccpas.co.uk).

29. These include appointing a treasurer; opening a bank account; decisions about signatories and authorized expenditure; methods of giving, bookkeeping, and auditing; budgeting; setting salaries; and overall financial accountability.

30. Some Christian agencies offer advice, including Stewardship Services (www.stewardship.org.uk) and the Charities Aid Foundation (www.cafonline. org). It is important to get current information as the law changes from time to time.

31. Related issues to which we cannot give attention here are the choice of a logo and style of any church website.

Chapter 7: Planting Churches: Who?

1. Books on church planting are usually written by those who have "succeeded" and confidently identify the reasons for their success. Research may suggest other more significant factors. Students on church-planting courses have learned much from honest sessions with those who have failed as church planters.

2. Such profiles and checklists are popular in North America, associated especially with the writings of Bob Logan and Charles Ridley, as are various assessment tools and processes to identity church planters. It is unclear how transferable some of their criteria are to European contexts (although the Assemblies of God uses a slightly adapted version of Ridgley's list). Several British books on church planting in the 1990s listed desirable characteristics of church planters, but these seem not to have drawn on any field research. Most denominations deploying church planters appear to operate relationally and to avoid formal assessment processes.

3. See especially 1 Corinthians 3:5-11; 4:9-17; 9:19-27.

4. We cannot engage here with various criticisms of this interpretation.

5. These guidelines are available as downloads from the Fresh Expressions (www.freshexpressions.org.uk) and Anglican Church Planting Initiatives (www.acpi.org.uk) websites.

6. A simple but very popular leadership matrix developed by John Adair; see John Adair, *Effective Team Building* (London: Pan, 1987), and www.johnadair.co.uk.

7. I have coauthored two short books on church planting with women, but I know of no others, except for one multiauthored book over twenty years ago, edited by a woman. See Stuart Murray and Anne Wilkinson-Hayes, *Hope from the Margins* (Cambridge: Grove, 2000), and Juliet Kilpin and Stuart Murray, *Church Planting in the Inner City* (Cambridge: Grove, 2007).

8. On this issue see further Stuart Murray, *Church Planting: Laying Foundations* (Carlisle: Paternoster, 1998), 243-48. It is discouraging to note how little has changed in the past decade.

9. A further issue that may influence the recognition of church planters is age. Some argue that younger planters will have more energy and greater flexibility, and may be willing to take more risks. Others counter that older planters may have greater experience, stability, and wisdom. There is general agreement that, regardless of age, church planters should have a proven track record in other areas of mission and ministry.

10. There is a parallel here with the feasibility/discernment process described in chapter 4.

11. David Shenk and Ervin Stutzman, *Creating Communities of the Kingdom* (Scottdale: Herald Press, 1988), 42-55.

12. See www.belbin.com.

13. See www.willowcreek.org.uk.

14. See www.myersbriggs.org.

15. For example, the resources offered by the McQuaig Institute; see www.mcquaig.com.

16. First coined by Bruce Tuckman in "Developmental sequence in small groups," *Psychological Bulletin* 63 (1965), 384-99.

17. See Acts 15:36-41 for a classic example. The team of disciples Jesus gathered and trained also argued about various things.

18. This is another reason why church planting often takes longer than anticipated.

19. Martin Robinson and David Spriggs: *Church Planting—the Training Manual* (Oxford: Lynx, 1995), 67.

20. See the appendix for further information.

21. A useful summary of common problems can be found at www.acpi.org.uk/articles/PlantersProblems.pdf.

22. See especially Michael Frost, *Exiles: Living Missionally in a Post-Christian Culture* (Peabody: Hendrickson, 2006), 108-29.

23. The terms used in this section—mentor, spiritual director, coach, and accompanier—are interpreted in various ways by different groups and often have overlapping roles.

24. Urban Expression and NEO teams have found such peer mentoring

very helpful. But it is striking how few teams deployed by planting churches have any links with other planting teams.

25. It may be helpful to take such external supporters around the area so they can visualize where the team is working and get a feel for the community. However, the planting team should gently but firmly discourage members of the planting church or other occasional visitors from "popping in" to see what is happening as the new church emerges.

26. Examples of urban mission agencies that operate as "mission orders" include InnerChange (United States), Urban Neighbours of Hope (Australia), and Urban Vision (New Zealand). Urban Expression is also moving in this direction. Three emerging churches with "new monastic" elements are Moot (London), mayBe (Oxford), and hOME (Oxford). Others drawing on monastic resources include the Northumbria Community, the Iona Community, and the Order of Mission associated with St. Thomas Crookes (Sheffield).

Chapter 8: Planting Churches: What Next?

1. Martin Robinson and Stuart Christine, *Planting Tomorrow's Churches Today* (Crowborough: Monarch, 1992), 298-312.

2. George Lings and Stuart Murray, *Church Planting: Past, Present and Future* (Cambridge: Grove, 2003), 21.

3. It is encouraging that the online guide, Share, www.sharetheguide. org, will be expanded to include sections on developing and sustaining fresh expressions of church.

4. A powerful image used by Ed Stetzer in *Planting Missional Churches* (Nashville: Broadman & Holman, 2006), 192.

5. See, for example, Tom Steffen, *Passing the Baton* (La Habra: Centre for Organizational Ministry Development, 1993).

6. www.acpi.org.uk.

7. See www.sharetheguide.org.

8. As noted in chapter 6: see www.x-pansion.net.

9. Ephesians 4:14.

10. See Stuart Murray, *Church after Christendom* (Milton Keynes: Paternoster, 2005), 165-74.

11. One of my doctoral students, Trevor Hutton, is currently research-ing this area, and I look forward to learning from his discoveries and recommendations.

12. Many churches planted in the 1970s and 1980s within the House Church (later New Church) movement went through these experiences in the 1990s. Some of today's emerging churches and fresh expressions are already encountering them, and others will no doubt do so at some stage.

13. Ephesians 4:13.

14. Ephesians 4:15.

15. The classic text on this phenomenon is David Garrison, *Church Planting Movements: How God is Redeeming a Lost World* (Midlothian: WIGTake Resources, 2004). See also Martin Robinson, *Planting Mission-Shaped Churches Today* (Crowborough: Monarch, 2006).

THE AUTHOR

Stuart Murray spent twelve years as an urban church planter in Tower Hamlets (East London) and has continued to be involved in church planting since then as a trainer, mentor, writer, strategist, and consultant.

For nine years he was Oasis Director of Church Planting and Evangelism at Spurgeon's College, London; he continues as an associate lecturer at the college.

He is chair of the Anabaptist Network and has a PhD in Anabaptist hermeneutics. Since September 2001, Stuart has worked under the auspices of the Anabaptist Network as a trainer and consultant, with particular interest in urban mission, church planting, and emerging forms of church.

Stuart is the founder of Urban Expression, a pioneering urban church-planting agency with teams in London, Glasgow, Manchester, and the Netherlands.

He has written several books on church planting, urban mission, emerging church, the challenge of post-Christendom, and the contribution of the Anabaptist tradition to contemporary missiology. Recent publications include *Post-Christendom: Church and Mission in a Strange New World* (Paternoster 2004), *Church after Christendom* (Paternoster 2005), and *Changing Mission* (CTBI 2006). This book was first published in the United Kingdom as *Planting Churches: A Framework for Practitioners* (Paternoster 2008).

Stuart is married to Sian, a tutor at the Baptist College in Bristol, where they live. He has two grown sons and a grandson.